"Using a wealth of everyday examples, Steven Reiss offers valuable insight into such matters as why some interpersonal relationships are enduringly satisfying, and others are not. His theory of motivation illuminates the important questions in our lives."
—Richard J. McNally,
professor of psychology, Harvard University

"Reiss shows us how to identify our own pattern of desires and how to compare and contrast the patterns in our relationships. The applications of this scientific extension of Maslow's hierarchy extend beyond the personal: Reiss's system can improve our working relationships and enhance our professional lives."
—Ruth Luckasson, J.D.,
regents' professor and professor of special education,
University of New Mexico

"An 'outside the box' approach to understanding individual behavior. Reiss clearly explains the sixteen basic desires, and shows how to easily plot one's own 'desire profile.' Readers of *Who Am I?* will gain valuable insight into their motivational styles—and have a lot of fun doing so."
—Edward Zigler,
sterling professor of psychology, Yale University

"Steven Reiss provides an exciting new way to think about ourselves."
—Ellen Langer, Ph.D.,
author of *Mindfulness* and *The Power of Mindful Learning*

"Well explained in lay readers' terms."
—*Library Journal*

Power

Independence

Curiosity

Acceptance

Order

Saving

Honor

Idealism

The 16
Basic Desires
That Motivate Our
Actions and Define
Our Personality

WHO AM I?

Steven
Reiss,
Ph.D.

Social Contact

Status

Family

Vengeance

Eating

Romance

Physical Activity

Tranquility

B

BERKLEY BOOKS, NEW YORK

A Berkley Book
Published by The Berkley Publishing Group
A division of Penguin Putnam Inc.
375 Hudson Street
New York, New York 10014

Published simultaneously in Canada.

PRINTING HISTORY
Jeremy P. Tarcher/Putnam hardcover edition / August 2000
Berkley trade paperback edition / March 2002

Berkley trade paperback ISBN: 0-425-18340-8

Visit our website at
www.penguinputnam.com

The Library of Congress has catalogued the Jeremy P. Tarcher/Putnam
hardcover edition as follows:

Reiss, Steven.
Who am I? : the 16 basic desires that motivate our behavior and define
our personality / Steven Reiss.
p.   cm.
Includes bibliographical references and index.
ISBN 1-58542-045-X
1. Motivation (Psychology).   2. Desire.   3. Meaning (Psychology).   I. Title.

BF503.R475   2000   00-027268
153.8—dc21

PRINTED IN THE UNITED STATES OF AMERICA

10   9   8   7   6   5   4   3   2   1

TO MIKE AND BEN

Contents

PART II

HOW THE BASIC DESIRES ARE SATISFIED

Introduction

Sometimes we become so consumed by our daily business that we forget to take a look at the larger picture of who we are and where we are headed in life. We go through the actions of work, children, and chores, and it takes an extraordinary event, such as a life-threatening illness, the death of a loved one, or a major career change, to focus our attention on the meaning in our lives. When we are faced with tragedy, we review what we have done, think about what we might have done, and wonder what it all means. We become clear on what it is we desire most. We learn who we are and what we truly value.

At least that was the experience I had in 1995 when I was diagnosed with a life-threatening illness. The whole thing was a big surprise. When I first started feeling tired, I thought it was just a flu and would pass in a few days. It continued, though, and so I went to see a physician. He ordered one round of tests after another with increasing urgency. Since I was a professor at the Ohio State University College of Medicine, it was easy for me to show up for the tests on the spur of the moment.

After I had undergone a scan for possible liver problems, a young doctor in a laboratory coat appeared. "You'll need a liver transplant," he said. I asked how anybody could possibly survive having his liver taken out and replaced by what once was somebody else's. "We do them all the time now," he answered, "Your chances of survival are ninety percent." Somehow hearing that I had "only" a 10 percent chance of dying seemed reassuring, so I asked when all this would happen. "In a few months," he said with a smile. "But don't feel sorry for yourself. I told several patients today that they would die. You at least have a chance."

After I had recovered from the shock, I went for second and third opinions and read up on liver transplants. The additional opinions not only confirmed that I needed a new liver but also indicated that I probably had a biliary tumor. Cancer in the biliary tract is a death sentence.

What a mess! I tried to take an objective look at my situation to plan my course of action. I had in hand multiple opinions from good doctors who had conducted many tests. They all came to the same conclusion, and none saw any likelihood of a mistake. The rare autoimmune disease they said I had was fatal if untreated, and the treatment was a risky liver transplant. Further, I had no chance at all if the dark spot on the films of my liver was in fact a tumor. I was in deep trouble.

Then one Saturday, my wife visited my hospital room and noticed that my color had changed from its usual yellow (I had jaundice from my failing liver) to something more akin to green. She called the nurse, who determined that my temperature was north of 104 and still rising. Realizing that a green appearance must be a symptom of something, she called the supervising doctor, who looked at me as if he were seeing a ghost. Even the dullest observer of human nature could discern from his facial contortions that things were not going well. "How serious is my situation?" I asked. "It's life-threatening," he answered. My temperature had reached 105. "You're dealing with a professor in the medical school," I warned. "If you lose me, you will be the one who has to tell the dean that there is nobody around to teach my students and finish the research on my grants. So please get my temperature back down."

Fortunately, that was as bad as things became. When I woke up a few hours later, my temperature was back down to 102 and my color had returned to yellow. Still, I was kept in the hospital for nine days just to be sure that the infection was completely gone. That gave me a lot of time to ponder the meaning of life.

When we are faced with the possibility of death, we try to make sense of what is happening to us. We search for meaning and start to psychologically prepare ourselves for death. I was starting to accept my fate until I considered the full implications for my relationship with my children. My wife and I had had children late in life, and my older boy had not yet started high school. When I realized that my sons might need me someday and I would not be there to help them, dying was no longer an option. I decided that I had to live. No matter what medical torture might be involved, I had to give myself every possible chance to survive.

After I left the hospital, I went to the library to read more about the illnesses I had, and I consulted with many researchers. I found some new, still experimental approaches to the treatment of my autoimmune disease. I chose one of them carefully, and was quickly scheduled for the procedure. Afterward, over the course of six months, my liver function gradually returned to normal.

THE PLEASURE PRINCIPLE

I recall my personal experience because it led me to rethink what it is that makes my life meaningful, which in turn led me to the research that formed the basis for this book. Many research psychologists have assumed that human behavior is guided by the desire to feel good, or what I call the Pleasure Principle. This principle says that above all, what people want is to maximize their pleasure and minimize their pain. N. M. Bradburn, the influential social psychologist, has said that the quality of a person's life can be measured by the excess of positive over negative feelings.[1] According to Bradburn, we are happy when we have more positive than negative feelings and unhappy when the opposite is true.

The Pleasure Principle implies that *everything* people do can be explained by a calculus of pleasure and pain. It suggests that people prefer optimism to pessimism because optimism is the more pleasurable of the two outlooks. Similarly, people prefer movies with happy rather than sad endings, even when the happy endings are unrealistic. How does this principle explain the fact that many people work at boring jobs? It implies that working at such jobs is the lesser of two evils, predicting that people would dislike unemployment even more than they dislike their current jobs.

Those who advocate the validity of the Pleasure Principle—variously called *pleasure theorists* or *hedonists*—say that nature uses pleasure and pain to prod us to do what is necessary for our health and survival. For example, nature uses hunger to tell us when we need to eat and thirst to signal when we need to drink. Since feeling hungry and thirsty are unpleasant, we are motivated to eat and drink when those things are essential for our health and survival.

So if everybody is maximizing pleasure and minimizing pain, why do workaholics spend little time relaxing, having fun with their families, or taking vacations? According to pleasure theory, it is because these people enjoy their work and feel restless when away from it. Pleasure theorists argue that workaholics are really doing what for them maximizes positive feelings or minimizes negative ones.

Is the desire to feel good all that motivates us? Are pleasure and pain the ultimate forces guiding our behavior? Although many researchers answer "yes," I say the answer is "no." I believe that behavior has meaning and value that goes beyond pleasure and pain. According to the extensive research I present in this book, the meaning, value, and purpose of life cannot be explained entirely in terms of pleasure and pain.

When I was faced with a life-threatening illness, in deciding how to proceed I did not give much consideration to how much pain I might experience. Instead, I was guided by my responsibilities to my children. When parents help their children, they aim for good things to happen to their children, not to themselves. Although parents take pleasure in their children's well-being, that does not mean that parents help their children for the selfish benefit of experiencing the joys of parenthood.

One morning in the hospital I experimented by thinking of what people were doing solely in terms of the pleasure or pain it brought them. When the nurse came in to take my temperature, I wondered why she was not doing something that would bring her greater pleasure. If having fun and feeling good are the goals of all behavior, as pleasure theorists say, who would want to work in a hospital? Hospitals are filled with people who are sick and some who are dying. In late mornings, I could hear patients awake from surgery, screaming in pain. Since nurses have the ability to find some other place to work, why wouldn't they do so if their overriding desire were to feel good?

Soldiers who sacrifice their lives are guided by a high purpose, not by their own selfish pleasure. Pvt. George Philips stood watch on 14 March, 1945, on the island of Iwo Jima. While his fellow soldiers slept after a day of heavy fighting, an enemy hand-grenade was suddenly tossed into the camp. Pvt. Philips threw himself over the grenade to absorb the explosion and save the lives of his comrades. His bravery earned him a posthumous Congressional Medal of Honor. I suppose a pleasure theorist could argue that Pvt. Philips was just trying to avoid a life of guilt at watching his fellow soldiers die, but such an explanation seems to me contrived and unconvincing. I think it is much simpler and more to the point to observe that, for Pvt. Philips, the desire for honor is what guided his decision to sacrifice his life. It was his duty to stand watch and protect his comrades, and he did exactly that. His sacrifice was a meaningful one, not a disguised effort to feel good.

The more I thought about this question, the more convinced I became that pleasure and pain do not drive our behavior to anywhere near the extent assumed by many psychologists. Pleasure is the *byproduct* of getting what we desire, it is not the aim of the desire. The goal of experiencing pleasure does not create the nurse's desire to help patients; rather, altruism prods nurses to make sacrifices for their patients. The goal of avoiding guilt does not create the soldier's desire to sacrifice himself for the good of his country; rather, honor motivates soldiers to make sacrifices.

When people face death and search for the meaning in their lives, they focus on their spirituality, families, relationships, achievements, and ideas. In the final calculation of what is valuable about our lives, pleasure and pain are not such an important part of the equation. You can discover this by reading philosophy and finding the logical error in hedonism (the inference that pleasure is the motivating cause of behavior because it is the universal consequence of satisfying desire), or through self-reflection and personal experience.

I left the hospital determined not only to overcome my liver disease but also to develop a new theory on human desire that is based on meaning, rather than on pleasure. As the head of the Nisonger Center at Ohio State University and an expert in personality and clinical psychology, I decided to begin a study of human motivation.

HISTORICAL PERSPECTIVE

If pleasure and pain do not drive our behavior, I wondered, what does? What really matters to us? According to Plato (427 B.C.–347 B.C.), the desire for truth (curiosity) is one of the greatest motivators in life, and wisdom is one of the greatest intrinsic joys.[2] Plato put forth the vision of an eternal world of ideals which indicate the essences of all things; when we discover these eternal ideals, we experience the joy of learning. Plato also placed high value on reason, moral duty, and public service.[3]

Sigmund Freud (1856–1939) put forth a very different view of human motivation. He said that, from cradle to tomb, what people want is sex, sex, and more sex. The reason we do not realize this, according to Freud, is because many of our sexual motives are unconscious, which means that they cannot be acknowledged without experiencing overwhelming guilt, anxiety, or embarrassment. Freud later modified his ideas to say that both sex and aggression drive our behavior.

If you have not read Freud or had the pleasure of knowing personally some of the old-time psychoanalysts, you probably do not realize just how serious these guys were about the psychological importance of sex. Freud was so impressed by the importance of sex that he even invented a new name for it, *libido*. He wrote that, in the unconscious mind, a pencil is a symbol for a penis, and a box is a symbol for a vagina.[4] He named the Oedipal Complex: the theory that boys 4 to 5 years old want to have sexual intercourse with their mothers. He believed that young girls developed an inferiority complex called "penis envy." When I was a graduate student in psychology at Yale, I heard a lecture from John Dollard, at the time one of the world's greatest psychoanalysts. Whatever else we do with our lives, advised Dollard, we should be sure to get enough sex. He pleaded with us to take this advice, lest we develop neuroses. Speaking before a group of young college students, Dollard had no trouble convincing his audience of the importance of this idea.

Many psychologists who were contemporaries of Freud, or who came after him, embraced much of what Freud said but differed with him on the importance of sexual motivation. For example, Carl Jung (1875–1961) thought that the will to live, a general life force, is the greatest human motivator. Alfred Adler (1870–1937) wrote about the desire for superiority and power.[5] Erik Erikson (1902–1994) developed a theory of ego development, or what might be loosely called a desire for human growth.[6]

Various schools of behaviorism have expressed different views on the question of what motivates people. Clark Hull (1884–1952) and Kenneth

Spence (1907–1967) developed an influential model of behavior that discussed human motives in terms of a series of learned and unlearned drives, such as the drive to eat when hungry or the drive to escape from anxiety.[7] This approach gave more emphasis to the energizing function of motives than to the roles of specific motives in guiding people toward some goals rather than others. The Hull-Spence theory had enormous influence during the period of about 1950 to 1975.

B. F. Skinner (1904–1990), another leading behaviorist, urged psychologists to pay little attention to finding the basic motives that guide our lives. Skinner believed that all motives, thoughts, and feelings (including pleasure and pain) are private. Only *you* know what your motives are, and if you do not tell us, we can only guess at them.[8] Since a person's motives cannot be known with scientific certainty, Skinner reasoned, psychologists should not pay attention to them. (If your spouse has stopped paying attention to your motives, thoughts and feelings, maybe it's because he or she has become a behaviorist.)

Carl Rogers (1902–1987) said that people are driven more or less by two desires, the desire to grow, called *self-actualization,* and the desire for self-acceptance.[9] According to this viewpoint, the key to happiness is to live our lives in accordance with our values. When people do things that are inconsistent with their values, they lose respect for themselves, stop growing, and become unhappy. Rogers's theory represented an original effort to reduce much of what is meaningful to us to a few overarching motives.

William James (1842–1910), the great American psychologist, philosopher, and educator, and William McDougall (1871–1938), the brilliant Harvard social psychologist, believed that behavior is guided by instinctual desires. In his epic work, *The Principles of Psychology,* James provided the following list of basic instinctual desires:[10]

- saving   the desire to hoard and collect

- construction   the desire to build and achieve

- curiosity   the desire to explore and learn

- exhibition   the desire for attention

- family   the desire to raise our children

- hunting   the desire to find food

- order   the desire for cleanliness and organization

- play   the desire for fun

- sex   the desire to reproduce

- shame   the desire to avoid being singled out

- pain   the desire to avoid aversive sensation

- herd   the desire for social contact

- vengeance   the desire for aggression

McDougall expanded and improved on this list.[11] Together, James and Mc-Dougall realized that human desire is multifaceted. They resisted the temptation to reduce everything to one or two supermotives, such as Freud's sex and aggression, or Adler's drive for superiority. James and McDougall were the first influential psychologists to develop a comprehensive theory of basic human desires.

After James passed away in 1910, McDougall was opposed by both behaviorists and psychoanalysts. Behaviorists rejected McDougall's idea that desires are inherited, arguing instead that they are learned. Viewing human behavior in terms of mostly sexual motivation, psychoanalysts argued that James and McDougall recognized too many instinctual desires. The influence of James and McDougall might have been lost altogether except that Harvard psychologist Henry A. Murray (1893–1988) restated McDougall's list of instincts as a list of psychological needs.[12] Murray's work was influential, partially because he developed a popular technique for assessing a person's motives.[13]

Another psychologist who made an important contribution to the study of human motivation was Abraham Maslow (1908-1970). Maslow was one of the few psychologists who looked at human nature primarily from a motivational perspective.[14] He made the important point that we are creatures of desire who are always wanting something. In this regard, Maslow analyzed human behavior very differently than did most psychologists. I embrace and even extend Maslow's thinking, arguing that a motivational approach to human behavior potentially can explain much more behavior than is generally realized.

BRIDGE BETWEEN PHILOSOPHY
AND PSYCHOLOGY

This book is based on original scientific research on the basic human desires that make our lives meaningful. Many people are not aware that the most famous analyses of human desire in history were not based upon scientific study. For 2,500 years, the greatest philosophers and scientists have produced many answers to the question, "What makes people tick?" Although the theories were brilliant and fascinating, few were based on any scientific research, and none was based on scientifically valid surveys of the kind reported in this book. What is perhaps most significant about the answer put forth in this book is that it is based on having actually asked large numbers of people what it is that is most important to them.

The research wasn't as easy as it may seem at first blush. In order to conduct scientifically valid surveys of what motivates people, my then-graduate student, Susan Havercamp, and I first needed to solve a number of technical issues concerning both the ideas we would use to guide our research and the methods we would use to collect our data. We addressed these problems by combining elements of psychology and philosophy. Psychologists have developed scientific methods for understanding behavior, whereas philosophers have developed many meaningful ideas. By combining the methods of psychology with the ideas of philosophy, we hoped to develop a new approach to the search for meaning and happiness.[15]

Our work made it possible to study human motivation in a comprehensive manner. During the past century, scientific research on motivation was conducted in a piecemeal fashion in which only one or two motives were evaluated in any particular study. The only group of psychologists that has studied motivation comprehensively was made up of psychodynamic researchers who used projective tests, such as inkblots, interpretation and storytelling procedures. However, these studies are not considered scientifically valid because they lacked objective measuring techniques.[16]

In this book, I will show you how to analyze your behavior—and the behavior of others—in new terms. Through surveys of more than 6,000 people from many stations in life, Susan and I discovered that there are 16 basic desires and values that drive nearly everything we do. The 16 basic desires presented here provide a powerful tool for self-discovery and self-awareness, and bring to attention aspects of behavior that we often overlook. This tool can help you understand how you react to others and how others react to you, and provides new insights into romantic relationships, careers, and spirituality.

Knowledge of these 16 basic desires can ultimately improve your ability to gain value-based happiness, which is the sense that life is meaningful—something we all want. This book will show you how to recognize the 16 basic desires in everyday life. It will describe how we fulfill them through relationships, work, family, sports, and spirituality. Ultimately, by learning about these desires and understanding which are most important to you, you will learn how to more meaningfully structure your relationships, home life, work, and daily life in order to achieve lasting value-based happiness.

PUBLIC ENCOURAGEMENT

On June 15, 1998, The Ohio State University issued a press release saying that Susan and I had found that 16 basic desires drive much of human behavior. Within a minute of the expiration of the news embargo, the lead science reporter for the BBC arranged for a series of interviews on U.K. national radio and their various international feeds. The story ran in the general news sections of the major U.K. papers (*The London Times, Telegraph, Observer, Scotsman*) and then spread to magazines and radio reports throughout the world, including national papers in India, Italy, and Canada.

Hundreds of people wrote to us about the press release. Only a few asked for self-help advice. Some asked how our results compare with the motivation theory of Abraham Maslow. Others asked how their own behavior fits into the 16 desires. They wanted to know where on our list is the desire to obey God, for example, and the desire for survival, and even the desire for shelter. The *Manchester Observer* quoted the work of evolutionary biologists to suggest desires we had supposedly overlooked. The *St. Louis Post-Dispatch* called to say they polled their editors to find out which desires were most important. The *Columbus Dispatch* ran the story on its front page, and the *Dallas Morning Star* ran a full-page piece, as did the Italian national newspaper, *Corte.* The European edition of *Time* reported our findings. ABCnews.com asked Internet surfers to prioritize the 16 basic desires, and nearly 10,000 people did so in a single day. Radio interviewers in Australia and the U.K. told me they had polls going with their callers on how to improve our list. Even the *Mirror,* a British tabloid, reported the story, complete with an obligatory nude who, incidentally, was not one of our research subjects.

A number of the reporters who interviewed me suggested that I write a book. I set out to write *Who Am I?* with the goal of explaining these research findings and their significance for helping people understand their lives better.

HOW TO READ THIS BOOK

An original theory of human motivation is presented in this book, which is divided into two parts. Part I explains the system of 16 basic desires and shows what is and is not included in each basic desire. Part II shows how we fulfill our basic desires in order to gain value-based happiness. I analyze relationships, careers, family, sports, and spirituality in terms of the 16 basic desires, and show how we have the potential to fulfill our basic desires through each of these areas of life.

In Chapter 1, you will learn the foundations of our research in terms of the definition of a basic desire, and you'll see how psychological research surveys really work. Each of the 16 basic desires is actually a category of closely related motives, and all or nearly all are seen in animals as well as people. The desires motivate nearly everybody, but not necessarily in the same ways. Chapter 1 explains why certain desires, such as the will to survive, are not considered to be basic desires.

A detailed description of each basic desire is presented in Chapters 2, 3, and 4. Then, in Chapter 5, the idea of a desire profile is discussed. Your personal desire profile is what makes you an individual. It shows how you rank, or prioritize, the 16 basic desires. Susan and I have developed a standardized psychological test, called the Reiss Profile of Fundamental Goals and Motivational Sensitivities, that assesses a person's desire profile.[17] You can estimate your own individual desire profile by the information presented in Chapters 2, 3, and 4, or by the questions summarized in Appendix A. The Reiss Profile can access more than two trillion different value profiles, only one of which describes you.

Chapter 6 explains the ways that your desire profile affects how you communicate with people, and how they communicate with you. Two types of misunderstandings that occur between people are discussed: ineffective communication and "not getting it." Misunderstandings that arise from ineffective communication can be resolved by supplying additional information, but "not getting it" occurs when two people have very dissimilar desire profiles. When "not getting it" occurs, additional information usually just sharpens the differences between the individuals. The idea of "not getting it" is a new take on the age-old question of whether or not we can truly know another person.

Part II shows how we can fulfill our basic desires through relationships, work, families, sports, and spirituality. The 16 basic desires suggest new ways of thinking about these areas of life.

In Chapter 7, you will learn the differences between two types of happiness, called *feel-good happiness* and *value-based happiness*. Feel-good happiness refers to the experience of pleasant sensations. In contrast, value-based happiness refers to the general feeling of meaning we experience when our basic desires are fulfilled. How much feel-good happiness you experience depends a lot on how fortunate you are—people who are rich, healthy, and beautiful generally will experience more feel-good happiness than people who are poor, ill, or less attractive. However, value-based happiness is the great equalizer. No matter who you are or what your circumstances, you have virtually the same opportunity for a meaningful life as does every other person on the planet.

Chapter 8 explains how you can satisfy your desires through a relationship with your spouse, partner, or close friend. I discuss how basic desires can either bind you and your partner or lead you in different directions in life as the years go by. A new way of evaluating compatibility in a relationship is discussed. Instead of looking at similarity of skills, I argue that it is more important to look at compatibility of basic desires, values, and goals. I distinguish between short-term and long-term relationships. In the short run, people can be attracted to each other for reasons pertaining to both feel-good and value-based happiness. As the years pass, however, the quality of the relationship is increasingly predicted by the factors influencing value-based happiness only, especially the compatibility of individual desire profiles.

Your desire profile affects your experience at work in several different ways, which we'll explain in Chapter 9. It affects how you are likely to think of your boss, and how your boss is likely to think of you. It affects how much you like your job. Careers provide opportunities for self-fulfillment. If you are thinking about changing jobs or careers, your knowledge of desire profiles can give you a practical, easy-to-use method of selecting work that is likely to be fulfilling.

In Chapter 10, I discuss how your desire profile affects how you relate to your children and your parents. The basic desire that binds parents to their children is different from the desire that binds children to parents. Furthermore, the principle of individuality applies to the parent–child relationship. Despite the commonality of some genes, you and your children can have very different desire profiles. When this occurs, your children will want to pursue paths in life you may not value. Your choice is between trying to change them or trying to accept them for who they are. If you try to change them, either they will become unhappy doing what you want (rather than what they want) or they will shut you out, possibly for a long time. By the time your children reach a certain age—approximately 14—your opportunity to mold them is largely behind you. You and they may be better off if you accept them for who they are than if you spend the rest of your life fighting with them.

In Chapter 11, I discuss how people fulfill their desires through sports. My thesis is that sports are more than games. They are opportunities for people to experience intrinsically valued feelings that satisfy basic psychological desires. You should have some fun with this chapter, which comments on the often asked (but rarely answered) questions of why Chicago loves the Cubs, Cleveland the Browns, and my father the New York Mets.

In Chapter 12, I comment on how the 16 basic desires can be fulfilled through spirituality. When Susan and I set out to find the basic elements of meaningful experience, we asked no direct questions about God or religion. Yet of the 16 basic desires that were identified by our research results, at least 12 define attributes of gods that various cultures have worshipped at different points in history. Furthermore, the world's major religions provide practices for satisfying all 16 basic desires. The strong connection between the 16 basic desires and spirituality suggests that these specific desires are truly the basic elements of a psychologically meaningful experience.

Finally, at the end of this book you'll find other possible applications for the system of 16 basic desires: implications for self-improvement, marketing, and psychological disorders. You will learn how some of the more memorable advertising slogans of our lifetime—such as Clairol's "Does she . . . or doesn't she?" and Nike's "Just do it"—connect to the 16 basic desires. I also outline some general guidelines for using your knowledge of the 16 basic desires for the challenge of change.

THE BASIC DESIRES THAT MAKE OUR LIVES MEANINGFUL

What Is a Basic Desire?

Although most people are not used to thinking about human behavior in terms of fundamental desires, knowledge of our 16 basic desires can help you gain insight into who you are and why you do what you do. The desires give you a new way of analyzing your behavior; when you learn the 16 basic desires, you can figure out how your behavior and life goals are connected to them. Because your desires indicate the path of psychological growth that you need to take to become who you want to be, they can help you think about what you need in order to gain value-based happiness.

The 16 basic desires also provide a powerful tool for analyzing the behavior of people you know. If we want to know what people will do, we should find out what they desire and predict that they will try to satisfy their desires. Desire may not tell us everything we want to know about ourselves or others, but what it tells us is very important for understanding behavior and happiness.

Here are the 16 basic desires. The order of presentation is without significance.

Power is the desire to influence others.

Independence is the desire for self-reliance.

Curiosity is the desire for knowledge.

Acceptance is the desire for inclusion.

Order is the desire for organization.

Saving is the desire to collect things.

Honor is the desire to be loyal to one's parents and heritage.

Idealism is the desire for social justice.

Social Contact is the desire for companionship.

Family is the desire to raise one's own children.

Status is the desire for social standing.

Vengeance is the desire to get even.

Romance is the desire for sex and beauty.

Eating is the desire to consume food.

Physical Activity is the desire for exercise of muscles.

Tranquility is the desire for emotional calm.

If you are interested in learning how to use these desires and do not require information on how our research was done, you can skip ahead to Chapters 2, 3, and 4, where the 16 desires are discussed in detail. The remainder of this chapter is concerned mostly with the underlying scientific research and philosophical analysis that led us to develop this particular list of basic desires and no other.

ORIGIN OF DESIRES

Let's consider where these 16 desires come from and how they are affected by experience and culture. William James and William McDougall said that our basic needs are genetically determined.[1,2] This means that we do not consciously choose what we want from life; rather, our deepest desires arise automatically, and as soon as we satisfy one of them, we automatically experience another and want something else.

According to William McDougall,

Every man is so constituted as to seek, to strive for, and to desire, certain goals which are common to the species, and the attainment of which goals satisfies and allays the urge or craving or desire that moves us. These goals . . . are not only common to all men, but also . . . [to] their nearer relatives in the animal world; such goals as food, shelter from danger, the company of our fellows, intimacy with the opposite sex, triumph over our opponents, and leadership among our companions.[3]

Each of the 16 basic desires that Susan and I found appears to fulfill McDougall's criterion of being common to the human species. For example, nearly everyone wants success (indicating the desire for power), self-determination (indicating the desire for independence), knowledge (indicating the desire for curiosity), and so on down the list. There are some minor exceptions to the universal nature of these goals, but we find that nearly everybody has each of these desires; the exceptions are rare.

The 16 basic desires are common not only to the human species but also to our nearest relatives in the animal world.[4] The expression in animals of nine of the basic desires is obvious—for example, the fact that animals explore their environments shows that they must have some degree of curiosity; animals who hoard food are motivated by the desire to save; animals socialize (indicating a desire for social contact), raise their young (indicating a desire for family), defend themselves (indicating a desire for vengeance), have sex (indicating a desire for romance), show fear (indicating a desire for tranquility), eat, and exercise. How the remaining seven desires connect to animal behavior is less obvious, but in Chapters 2, 3, and 4, I present observations to support these connections. For example, animals' common practice of licking themselves clean falls under the desire for order. The young bird's desire to gain attention in the nest may be the origin of the instinctual human desire for social status.

The fact that all (or nearly all) of the 16 basic desires are seen in animals lends credibility to the claim that the list is important. When Susan Havercamp and I conducted the surveys from which we developed this list of desires, we did not ask people to tell us what values they shared with animals. We did not ask any questions at all about animals. Yet the desires that emerged from our survey research are largely those that are seen in animals.

In fact, it can be argued that these desires have survival value in the wild and, thus, evolutionary significance.

Although almost everybody embraces the 16 basic desires, individuals vary in how intensely each desire is experienced. These individual differ-

TABLE OF BASIC DESIRES

BASIC DESIRE	EVOLUTIONARY (INSTINCTUAL) BASIS	ASSOCIATED EMOTION	BEHAVIOR
Power	Dominant animals push others away from food	Competence, influence	Leadership, achievement
Independence	Animals leave nest, increasing area over which food is sought	Freedom	Self-reliance
Curiosity	Animals like to explore novel stimuli	Wonderment	Truth-seeking, problem-solving
Acceptance	Unclear	Self-confidence	Assertive behavior
Order	Animals have instincts to lick or clean themselves	Security, stability	Makes many rules, clean, "perfect," compulsive
Saving	Hoarding of food or essential supplies	Ownership	Collecting, frugality
Honor	Avoid being stared at or singled out—keeps animal close to herd	Loyalty	Character, morality, principled behavior

TABLE OF BASIC DESIRES (continued)

BASIC DESIRE	EVOLUTIONARY (INSTINCTUAL) BASIS	ASSOCIATED EMOTION	BEHAVIOR
Idealism	Altruism	Compassion, sense of justice	Social causes, fair play
Social Contact	Herd instinct	Happiness, belonging	Party, join clubs/groups
Family	Maternal/paternal instincts	Love	Parent, homemaker
Status	Attention helps survival in nest	Self-importance, superiority	Concern with reputation, showing off
Vengeance	Aggression	Anger, hate	Revenge
Romance	Reproductive sex	Lust, appreciation of beauty	Sex, courting
Eating	Hunting instinct	Hunger	Eating, dining, cooking
Physical exercise	Strong animals survive	Vitality	Physical activity, participatory sports
Tranquility	Animals need to avoid danger to survive in wild	Safety, sense of peace	Avoids stressful situations

ences in desire partially reflect genetic variations across individuals. For example, some people are born with the potential for very strong tendencies toward aggression (indicating a desire for vengeance), whereas others are born with the potential for only weak aggressive tendencies. Some people are born with the potential for enormous curiosity, whereas others are born with the potential for little curiosity. No two people have exactly the same potential for a particular desire. Across all 16 basic desires, the strength of desire varies significantly, depending on both the individual and the desire in question.

The 16 basic desires make us individuals. Each person has his or her own hierarchy of basic desires, and in part this reflects the importance of each desire for the person's happiness. When we learn our desire hierarchy, also called a *desire profile,* we can gain insight into how we each prioritize the 16 basic desires. We learn which ones are stronger in us as compared with the average person, and which ones are unusually weak. It is how we experience the strength of the 16 basic desires in comparison to how others experience them that is most important in understanding how we relate to other people, and how they relate to us.

We are individuals to a much greater extent that many people realize. Because of genetic variations in basic desires, no two people enjoy the same experience in exactly the same way. Your boss experiences the basic desires differently than you do. Parents experience the basic desires differently from each of their children. Wives experience the basic desires differently than do their husbands. According to the theory of 16 basic desires, for example, sex is a much more intensely pleasurable experience for some people than for others, based partially on individual variations in the genes that make sex a motive. Similarly, parenthood is a significantly greater potential joy for some than for others. Since we cannot experience the intensity of another person's enjoyment of sex or parenthood, we sometimes do not appreciate the extent to which these desires are or are not motivational for other people. We are prone to misunderstand why some people react to sex or parenthood differently than we do because we do not realize how the genetic differences between us have resulted in differences in intensities of pleasure.[5] Often the consequence of this misunderstanding is a process I call "not getting it," which is discussed in more detail in Chapter 6.

Because our basic desires have a genetic origin, we tend to have the same basic goals throughout most of our lives. People do not change very much in what they fundamentally desire. Curious children tend to become curious adolescents, who tend to become curious adults. People who have strong appetites tend to struggle with their weight all their lives. People who like to organize and plan things when they are adolescents will probably still enjoy organizing and planning things when they are adults. The underlying genes that influence these desires do not change much as we grow older.

Can people change, or does a genetic origin of the 16 basic desires imply that our basic personalities are determined at birth? Genes are not the only important influence on basic desires and how we satisfy them. However, the genetic factors in our desires provide significant stability to our behavior. I suspect that people can change, but to a certain degree and not very easily.

ROLE OF CULTURE AND LEARNING

To what extent can culture or experience change our basic desires? According to James and McDougall, desires occur automatically, but how we go about satisfying them is determined by our upbringing, culture, and experiences. For example, parents instinctively love their children, but how they express that love and rear their offspring depends on their culture and learned habits, not on their instincts. People instinctively desire sex, but how they satisfy that desire varies considerably from one culture to the next. Kissing is a good example of cultural differences in how the desire for romance is satisfied. In some cultures, emphasis is given to sniffing and smelling while kissing a lover.[6] In Mongolia, a father does not kiss his son; he smells his son's head instead. Inuits and Polynesians rub noses. French kissing may have evolved as a symbolic effort to unite two souls.

Achievement motivation (part of the desire for power) is a good example of how culture can affect a basic desire. Schoolchildren in the United States lag behind their counterparts in Japan and Taiwan from the day they enter school.[7] The results of standardized achievement testing show significant advantages in favor of Japanese students in both math and reading. Within the United States, Asian-American young people seem to enjoy disproportionate educational achievement. Japanese-Americans score higher than average on standardized achievement tests and are disproportionately represented at elite colleges such as Harvard and Stanford.

What accounts for the great achievement orientation of Japanese students? Some experts say it is the emphasis Japanese culture places on academics. Japanese parents have higher expectations of the school system than do American parents. Furthermore, Japanese students spend 240 days a year in school, compared with 180 for most American students.

Can culture modify the strength of a desire as well as the way in which the desire is satisfied? Are some societies more status-oriented than others? Are some more idealistic? Some experts provide affirmative responses to these questions. Many psychoanalysts say, for example, that cultural differences in child-rearing influence the degree of anxiety adults experience and, thus, people's motivation to seek tranquility. One of the influential psychoanalytic studies that supports this viewpoint was conducted by former Harvard University Professor of Education John Whiting and former Yale University Professor of Psychology Irving Child.[8] These researchers, who studied anthropological reports of 75 different cultures, concluded that how much anxiety and fear people experience as adults depends on the society's child-rearing practices.

It's important to note that this book is based on research with Americans, Canadians, and Japanese. Although the research participants reflected some of the multicultural nature of these countries, we did not conduct research with other nationalities and cultures. Thus, we do not know the extent to which the 16 basic desires affect people in other cultures. But even if the average strength of the 16 basic desires were found to vary across cultures, I expect that the definitions of the 16 basic desires presented in this book would be proven to be universal. I base this expectation partially on the genetic origin of the desires.

An individual's learning experiences also can influence the intensity of the person's 16 basic desires. For example, prudish parents can cause an adolescent child to feel guilty about sex. Although guilty feelings do not reduce the strength of the adolescent's sexual desire, they may combine with the adolescent's sex drive in such a manner that the overall (or net) motivation for sex is lowered. The individual will likely feel ambivalent about sex, sometimes feeling strong desire mixed with guilt feelings. This may not be the same as a person who is born with a potential for a weak sex drive, but we might see somewhat similar effects in terms of how strongly the individual is motivated toward sexual activity.

A person's beliefs can influence desires significantly. In fact, some experts say that the quickest way to weaken or strengthen our desires is by examining what we believe about them. Albert Ellis, one of the founders of cognitive therapy, has put forth the idea of "must" beliefs.[9] The belief that "everything must be in its place," for example, strengthens the basic desire for order. So does the belief that "rules must be followed." If the desire for order has become so strong that it causes problems in a person's life—such as a compulsive tendency to clean up—Ellis advocates challenging the person's "must" belief on the grounds that the belief is irrational. He has reported many clinical cases in which he has used his cognitive therapy to help clients solve their problems.

These considerations show how complex human motives can be. Our basic desires have an evolutionary origin, but they are significantly modified by culture, beliefs, and individual experiences in ways that are still not well understood. What we desire is largely determined by our genes, but how we fulfill our desires is largely determined by culture and experience.

HOW OUR SURVEY WAS CONDUCTED

The surveys Susan and I conducted were not straightforward polls such as the ones conducted by marketing firms when they need to evaluate a product. We did not ask people to tell us whether power or tranquility was more important to them. At no point did we attempt to determine which of the 16 basic desires are most important to the largest number of people. Rather, the aim of our research was to learn what basic desires make our lives meaningful.

I don't want to sound critical, but I must question the validity of a marketing approach to human desires, if only because so many people initially told us that this is what they thought we were trying to do. Let's take a look at a research study that actually adopted this marketing approach and see why the methods are invalid.

On April 30, 1999, my local newspaper, the *Columbus Dispatch,* carried an Associated Press story of a survey of desires conducted by a group of medical researchers at Columbia University. In a poll funded by the prestigious National Institutes of Health, the Columbia University researchers asked 500 adults about the importance of various aspects of life. The researchers found that 99 percent considered it very important to have loving family relationships, 98 percent considered that financial security was very important, and 82 percent thought that sex was very important. Ninety-four percent, about equally divided between men and women, agreed with the statement: "Enjoyable sexual relations add to a person's quality of life."

The story was reported under the headline, "Good Sex Beats Good Job, but Family Ranks First." Having asked thousands of people about their desires for sex and family, I do not believe for a moment that the headline is a valid description of the relative importance of these desires. If family were a stronger desire than sex, few societies would need to adopt social policies to punish parents who have abandoned their responsibilities to their children. Furthermore, statistics on teenage pregnancy suggest that some men are much more motivated to have sex than they are to raise the child who is born as a consequence. History teaches that infanticide was common during ancient times—and still may exist in some primitive societies today—and social researchers say that child abuse remains far too common. People beat children, burn them, and kill them. Given these facts, I do not see how anybody could suggest that family is the greatest desire and is preferred by 99 percent of the population.

How did this poll produce such flawed findings? It is because the results depend entirely on how the questions were worded. Although virtually everybody endorses the statement, "sex is important," only a minority of people endorse the statement, "sex is the most important goal in my life," and hardly anybody endorses the statement "I would rather die than live without sex." Although nearly everybody agrees that "family is important," fewer people agree that "my children are the most important people in my life," and even fewer would say, "my greatest goal is to raise children." Depending on how the questions are worded, the results of a poll could show that family is more important than sex, or that sex is more important than family, or that both are important to 99 percent of the population, or that the majority of people do not think that either is important.

The research methods that Susan and I used to study basic desires were very different from those used in a consumer poll. We began by developing a comprehensive list of all the important goals we could think of. Over a period of about three months, we asked friends and colleagues to help us develop the list. We included only those goals that people might intrinsically value and that we considered psychologically significant. We placed more than 400 goals on our initial list—far too many to be of practical use in analyzing human behavior. We pared the list down to 328 goals by eliminating apparent redundancies and psychologically insignificant goals that account for a relatively small amount of our behavior. We cut out many basic biological needs, such as drinking water, because they are not relevant for understanding who we are. People spend relatively little time drinking water, and the behavior of drinking water is very similar from one person to the next. Our culture says very little if anything about drinking water. Although drinking water is important in biology and essential for life, it is not important in psychology. In contrast, eating is an important topic in psychology. People spend a great deal of time preparing and consuming food, many cultures and religions have dietary rules, and many people have eating disorders. Since our eating habits are important to who we are, but our habits of drinking water are not, we kept on our list the desire to eat but we eliminated the desire to drink water.

We then asked a group of 401 adolescents and adults from diverse stations in life to rate how much they like or dislike each of the remaining 328 items. The participants were sampled from six sources (three universities, a high school, a seminar for persons in community agencies serving people with mental retardation, and a church group) in Ohio and in Pennsylvania. About one-third of the participants were male, and three-fourths were under the age of 55. A total of about 10 percent were African-American, Asian-American, or Hispanic. The participants did not represent a random sample of a population of interest because that is rarely required for the kind of research that we did; generally, it is sufficient to work with a group of at least 300 people of diverse backgrounds, ages, and ethnic groups.[10] The results of the research have been reproduced three times with different samples from various parts of the United States and Canada.

After the data we received from questioning the 401 participants were entered in a computer, we used a mathematical technique called *factor analysis* to search for the root meanings of people's responses to our questionnaires. We instructed the computer to reduce the 328 goals to 10 categories based on root meanings. The computer evaluated thousands of possible ways to do this and then selected the 10 categories that embraced the largest number of goals. We then started all over again, this time instructing the computer to create 11 categories of desires based on root meanings. Again, thousands of possible root meanings and combinations were evaluated and compared until the 11 categories that embraced the largest number of goals were found. The process was repeated for up to 20 categories of desires. We then studied each result to determine which one offered the most powerful categories of basic desires based on root meanings. Eventually, our results showed that 15 or 16 categories summarized the 328 goals with an unusual degree of accuracy and comprehensiveness. Adding another category gave us only slightly greater accuracy, which was not worth the added complexity of a seventeenth category. Using only 14 categories left out several important basic desires. The results were clear: about 16 categories was the best description of basic motivation.

Once we had identified the 16 basic categories of human motivation, we conducted research designed to measure these categories in the most efficient and accurate manner. This work used literally thousands of additional research volunteers from many walks of life, and resulted in the Reiss Profile of Fundamental Goals and Motivational Sensitivities, a 128-item questionnaire, or psychological test, that takes about 15 minutes to complete and can reveal a person's hierarchy of desires and motives. This test enables us to study motivation comprehensively (we can profile 16 categories of goals), objectively (our questionnaire not only meets but exceeds conventional requirements for a standardized test), and scientifically (our conclusions lead to numerous predictions so that people can accept or reject our ideas based on what they themselves can observe). The Reiss Profile is a reliable tool that can help us understand relationships, choose jobs, figure out why our kids do what they do, and analyze personality problems.

The Reiss Profile can help you identify your most important basic desires. Professional ethics restrict the use of the test to professionals who have expertise in how to score and interpret it. However, I have developed for this book a series of general questions that will help you find those basic desires that are most and least important in driving your behavior. These questions are presented in Chapters 2, 3, and 4, and are summarized in the Appendix.

If you wish to take the test itself, you may do so through a licensed psychologist, school counselor, vocational counselor, or marriage counselor.

People who are skeptical about the validity of psychological tests have asked Susan and me how we know that the research participants answered our questionnaire truthfully. We completed the studies twice—first by asking people to rate themselves, and a second time by asking observers to rate them. We received similar results from both the self-report and observer methods. Further, we administered psychological tests of faking to our subjects. The results showed only trivial levels of faking, indicating that the subjects did not become defensive when we asked them about their desires. Based on these considerations, we can be confident that people responded accurately to our questionnaires.

Along similar lines, we are often asked if the answers people give on the Reiss Profile have any significance beyond the test itself. "Maybe people are just saying things that have no relationship to how they actually behave," some people say. This is a valid point. All psychological tests need to be studied carefully to determine the degree of correspondence between the answers provided on the test and the actual behavior of the people in the "real world."

Susan and I, and others, have been looking carefully into this issue of the predictive value of test scores. Generally, our results are showing a good degree of predictability. How a person scores on the Reiss Profile can predict such important behaviors as a person's college major, membership in a club or interest group, and scores on various other psychological tests known to be valid measures of personality or anxiety. Later in this book I present evidence that Reiss Profile scores can predict how religious or athletic a person is, perhaps imperfectly, but at a statistically significant, above-chance level. The scores also vary systematically with the presence of certain genetically determined clinical disorders. Based on this evidence, it is unlikely that a person's scores on the Reiss Profile are unrelated to that person's behavior. Research evidence shows that this is not true of large numbers of test-takers.

In this book, I use the term *basic desires* to refer to the 16 categories of goals that were the result of our research. By definition, a basic desire is a category of more narrowly defined goals and motives that have a common theme. Further, each basic desire is largely unrelated to all other basic desires.[11]

MEANS AND ENDS

When I discuss basic desires in this book, I am always referring to end goals. The idea of an end goal dates back to Aristotle (384 B.C.–322 B.C.), who divided human motives into means and ends. *Means* are things done because they produce something else, whereas *ends* are what we intrinsically value (desire for its own sake). For example, when a person swims for the fun of it, swimming is an end. When a swimmer competes in a meet, however, swimming is an intermediate step toward the end goal of winning the competition. In order to understand why people swim for the fun of it, we need to study the basic desire for physical exercise. In order to understand why people want to win swim meets, however, we need to study the motive of competition (which falls under the basic desire for vengeance.)

Aristotle noted that means are intermediate steps toward accomplishing a goal, whereas ends are the last step, or the ultimate goal. Although the number of means in life is limited only by our imagination, the number of potential ends is determined by genetics. The questions Susan and I asked ourselves, therefore, are how many ends guide our behavior and what they are.[12]

There is more to the idea of an end goal than meets the eye. End goals are just that, namely, the end of an explanation of human behavior, and this point is often misunderstood. For example, I had a discussion with a colleague concerning my idea that vengeance is an end goal. I was talking about Eric Harris and Dylan Klebold, the two students who opened fire on their classmates and teachers at Columbine High School in Littleton, Colorado.

"The students' behavior can be explained as vengeance," I asserted.

"They obviously wanted vengeance," declared the colleague. "A four-year-old could figure that out. There must have also been more at work than that—maybe they were brutally attacked as children and were trying to get even with the attacker. Maybe their parents made them feel unim-

BASIC DESIRE	END GOALS
Power	Achievement, competence, leadership
Independence	Freedom, ego integrity
Curiosity	Knowledge, truth
Acceptance	Positive self-image, self-worth
Order	Cleanliness, stability, organization
Saving	Collection, property
Honor	Morality, character, loyalty
Idealism	Fairness, justice
Social contact	Friendship, fun
Family	Children
Status	Wealth, titles, attention, awards
Vengeance	Winning, aggression
Romance	Beauty, sex
Eating	Food, dining, hunting
Physical exercise	Fitness
Tranquility	Relaxation, safety

portant and powerless, and they were trying to prove their worth or get attention."

"Simplicity is a virtue in explaining behavior," I protested. "When I say that vengeance is an end goal, I mean it has intrinsic value. Although we hate to admit it, getting even is fun for many people and a need for many others. In the warped minds of the attackers, they were having 'fun.'"

"But people are interested in the non-obvious, in what is hidden below the surface," the colleague persisted. "Everybody knows that the students killed out of vengeance."

"But everybody does not realize that there might be no deeper explanation. The desire to get even is a basic human need. It may have been stronger in these two students than in most people. These people were born to hate."

There is no obvious way to predict such behavior before it happens, but the system of 16 basic desires predicts certain behaviors better than any other tool I know. If you want to predict who will become a hater, look at who strongly values vengeance. People who say they strongly value vengeance as its own reward—for no other purpose—are your current or future haters. Of course, knowing that somebody is born to hate does not mean that the person will become a killer, but I suspect it is an important first step in that direction.

WHY SURVIVAL, WEALTH, AND EVEN KNOWING GOD ARE NOT BASIC DESIRES

One of the first questions that occurs to many people when they look at the list of 16 basic desires is, "Why didn't you include the desire for survival? Or the desire for money? Or the desire for shelter?" Many people think, "I have a real need for the presence of God in my life. Isn't religion a basic desire?" These are certainly valid questions.

Our research on basic desires was aimed at finding the fundamental psychological elements of meaningful experiences. We sought a list of desires that would allow us to take a totality—for example, a romantic relationship or satisfaction with a job—and analyze it into its psychologically meaningful components. In a sense, we are looking for the building blocks of psychological meaning.

Although the desire to know God is a profoundly meaningful experience, it cannot be reduced to one part of a totality. Rather, the desire to know God is the totality itself. In this book, I treat spirituality as a totality and show how it is connected to all 16 basic desires.

Spirituality is such a deeply personal feeling that some readers might agree with my position while others might disagree. Whatever your initial reaction, I hope you hold off coming to a firm conclusion until you have read Chapter 12.

What about the will to survive? It does not meet the criteria for a basic desire for the following reasons: First, it is not unrelated to the other basic desires. Eating and the will to survive, for example, are not unrelated. When a person no longer cares if he or she lives, the person may not care about eating. Second, little meaningful behavior can be explained in terms of the will to live, and by definition, a motive must have significant explanatory value to be considered a basic desire. Look at the topics that comprise what we call psychology—relationships, family, human growth, mental illness, and so on. The will to live is not highly relevant to these topics. Biologists talk much more about the will to live than do psychologists. If you want to understand meaningful human behavior—and to keep the list of basic desires to a workable minimum—the will to live lacks the generality of explanatory significance needed to make the list.

Since the need for shelter, which helps us maintain a constant body temperature, has little significance in explaining human behavior, it was not included in our initial list of 328 goals, and it is not considered a basic desire. Shelter doesn't motivate much behavior; for example, it is not relevant to interpersonal communication, romantic relationships, parent-child relationships, career counseling, spirituality, or mental illness. Again, the desire for shelter is more relevant to biology than it is to psychology.

What about the yearning for wealth, or for freedom? As we shall see, these motives are included in the 16 basic desires. The desire to be wealthy for the sake of being rich falls under the desire for status, and the desire for freedom falls under the desire for independence.

Keep in mind that the system of 16 basic desires is a scientific theory. In the final analysis, what matters is the factual validity of the theory and how accurately the 16 desires can be used to predict behavior.

Some readers may enjoy trying to think of a seventeenth desire that Susan and I overlooked. For readers who are interested in this challenge, here are the ground rules. You need to look at these criteria:

1. The desire you are thinking of must be valued intrinsically rather than for its effects on something else. That is, it must be sought for its own sake.

2. The desire must have explanatory significance for understanding the lives of nearly everyone.

3. The desire must be largely unconnected to the 16 basic desires already on the list.

Only if all three of these criteria are met can we consider the possibility of a seventeenth basic desire. And if all three ground rules are met, we must still determine if a system of 17 basic desires can predict meaningful behavior significantly more accurately than can the present system of 16 basic desires. Although not impossible, it is a formidable challenge to be able to find a desire that should be added to our list.

Why My Dog
Saves Socks

This chapter and the next two are devoted to a detailed discussion of each of the 16 basic desires that make our lives meaningful. Once you learn how to identify the desires, you will see many examples of them in your life.

An important part of these three chapters is the specific questions intended to help you determine whether a particular desire is very important, important, or less important in your life or the life of a person of interest to you. What you are looking for in trying to understand a person—yourself, a significant other, a friend, or someone from work—are those basic desires that are *very* important to the individual and those that are *less* important. In contrast, the ones that are of *average* importance are of little consequence. You can use the form on page 261 to keep track of your answers, which you can chart after you have rated yourself on all 16 basic desires.

In determining your "desire profile," you'll probably find that anywhere from 3 to 10 of the desires are very important to you. You shouldn't expect to have strong feelings about every desire; most people are motivated strongly by only a few of the 16.

Let's begin our discussion with the desire for power.

POWER

We all desire a certain amount of power, which is the desire for influence (to impose one's will on others or on the environment.) Power creates a periodic need to experience feelings of mastery and competence, and it motivates efforts to pursue challenges, ambitions, excellence, and glory. In animals, power is expressed primarily as dominance behavior. Animals who can dominate others will push them away from scarce food, increasing their own chances for survival. Power has been suggested to be an aphrodisiac in animals, although scientists now say that this may often not be true.

J. Edgar Hoover (1895–1972) was an excellent example of someone who had a strong desire for power throughout his adult life.[1] He liked the following peom, which idealized power:

> . . . *only the Strong shall thrive;*
> *That surely the weak shall perish, and only*
> *the fit survive.*

Hoover was named Director of the Federal Bureau of Investigation (FBI) on December 10, 1924, and held the position until his death in 1972. He built the agency into a significant arm of the federal government. Early in his career, he learned how to create a secret system of files that few in government could access. Under the guise of investigating subversive activity, he ordered FBI agents to conduct political espionage.

Hoover became so powerful that even U.S. presidents were afraid to fire him. When President Lyndon B. Johnson was asked about his support of Hoover, he explained, "I'd rather have him inside the tent pissing out than outside the tent pissing in."[2] President Richard Nixon worried that if he fired Hoover, "We may have on our hands here a man who will pull down the temple with him, including me. . . ."[3] The presidents came and went, but Hoover stayed as captain of a federal police force with semi-secret activities.

As shown by Hoover's example, the desire for power can be so strong that it dominates an individual's personality. Powerful people intrinsically enjoy imposing their will on others. They can be as tough as nails when running an office, business, military unit, or other agency.

The desire for power can be satisfied in a number of ways. One of the most common is through achievements, both great and small. This is because achievements are a form of influence. For example, powerful people enjoy having impact on a profession by becoming great lawyers, baseball players, doctors, artists, or musicians. When the desire for power is more ordinary, so are the person's ambitions, such as the ambitions of doing well in a bowling league, finishing a local marathon, or building a wooden table.

Leadership is another common way of satisfying the desire for power. Powerful people like to be in charge of things. When a person who has a strong desire for power lacks the social skills necessary to influence other people gracefully, the individual will simply dominate them. Powerful people, for example, often are described as authoritarian, domineering, autocratic, manipulative, and exploitative. They take command at both home and work, telling everybody what to do and how it should be done. They even dominate conversations, sometimes speaking loudly so they can be overheard by (and influence) others not part of the conversation. As the nineteenth-century philosopher George Ramsay put it, some people cannot bear to see a person going in one direction without urging him or her to go in another.[4]

Some people are essentially addicted to power. Napoleon Bonaparte was not satisfied when he became the ruler of France; he wanted even more power. He conquered one country after another until he was stopped at the battle of Waterloo. Generally, powerful people are willful and determined.

The psychoanalyst Alfred Adler argued that power is the overarching psychological goal of all people.[5] He thought that infants and children develop an unconscious feeling of inferiority because they compare themselves to their bigger, more powerful parents. He concluded that people spend their adolescent and adult lives striving for superior power to compensate for these deep-seated feelings of inferiority.

According to the system of 16 basic desires, nobody desires to experience power every moment; instead, what we desire is a certain amount of power. When we experience more power than we want, we may seek out the opposite experience, submission, to restore the desired balance. A good case in point is the businessman who is the boss at work but behaves submissively at times at home or who prefers to be submissive sexually. Each of us is an individual in terms of how much power we seek and how often we use submission for balancing purposes.

Rate your desire for power as *very important* to you if any of the following statements is generally true:

1. You are highly ambitious compared with other people your age.

2. You usually seek leadership roles.

3. You usually dominate in social situations with people your age.

Rate your desire for power as *less important* to you if either of the following statements is generally true:

1. You are noticeably less ambitious than other people your age.

2. Generally, you prefer being submissive in social situations.

Rate your desire for power as of *average importance* if you have not rated it as very important or less important, or if you have endorsed statements indicating that power is both very and less important to you. After you have rated yourself, you may wish to rate the other people in your family or life. Keep track of the ratings on page 261 and refer back to them when you read Part II of this book.

INDEPENDENCE

Independence, the desire for self-reliance, creates a periodic need to feel free.[6] Its primal roots are instincts that drive animals to leave the nest and set out on their own. This gives the species a better chance of survival by increasing the territory over which food is sought. In human beings, independence prods adolescents to set out from their parents' home and make homes of their own. Independence is what may motivate a teenager to get his own car and become "his own person;" unfortunately, it does not necessarily motivate him to get his own job, which some parents view as a defect of the evolutionary process regarding this desire.

People who are highly independent-minded generally dislike having to rely on others to meet their needs. Although most students appreciate help from a teacher, independent-minded students prefer to do things with minimal or no assistance. They especially dislike receiving assistance for anything they feel they can do by themselves. It is very important to them that their term papers or class projects reflect their own ideas and their own work.

I witnessed a memorable example of a fiercely independent child while I was waiting in line to buy a plane ticket. A six-foot man in line in front of me accidentally moved ahead of a four-year-old child with his mother. The child, who barely made it up to the man's kneecap, indignantly yelled "Hey," pushed the man's knee, and tried to reestablish his ground. This child's natural tendency was to defend his turf by himself, fearlessly ignoring the obvious difference in size between himself and the man.

Because independence is a basic desire, there is a natural tendency for some people to resent people who help them. Helpers may mean well, but they can frustrate our desire for independence. Similarly, children resent parents who discourage them from growing up and becoming independent. This resentment is called *dependent hostility,* meaning anger directed at those who keep us in a state of dependency.

Elderly people who are independent-minded can hate becoming residents of nursing homes, where they will be dependent on nurses and others. If they become bedridden, they must wait for an aide to get them a drink of water or to take them to the bathroom. For people who dislike being in need of others, such experiences can be humiliating.

Many people do not want to become as indepedent as possible; rather, they seek a certain degree of independence with which they are comfortable. When we encounter situations that require us to be more independent than we want to be, we temporarily experience freedom as more of a burden than a joy. We can use *interdependent* relationships to balance the feeling of too much freedom. A capitalist who must be very self-reliant at work, for example, can easily experience a burdensome level of freedom. A common antidote is a supportive spouse or family who provide feelings of interdependence to balance things out by the end of the day or week. How much freedom is too much depends entirely on the individual. Both independence (the joy of self-reliance) and interdependence (the joy of trusting others to help us) are normal, healthy states.

Is psychological independence consistent with romantic love? Can we love someone and yet desire to be separate (independent) from him or her? Or does true love necessarily motivate us to want to become one with the person we love? Canadian psychologists Kenneth L. and Karen K. Dion have taken a thoughtful look at these questions.[7] They suspect that true romance can imply a desire to lose one's independence and unite with another. Lovers can desire to reduce to zero the psychological distance between them, replacing the intrinsic value of independence with the interdependence of romantic love.

L. Takeo Doi, the Japanese psychiatrist, has discussed the concept of *amae,* which means to presume another's benevolence.[8] According to Doi, amae has a positive connotation in Japan. The Japanese recognize the desire for interdependence as an accepted part of intimate relationships. This viewpoint implies that the use of interdependence to balance feelings of freedom is a culturally influenced behavior. The theory of 16 basic desires essentially embraces this viewpoint.

Rate your desire for independence as *very important* to you if either of the following statements is generally true:

1. You usually resist advice and guidance from others.

2. Self-reliance is essential to your happiness.

Rate your desire for independence as *less important* to you if either of the following statements is generally true:

1. Compared to other people your age, you are noticeably more devoted to your spouse or partner.

2. You dislike being on your own.

Rate your desire for independence as of *average importance* if you have not rated it as very important or less important, or if you have endorsed statements indicating that independence is both very and less important to you. After you have rated yourself, you may wish to rate the other people in your family or life. Keep track of the ratings on page 261 and refer to them when you read Part II.

CURIOSITY

Curiosity, which is the desire to learn for learning's own sake, is one of the great joys in life. It prods animals both to explore environments and to learn from experience. By exploring environments, animals can find food, water, and other essential materials. Learned habits help animals gather food more efficiently and avoid danger. In human beings, curiosity includes the desires to read, write, and think, in addition to the primal desire to explore new places.

Benjamin Franklin, one of our country's founding fathers, was an excellent example of a highly curious person.[9] Throughout his life, Franklin loved to read and write, and he had a phenomenal memory. He studied philosophy and enjoyed intellectual debate and conversation. He founded a debating club in 1727, started a printing business in 1728, and became a newspaper publisher in 1729. He started the first subscription library in North America in 1731, and a year later he published the first edition of *Poor Richard: An Almanac.* He invented the Franklin stove, and founded what is now the University of Pennsylvania. Franklin had such an active mind that he was still publishing one month before he died at age 84.

Abraham Lincoln is another example of a highly curious person. "He wanted to learn, to know, to live, to reach out; he wanted to satisfy hungers and thirsts he couldn't tell about."[10] As a child, he borrowed books from his neighbors and read them from cover to cover. As a teenager, he borrowed the textbooks of neighbors who returned from college. He boasted that he had read Aesop's *Fables* so often he could rewrite the text from memory without loss of a single word.

Curiosity should not be confused with intelligence. Intelligence refers to how easily a person learns things, whereas curiosity refers to how much a person *enjoys* the process of learning.

Nor should it be confused with the desire for achievement. As noted previously, achievement motivation is part of the desire for power (the joy of having influence), which is largely unrelated to the desire for curiosity. The need to get straight A's (indicating a desire for power) is very different from the need to understand how things work (indicating curiosity). An achievement-oriented child may want to read only those books that are required by a teacher as part of a formal class, whereas a curious child wants to read any interesting book. If schools gave no diplomas, curious people would show up anyway, hoping to learn and enjoy themselves.

Truth-seeking is perhaps the purest example of curiosity. The curious person is not satisfied with the joy of intellectual activity, but feels an additional need to distinguish between truth and falsehood. Some professors who have a thirst for knowledge do not like to play bridge, chess, or other intellectual games because the games do not involve a search for truth. The search for truth can dominate a person's life. Teachers who want to mark children for future success in academia should look for truth-seekers, because they have the motivation required to make years of sacrifice to discover something.

Highly curious people are intellectual forces. They have an enormous desire to analyze things, and they want to think about virtually everything imaginable. Leonard, for example, is one of the most curious people I have ever met. A professor at one of the world's best universities, he rises early and goes to work, where he teaches, reads, and thinks about his research. When he meets a colleague in the elevator, he discusses the person's latest book. When he cannot be found in his office writing and thinking, he is in class lecturing or answering undergraduates' questions. Dinner, for him, is an opportunity to meet with a colleague and learn about the person's latest research. A vacation is an opportunity to explore a national forest or visit a European city to learn about its rich history. Most people would find such a lifestyle too intellectually intense. Leonard devotes nearly ten hours a day to learning, whereas I suspect many people would rather devote about half an hour a day to it.

When our learning experiences are more intense than we enjoy, we try to balance things by engaging in mindless or frivolous activities. A good example is the high school or college student on summer break or during the week following final examinations. The vast majority head for the beaches, movie theaters, athletic fields, and so on, where they aim to party, play, or exercise. For the time being, these students have had their fill of learning, and it is only after a long break that their curiosity will, hopefully, emerge anew.

Curiosity is a psychologically significant motive; young people spend a third of their waking hours in school and doing homework, and adults frequently seek out clubs or programs to learn new skills. Scientific curiosity, or the desire to explore new ideas, has produced much of our technology. On an everyday basis, people like to think about the meaning in their lives or to debate politics.

Rate curiosity as *very important* in guiding your behavior if any of the following statements are generally true:

1. You have a thirst for knowledge.

2. Compared to your peers, you ask a lot of questions.

3. You think a lot about what is true.

Rate your curiosity as *less important* in guiding your behavior if either of the following statements is true:

1. You dislike intellectual activities.

2. You rarely ask questions.

Rate your curiosity as of *average importance* if you have not rated it as very important or less important, or if you have endorsed statements indicating that curiosity is both very and less important to you. After you have rated yourself, you may wish to rate the other people in your family or life. Keep track of the ratings on page 261 and refer to them when you read Part II.

ACCEPTANCE

Acceptance, the desire for inclusion, motivates people to avoid rejection and criticism. Its primal origins are unclear. Although pets clearly react to being accepted or rejected by their owners, I cannot say with any confidence that such behavior expresses what I mean by acceptance. As I use the term, I am referring to a desire that is closely associated with our self-concept and self-esteem.

We all need to be accepted for who we are. This is the greatest gift parents can give to their children because it is what children need most. Accepted children develop a basic sense of self-confidence and worth, whereas rejected children lack self-confidence and feel unworthy. Parents who reject their children virtually guarantee that their children will have significant psychological adjustment problems for a large part of their childhood and probably much longer. Peer and community acceptance also are important for healthy development.

People who are strongly motivated to seek acceptance tend to lack self-confidence, feel insecure, and show anxiety in social situations. They seek a high degree of acceptance from others. They overreact to criticism, going to unusual lengths to avoid situations in which they might be evaluated. For example, some children rarely raise their hands in class for fear of giving the wrong answer and being rejected by the teacher or class. Many adolescent boys miss opportunities to ask girls for dates because they are afraid and shy. Some adults do not try for promotions or challenging jobs because they are afraid of being rejected. Some people stop trying to make themselves physically attractive—they let themselves gain weight, or wear unflattering clothes. Since they are not trying to look good, expectations are low and rejection loses some of its sting.

Child psychiatrist Stella Chess reported a case example of Allen, a boy who was highly sensitive to rejection and criticism.[11] Even minor criticism caused him to quit an activity. He stopped playing basketball when he missed some shots, and he dropped academic projects when his teachers pointed out small errors. In play therapy, Alan did fine until something went wrong, after which he became upset and wanted to stop playing. Although his parents and teachers had assured him that his mistakes were minor, he felt they were terribly significant.

Interestingly, the desire for acceptance is the only basic desire that is closely related to a person's self-concept or self-esteem. Originally, Susan and I had thought that people showed three distinct desires: the desire for positive self-regard, the need to be romantically loved by someone, and the need to minimize criticism. These expectations were not borne out in our studies. Instead of a number of desires expressing issues psychologists generally associate with the self-concept, our results indicated only one such desire. If future researchers succeed in demonstrating a seventeenth basic desire, my guess is that it will be a desire closely linked to self-concept issues but clearly distinct from the desire for acceptance.

Many common examples show how the desire for acceptance can lead to an undue sensitivity to criticism. For example, some people are afraid to speak up in a restaurant when served cold or poorly prepared food. Rather than complain about it, they say nothing to avoid conflict with the waiter. They are afraid that the waiter will not accept them if they complain. Another common example is when a person is nonassertive with a car mechanic. The mechanic tells the person that it will cost $125 to fix the car, but when the bill is presented later, it is for $175. The nonassertive person does not ask about the discrepancy, instead avoids conflict and the possibility of being disliked or criticized by the mechanic.

Sensitivity to rejection is sometimes the root cause of extreme shyness. Some shy people are quick to think that they are being criticized or that other people are noticing their negative features or qualities. They indulge in negative thinking about what other people conclude about them, and they often are afraid to speak in public.

The desire for acceptance can lead to test anxiety in schoolchildren and college students. Students may worry that if their grades do not meet expectations, they face a loss of acceptance from parents, teachers, or peers. Advocates of the self-esteem movement have sought to protect children from test anxiety by rigging success, not giving tests, or not grading tests. According to the results of a recent study by Ohio State University graduate student Linda Park and myself, however, protecting children from failure may not lead to lessened test anxiety. Test anxiety, we found, had little to do with how much failure students had experienced and everything to do with how much pressure they put on themselves to perform. An honor student who never fails a test can show much more test anxiety than a juvenile delinquent who only rarely passes tests: The honor student can worry that a grade of "B" will precipitate criticism, whereas the juvenile delinquent figures that another failed test will cause no additional loss of acceptance or esteem. These results suggest the futility of trying to protect children from the possibility of failing or doing poorly on a test; what is needed to reduce test anxiety and improve esteem is to teach students that poor test performance will not lead to a loss of acceptance among those who really matter in their lives.

The desire for acceptance is evident in any group that has been stigmatized or excluded from society. A good case in point is the group of people who have mental retardation. These people have feelings just like everybody else, but often they are treated as if they have no feelings at all. They are criticized for having low IQs with epithets such as "retard" and "dummy." Many people with mental retardation develop an extreme sensitivity to such criticism. They become so insecure that they rely on other people to help them even when help is not needed, a phenomenon called "outerdirectedness" by Yale University Professor of Psychology Edward Zigler.[12] "Call me anything you want," one young man once told me, "but don't call me retarded."

Rate acceptance as *very important* to you if any of the following statements is generally true:

1. You usually set easy goals for yourself.

2. You are a quitter.

3. You have great difficulty coping with criticism.

Rate acceptance as *less important* to you if either of the following statements is true:

1. You have a lot of self-confidence.

2. You handle criticism noticeably better than most people—that is, you do not become unduly upset.

Rate your desire for acceptance as of *average importance* to you if you have not rated it as very important or less important, or if you have endorsed statements indicating that acceptance is both very and less important to you. After you have rated yourself, you may wish to rate the other people in your family or life. Keep track of the ratings on page 261 and refer to them when you read Part II.

ORDER

The desire for order is apparent when we organize things, make plans, make up a schedule, write down a list, set rules, and make things neat or clean. Its primal roots are in cleaning rituals, which are seen in many animal species. Dogs and cats, for example, lick themselves clean. The survival value of these rituals is apparent—they prevent disease. In human beings, order includes the enjoyment of rituals and traditions. Order gives people a sense of stability and control. The absence of order can be upsetting because it implies chaos, unpredictability, and flux.

Each person has a certain degree of order with which he or she feels most comfortable. Organized people are those who prefer a relatively high degree of order, whereas flexible people are those who prefer a low degree of order. When the amount of order we experience is other than what we prefer, we are motivated to reestablish the desired level. When we have experienced more order than we desire, we seek out activities with a high degree of ambiguity, such as playing a game of chance; when we have experienced less order than we desire, we try to reduce unpredictability in our daily life, perhaps by making a list of things to do.

In the movie *The Odd Couple*, Felix Unger and Oscar Madison provide a good example of two people with dramatically opposite degrees of desire for order. Felix has moved into the apartment of his good friend Oscar because his wife can no longer put up with him. Oscar is a slob, but Felix is neat as can be. Oscar leaves spilled milk in the refrigerator and a pile of dirty dishes in the sink, and wipes greasy fingers on his shirt. He keeps no discernible schedule, sometimes eating dinner as late as 3 A.M. Felix follows a precise schedule, squares pictures hanging on walls, and lives by inflexible rules. He wears a formal shirt and tie to poker games, disinfects the air after people smoke, and even cleans and disinfects the playing cards. When the two of them live together, Oscar cannot relax in his own home, and Felix feels that Oscar doesn't appreciate his efforts to keep the house clean and organized. Oscar becomes more and more angry while Felix struggles to maintain control.

"I put order into this house," Felix boasts.

"You're not going to make any effort to change? This is the person you'll be till the day you die?" asks Oscar.

"We are what we are," replies Felix.

My wife, Maggi, and I provide another example of two people who differ in how much order we desire. Maggi pays attention to details and likes to organize and clean. Whenever she gets nervous, she will straighten things. She has developed detailed schedules by which various things in our house are periodically cleaned.

In contrast, I have a very high desire for flexibility (low desire for order) and a high tolerance of ambiguity. It astonishes me that Maggi or anybody else would even think to spend time developing a cleaning schedule for a house. I hate planning so much that I don't even enjoy planning a vacation. My preference is to get on a plane or drive a car wherever I feel like going on the day I start my vacation. I like being disorganized.

I sometimes avoid doing things if it requires that I develop a plan. When I started writing this book, I just went at it and only developed a plan after I had already written a draft of the entire book. I also dislike rigid rules. I realize that rules are important, but I like to interpret them flexibly. I have great trouble following a daily schedule. Whenever anything is well organized, it makes me feel uncomfortable.

The desire for order has explanatory significance in psychology. Differences in how strongly people desire order can be a major source of conflict in relationships and families. "Odd Couple" spouses will argue over how clean or messy the house is. If a highly organized parent sets many rules and rigidly enforces them, a child may rebel. When a boss is disorganized, he or she creates stress for subordinates who hate ambiguity. Furthermore, very strong desires for order are associated with obsessive-compulsive disorder (OCD). OCD is an anxiety disorder in which a person's extreme concerns about cleanliness or ritual interfere with his or her ability to meet the obligations of everyday life.

Rate your desire for order as *very important* in your life if any of the following statements is generally true:

1. You are noticeably more organized than most people.

2. You have many rules and try to follow them religiously.

3. You enjoy cleaning up.

Rate your desire for order as *less important* in your life if either of the following statements is generally true:

1. Your office/workplace is usually a mess.

2. You hate planning.

Rate your desire for order as of *average importance* if you have not rated it as very important or less important, or if you have endorsed statements indicating that order is both very and less important to you. After you have rated yourself, you may wish to rate the other people in your family or life. Keep track of the ratings on page 261 and refer to them when you read Part II.

SAVING

Saving is the desire for collecting. Its primal origins are animal instincts to hoard food and materials essential for survival.[13] In human beings, this desire motivates people to save money and to hoard items of interest. It makes frugality an intrinsic value.

The value of frugality motivates us not to waste anything, not even time. Frugal people aim to save everything and throw away nothing, so long as it is possible to make any use of it at all, however trifling that use may be. They try to save money, no matter how much or little they have to live on. Savers tend to have few or no credit cards, and when they do, the cards are usually from the less expensive stores.

An excellent example of the attitude of a saver was expressed by the book *The American Frugal Housewife,* first published in 1828. This book was intended to help people overcome what the author, a Mrs. Child, saw as the greatest national problem of the 1820–1830 era in America, namely, extravagant family spending. "There is no subject so much connected with individual happiness and national prosperity," observed Mrs. Child.[14] What is wrong with the country, she explained, was that few young people had learned the virtue of saving. She could barely contain herself when she saw a 16-year-old girl playing a piano while the girl's mother was sewing. Mrs. Child asked why the family did not have a more profitable use for the girl's time. Mrs. Child was not much impressed with what was happening with American boys in the 1820s, either. She told the tale of a lad who was too embarrassed to return bottles to the grocer. Another sure sign of the erosion of American values, thought Mrs. Child.

Each individual is most comfortable with a certain balance between frugality and extravagance. People who have a strong desire for saving favor frugality, and those in whom this desire is weak favor extravagance. When experience is significantly different from the desired balance, people are motivated to save or to spend to restore the balance.

Misers are people dominated by the desire to save. Hetty Green, for example, was one of the richest women in America at the beginning of this century. Her net worth was more than 110 million dollars, a near-inconceivably vast sum at the time. Yet she refused to hire a doctor when her son, Ned, dislocated his knee in a sledding accident.[15] Although she believed in medicine, she was too "frugal" to hire a doctor. She gave Ned homemade remedies which, unfortunately, did not work. When Ned lost his leg, Hetty became upset, but apparently not as upset as she would have been if she had had to pay for a doctor.

My dog, Rusty, saves socks. I don't understand why he does it, but the activity is very important to him. Rusty will quickly sneak into rooms when a person is taking a shower. He'll make off with the person's socks, and take them under the dining room table, where he collects them. Rusty guards his socks the way a miser guards money. He growls if anybody comes near his cache.

These examples show that collecting can be its own reward. Hetty collected dollars, and Rusty collects socks. Other people collect antiques, art, autographs, automobiles, books,[16] clothes, coins, firearms, furniture, jewelry, magazines, military memorabilia, music, photographs, sports memorabilia (such as baseball cards), stamps, tools, or toys.

Some marketers have tried to take advantage of the joy of collecting while promoting their products. During the 1950s, for example, consumers collected "green stamps" when they made purchases at participating stores. The stamps were pasted into books and saved until a consumer had enough (perhaps 50 to 100 books) to exchange for a prize, such as a toaster, lamp, or radio. Recently, McDonald's Beanie Babies have become collectors' items. Some people save airline frequent-flyer miles not just because they can exchange them for trips, but because they enjoy the act of collecting the credits.

The pursuit of wealth comes under the desire for saving, but it must be analyzed in each individual case if it is to be properly understood. Sometimes the end goal of wealth is saving, but other times it is status. When people save money to watch their bank accounts grow—like Hetty Green or the Charles Dickens character Scrooge—the end goal is saving. When people save money to buy expensive things or to impress others with their wealth, the end goal is status.

Culture and experience can have a strong influence on attitudes toward saving. Today, Americans have a relatively low saving rate compared with people from other nations. Modern baby boomers save a lower percentage of their incomes than did their parents. Some experts say that it is our consumer-oriented economy that has led to the low savings rate, but others attribute it to people's confidence that our relatively prosperous economy will remain strong.

The desire to save is a psychologically significant motive that can explain meaningful behavior. For example, many married couples quarrel over how much money to save and how much to spend. One spouse may want to buy a new car, but the other may think it more prudent to save the money. The psychological significance of saving is also suggested by economic theory. Capitalism for example, requires a populace that is willing to save and invest its money. Furthermore, some experts say that OCD symptoms can be motivated by a very strong desire to hoard.

Rate your desire for saving as *very important* to you if any of the following statements is generally true:

1. You are a collector.

2. You are a miser.

3. You are noticeably more tight with your money than other people are with their money.

Rate this desire as *less important* to you if either of the following statements is generally true:

1. You are a free spender.

2. You rarely save anything at all.

Rate your desire for saving as of *average importance* if you have not rated it as very important or less important, or if you have endorsed statements indicating that the desire to save is both very and less important to you. After you have rated yourself, you may wish to rate the other people in your family or life. Keep track of the ratings on page 261 and refer to them when you read Part II.

Why Kids and Elephants
Will Make You Wet

Five basic desires that pertain mostly to social behavior—honor, idealism, social contact, family, and status—are discussed in this chapter. As in the preceding chapter, you will learn that each desire has intrinsic value, motivates nearly everyone to some degree, and is a psychologically significant motive capable of explaining a lot of behavior. Further, individuals differ in how strongly they embrace each desire.

HONOR

Honor is the desire to be loyal to one's parents and, by extension, to one's heritage, ethnic group, culture, moral code, religion, city, or nation. For example, we honor our parents when we are loyal to the moral principles and religion they taught us when we were children. We honor our forefathers when we practice the traditions and customs of our ethnic groups, and we honor our nation when we show patriotism. People with a strong desire for honor tend to place a high value on character, religion, ethnic traditions, and patriotism.

The desire for honor motivates people to place a high value on duty. Some people have such a strong sense of duty that it takes precedence over everything else they do. We recognize a child's duty to parents, a judge's duty to the law, and a soldier's duty to country. People who uphold their duty bring honor to themselves and are a credit to their parents.

People differ considerably in how loyal and principled they are. Although some passengers on the *Titanic* gave up their seats in lifeboats so that others might live. In contrast, a passenger named Masabumi Hosono jumped into a lifeboat from the deck of the ship, taking a place that was supposed to have gone to a woman or a child.[1] He lived the rest of his life in shame.

People who have a strong desire for honor tend to experience shame and guilt when they behave dishonorably. Shame is the emotion people experience when they fail to do their duty, whereas guilt is the feeling people have when they violate their principles.[2] Because people with high honor do not want to live with shame or guilt, they are motivated to do their duty and to treat others morally. In contrast, people with low honor lack the potential to experience much shame or guilt. These people have little sense of duty or moral principle.

The primal roots of the desire for honor may be related to the emotion of shame. Some predators do not attack animals that are part of the herd but will stare at, stalk, and attack an animal who is singled out.[3] Since the animal who experiences shame when stared at may run back to the herd before the predator attacks, shame can have survival value.

The system of 16 basic desires distinguishes among loyalty to parents, spouse, friends, and children. Of these, only loyalty to parents satisfies the desire for honor. Loyalty to spouse satisfies the desire for romance, loyalty to friends is motivated by the desire for social contact, and loyalty to children is part of the basic desire for family. The actions of Linda Tripp are a good example of the difference between loyalty to moral principles and loyalty to friends. Although Tripp is known among her associates as a person of principle, she was a poor friend to Monica Lewinsky, whom she tape-recorded for prosecutors in the Clinton affair. The reason she could be loyal to a moral code and yet betray her friend is that the two behaviors are related to different basic desires and values. Although Tripp exhibited a strong desire for honor and duty, she showed only a weak desire for social contact.

Since one's school can be a psychological symbol for one's parents— the words "alma mater" are Latin for foster mother—alumni and students can satisfy their desire for honor by showing school spirit. The lyrics of many college fight songs, for example, express the idea that being loyal to one's college is a matter of honor. The Ohio State University Buckeyes sing:

> Her honor defend,
> we'll fight to the end,
> for O Hi O.

By rooting for our school's teams, we experience loyalty, which partially satisfies the desire for honor.

The desire for honor can motivate people toward self-discipline, which can be important for adherence to strict moral and honor codes. The Indian nationalist Mohandas K. Gandhi held that self-discipline is essential to moral duty.[4] Many other moral philosophers have agreed with this general idea.[5]

Differences in the desire for honor can be a source of conflict in a marriage. It is not uncommon, for example, for couples to fight over loyalty to their respective families or heritage. This is especially common in interfaith marriages, where the couple must resolve issues of how to raise children and observe various religious holidays.[6] Couples with different faiths must come to grips with the sense of separateness that is created between them when each partner worships in his or her religion.

Rate your desire for honor as *very important* to you if either of the following statements is generally true:

1. You are known as a highly principled person.

2. You are known as a very loyal person.

Rate your desire for honor as *less important* to you if either of the following statements is generally true:

1. You believe that everyone is out for him- or herself.

2. You do not care much about morality.

Rate your desire for honor as of *average importance* if you have not rated it as very important or less important, or if you have endorsed statements indicating both a high and a low desire for honor. After you have rated yourself, you may wish to rate the other people in your family or life. Keep track of the ratings on page 261 and refer to them when you read Part II.

IDEALISM

Idealism, which is the desire for social justice or fairness, motivates people to get involved and contribute to the betterment of humankind. Its primal roots are unclear. Some say that idealism is related to altruistic behavior seen in animals, but others say that animals do not show true altruism except possibly in isolated examples.[7] In human beings, idealism motivates people to join service organizations, volunteer for programs for the needy, give to charity, or work toward the improvement of their community. Some people join the clergy for idealistic reasons.

Many people devote a large portion of their careers to making the world a better place. Some physicians devote their time and energy to improving public health in third-world countries instead of building a lucrative private practice at home. Other physicians work on policy issues while they could have higher-paying jobs at hospitals.

There is no significant correlation between the desire to help society and the way in which people behave toward others. Some very famous humanitarians make poor personal friends and do not even spend much time with their own children. Because idealism, family, and social contact are three distinct desires, it is possible for some people to care much more about social causes than about the key realtionships in their lives.

Idealism motivates people to intrinsically value fairness and justice. Human beings almost universally develop a sense of fair play—for example, in all cultures people feel some obligation to return personal favors and to keep promises. This primal sense of fairness is the psychological foundation for more complex ideas of social equality and equality under the law. Idealistic people can place so much value on social fairness that they essentially determine how important everything is by how it relates to social justice.

Individuals differ considerably in how motivated they are by idealism. Examples of people with a weak desire for idealism include politicians who betray the public trust and steal from their communities. In the motion picture *Gone With the Wind,* Scarlett O'Hara goes looking for a doctor to deliver her friend's baby. She is so oblivious to the devastation of the Civil War that she literally steps over wounded soldiers lying in the streets of Atlanta. This scene dramatically reveals Scarlett's focus on her personal concerns and her lack of attention to what is happening in her society.

In contrast, idealistic people are attuned to the social significance of what they do. They may think that improving society or working toward some social cause is the most important thing in life. Often they will take personal risks to promote their ideals. Former President Jimmy Carter has built houses for the poor through Habitat for Humanity, and has traveled throughout the world to monitor elections and work for peace. Before Carter decides to do something, he considers how the activity connects to his ideals.

Other examples of people with a strong desire for idealism include Mother Teresa, who fought poverty in India; medical researchers who work selflessly to improve health care; and Peace Corps workers who volunteer to help people in other countries. Entrepreneur Ted Turner made a $1 billion gift to the United Nations and urged his fellow billionaires to do more for charity. In these people, we see a lifelong commitment to social justice and sometimes even a willingness to die if necessary to achieve that goal.

Martin Luther King, Jr., who was born in 1929, is another excellent example of a person who spent his life seeking social justice. In 1955, King was the minister at Dexter Avenue Baptist Church in Montgomery, Alabama. At that time, Montgomery was a segregated city, as was much of the South.

On December 1 of that year, a weary African-American woman named Rosa Parks took a seat on a bus near the front of the section reserved for African-Americans, and refused to give up her seat to white passengers. The black ministers of the city, including King, organized a boycott of the city's buses, and King spent the rest of his career using nonviolent tactics to end segregation in America, which was his ideal.[8]

Rate your desire for idealism as *very important* to you if any of the following statements is true:

1. You make personal sacrifices for a social or humanitarian cause.

2. You have repeatedly volunteered time to community-service organizations.

3. You have repeatedly made generous contributions to the needy.

Rate your desire for idealism as *less important* to you if either of the following statements is generally true:

1. You pay little attention to what is going on in society at large.

2. You do not believe in charity.

Rate your desire for idealism as of *average importance* if you have not rated it as very important or less important, or if you have endorsed statements indicating that idealism is both very and less important to you. After you have rated yourself, you may wish to rate the other people in your family or life. Keep track of your ratings on page 261 because you may wish to refer to them when you read Part II.

SOCIAL CONTACT

This is the desire to spend time with peers or friends. Seeking fun is part of this desire, since the results of our studies show that fun is something that occurs primarily with other people. Even animals prefer to have playmates when seeking fun. For example, African elephants run, twirl, flap ears and trunks, spray water on each other, and utter loud play sounds.[9] Children generally prefer playing with others to playing alone. Young kids are often seen in summer running around squirting each other with water guns while laughing and making noise, not unlike African elephants.

The Three Musketeers, from Alexandre Dumas's novel, are a good illustration of the joy of social contact. Their motto, "One for all, all for one," speaks directly to the pleasure of bonding with peers. D'Artagnan and his three friends were fun loving. They loved to drink, joke with each other, cause mischief, and pull pranks. They liked people and readily initiated conversations with strangers.

The friendship which united these four men, and the need they felt
for meeting three or four times a day, whether for duels, business,
or pleasure, caused them to be continually running after one an-

other like shadows, and you constantly met the inseparable looking one for the other. . . .[10]

Sociability is highly correlated with being cheerful and having goodwill toward others. In Woody Allen's movie *Annie Hall,* for example, Alvy Singer provides a humorous example of a person who does not make friends easily. Alvy has such a depressing viewpoint that he thinks "everything is divided between horrible and miserable." His lover, Annie Hall, is a much more upbeat, positive, and sociable person. Their differences drive them apart when Annie leaves Alvy to seek fun, parties, and romance in southern California.

Sociable people need to be around others, not only for fun, but also for a basic sense of happiness. They are motivated to seek out others, get to know others, and make themselves interesting to others. They cannot stand to be alone for long periods of time. When they are with other people, they seek out the fun in a situation.

Everybody seeks a certain amount of socializing, which varies depending on the individual's nature. When people experience what they consider to be too much socializing, they feel burdened by the demands of interacting with others. After a few days of attending meetings, for example, a businesswoman who has had her fill of socializing wants to spend some time alone. When people socialize less than they would like, they feel lonely. After teaching all day in an elementary school, a teacher may long for adult contact and seek out a party or visit a friend. In these examples, both the businesswoman and the teacher are aiming to maintain some balance between socializing and privacy.

A desire for privacy does not necessarily indicate that a person is shy.[11] Whereas a private person has a low desire for social contact, a shy person desires social contact but is afraid of being rejected. Although shy people actually have at least an average desire for social contact, they are also easily embarrassed (indicating a high desire for acceptance). They may act as "stuffed shirts," afraid to have fun because of a fear of appearing foolish.

Many clinical psychologists regard the ability to make and keep friends as an important component of mental health. Social isolation can be a symptom of various psychological disorders, such as depression, schizophrenia, and autism. Both people with clinical depression and those with schizophrenia are socially withdrawn. Children who have autism prefer to play alone. They do not show normal interest in receiving attention from their parents.

According to the theory of 16 basic desires, the desire for privacy is a normal emotion that can be distinguished from the patterns of social withdrawal seen in clinical disorders. We all need to be alone at times, although some people experience this need more intensely than do others. It is only when the desire for privacy occurs in the context of feelings of profound sadness, or when other signs of mental illness are present, that we need to be concerned about the possibility of a serious psychological disorder.

Social contact can be sought both as a means and an end. When people join a country club or social group in order to network for business purposes, social contact is a means to career success (satisfying the desire for power). When people join a country club for prestige, social contact is a means of impressing other people (status). According to the results of Susan Havercamp's doctoral dissertation, college students join fraternities and sororities primarily to gain prestige, not to enjoy the company of the other people in these clubs. The basic desire for social contact is indicated only when a person seeks friendship for no apparent reason other than to enjoy being with other people.

Rate your desire for social contact as *very important* to you if either of the following statements is true:

1. You feel that you need to be around other people a lot to be happy.

2. You are known as a fun-loving person.

Rate your desire for social contact as *less important* to you if any of the following statements is generally true:

1. You are a private person.

2. You hate parties.

3. You do not care much about other people except for family and a few close friends.

Rate your desire for social contact as of *average importance* if you have not rated it as very important or less important, or if you have endorsed statements indicating that social contact is both very and less important to you. After you have rated yourself, you may wish to rate the other people in your family or life. Keep track of the ratings on page 261 and refer to them when you read Part II.

FAMILY

The desire for family is, essentially, a desire to raise and love your own children. In animals, this desire is expressed as paternal and maternal instincts. In one documented example, an elephant risked her life repeatedly in a determined and persistent effort to save her calf from drowning.[12] In human beings, family motivates the desire to take care of, and to sacrifice for, one's children—it is much more than a desire to have children. The desire is important for human beings because of the great amount of nuturance, protection, and education children need prior to becoming independent adults.

Some psychologists have said that family is part of a more basic need to nurture.[13] According to this idea, a nurturing person enjoys being needed and loves to watch children, animals, and even plants grow. The results of our research, however, show that nurturance is not a basic desire. People with very strong parenting instincts can have no need at all to raise other people's children and may not enjoy pets or taking care of plants. Like animals, people have a basic desire to look after their own. The basic motive is much more narrowly focused on one's own children than has been thought by those who have put forth the idea of a more general desire to nurture.

If you are a person who is nurturing, or if you know of such a person, you may think I must be wrong in saying that the basic desire for family is limited to taking care of one's own. Keep in mind, however, that basic desires are common motivators. When I say that parenting is a basic desire, I mean that parenting is a basic need associated with the species—if it were not, we probably would not be here. When I say that nurturance is not a basic desire, I do not mean that nobody is nurturing. Although some people need to nurture, this need is not basic to the human species.

Many parents devote significant time, effort, and expense to raising their children. They may stay at jobs they do not like because they need the money for their children. Many people work several jobs or put in overtime so that they can afford to send their children to college. Some parents donate healthy organs for transplantation to their children who need them. At an enormous commitment of time and effort, some parents take care of children who have disabilities or chronic illnesses. Yet most parents say that despite all the sacrifices and responsibilities, raising a family is one of the greatest joys of life.

The parent–child bond is commonly recognized as special. America was outraged when independent prosecutor Kenneth Starr forced Marsha Lewis, Monica Lewinsky's mother, to testify against her daughter. Many people thought that the mother–daughter relationship is too personal to be invaded by legal proceedings, even when criminal issues are being investigated.

Individuals differ considerably in their desire to raise a family. Some people desire a lot of children and spend much of their time taking care of them. Mia Farrow, the movie actress, is an excellent example of a person who has a strong desire for family.[14] She is the mother of 14 children, 10 of them adopted. In explaining why she only works in the summer, she told a reporter, "I want to be a mom to my kids. I can't leave it to somebody else."

In contrast, some parents show little interest in their children after they are born. A good example of someone with a weak desire for family was entertainer Jackie Gleason, the star of the television show "The Honeymooners." Gleason told his biographer that he used work as an excuse because he really did not want to spend much time at home with his kids.[15] He did not like himself for feeling that way, but he just could not enjoy raising his kids, even though he felt a sense of obligation. Some parents who have similar feelings sometimes delegate the responsibility for raising their children to grandparents or to hired help.

Rate your desire for family as *very important* to you if either of the following statements is generally true:

1. Raising children is essential to your happiness.

2. Compared with other parents you know, you spend much more time with your children.

Rate your desire for family as *less important* to you if either of the following statements is generally true:

1. You find being a parent or the idea of it mostly burdensome.

2. You have abandoned a child.

Rate your desire for family as of *average importance* if you have not rated it as very important or less important, or if you have endorsed statements indicating that family is both very and less important to you. After you have rated yourself, you may wish to rate the other people in your family or life. Keep track of the ratings on page 261 and refer to them when you read Part II.

STATUS

Status is the basic desire for prestige. In animals, it is expressed as a desire for attention. Newborn birds and other animals call attention to themselves in order to get their parents to address their needs. If the need for attention is especially strong in a baby bird, it may increase the chances for survival as compared with other members of a nest. In human beings, status also has apparent survival value because it leads to better nutrition and health care and to privilege during times of emergency. For example, upper-class passengers were given the first opportunity to fill the lifeboats when the *Titanic* started to sink.

People who are driven by status seek to move "up" in this world. They want to become "somebody"; they hope to become wealthy and impress other people with how rich they are. People with a high need for status are impressed by expensive homes, clothes with designer labels, and expensive cars. They are impressed by royalty, celebrities, and high society. They care a great deal about their reputations and are highly attentive to what others think of them. They may feel important and even a bit superior to most people. They may enjoy the attention that their status gains them. On the other hand, people with a low need for status are unimpressed by expensive things and celebrity status. They may not care much if other people draw the wrong conclusions about them because they do not care that much about their reputations.

Because status is highly valued in most societies, rich people rarely seem to marry poor people. Although rich people sometimes fall in love with poor people, their desire for status and their attitudes about social class can discourage them from entering a marriage that may be viewed by their contemporaries as "beneath" them. On the other hand, poor people often fantasize about marrying rich people. One of the most enduring themes of fiction is the tale of a rich person falling in love with a poor one—will the rich person's love overcome the desire for status? It happened for Cinderella, of course.

Status is so important to some people that they seek it even in death. I once overheard a conversation between two people attending a funeral. One was telling a relative that his parents were to be buried in the prestigious section of the cemetery. He observed that the plots cost more in that section of the cemetery, but his parents had felt that only the best would do when it came to their final resting place. They allotted money they could have spent while they were alive to be used for prestigious burial plots after they were dead. What better proof could there be that status is an intrinsic value (sought for its own sake)?

Generally, people seek the degree of status that makes them feel most comfortable. Social climbers strive for a high status, and egalitarian people seek lower status. These two groups have opposite desires regarding status—the one is strongly motivated to gain status, the other to avoid it. Most people aim for moderation, however, seeking to balance their feelings of importance (high status) and humility (low status). When people experience more status than they like, they seek humbling experiences to balance things out; when they experience more humility than they like, they seek experiences of prestige.

Status is a psychologically significant desire that affects many aspects of life. Although all human societies have status hierarchies to indicate a person's place in life, in some societies the hierarchies are much more detailed and clearly defined than in others. The caste system in India is a striking case in point. There, membership in a caste determines what jobs people can take, whom they can marry, what they can eat, and with whom they can socialize. There are about 3,000 castes organized into four large classes. At the top of the hierarchy are the brahmans (priests or scholars), followed by kshatriyas (warriors and rulers), vaisyas (merchants, traders, and farmers), and sudras (artisans, laborers, servants, and slaves).

According to Paul Fussell's book *Class*,[16] Americans are highly status-conscious. In corporate parking lots, for example, people with high status are assigned spaces closer to the building than are those with low status. High-status people are given bigger offices, located closer to the boss, than are low-status people. Nearly all large corporations have different ranks that confer status. In our private lives, status is conferred by living in an exclusive neighborhood, belonging to a country club, wearing expensive clothing, and owning a luxury car.

Employers often use job titles to add or subtract status from a position. When professional people with a strong desire for status are offered a new job, they may spend more time negotiating their job title than their salary and benefits. Many people look at their job title more than their salary to evaluate how well their career is going. In academia, Ivy League schools are well known for paying their faculty less than they would earn at another university. The difference in pay is supposedly made up for by the prestige of teaching at such a school.

During the 1950s, suburbia was a place where people felt they had to "keep up with the Joneses." When one family could park a brand-new Oldsmobile outside their house, their neighbors thought they needed to buy a new car, too, just to show the rest of the block how well they were doing financially. Over the years, the game was played with country club memberships, professionally manicured lawns, in-ground pools, and backyard balconies.

Another indicator of the significance of prestige is that it adds value to consumer products. A Mercedes-Benz and a Ford Crown Victoria are both excellent automobiles that will get you where you want to go, but the Mercedes will cost anywhere from three to five times as much as the Ford. Why? Part of the greater cost is superior components, but most of it is the prestige factor. Many people will pay more for the prestigious or brand-name product even if they can get roughly equivalent quality with a generic or less-expensive product. This shows that status is highly valued by a great many people.

Royalty represents the highest possible social rank. The status of those with "royal blood" is unrelated to their accomplishments—royalty reigns by birthright. Because the desire for status is associated with the need for attention, royals become a spectacle. They build lavish, ostentatious palaces, wear expensive jewelry, and dress in attention-grabbing garb. If you doubt the connection between status and attention, try to attend a function presided over by a royal person. I once went to a speech given by Prince Charles. Everybody, including me, stared at him as if he were somehow a different kind of human being. What impressed me was the dignity Prince Charles maintained while he was being stared at. I recall thinking to myself that this is what royalty is all about, to have people stare at you and not become embarrassed, as if it were a natural state of affairs.

Rate your desire for status as *very important* to you if any of the following statements is generally true:

1. You almost always want to buy only the best or most expensive things.

2. You often buy things just to impress other people.

3. You spend a great deal of time trying to join or maintain membership in prestigious clubs or organizations.

Rate your desire for status as *less important* to you if any of the following statements is generally true:

1. You usually do not care what most people think of you.

2. You are significantly less impressed by wealth than most people you know.

3. You are not at all impressed by upper-class status or by royalty.

Rate your desire for status as of *average importance* if you have not rated it as very important or less important, or if you have endorsed statements indicating that status is both very and less important to you. After you have rated yourself, you may wish to rate the other people in your family or life. Keep track of the ratings on page 261 and refer to them when you read Part II.

Why a Secretary
Feared Heights

In this chapter, you will learn about the remaining five basic desires: vengeance, romance, food, physical exercise, and tranquility.

VENGEANCE

The desire to get even with people who offend us is associated with feelings of anger or hatred. Its primal origin concerns an animal's need to defend itself when attacked. Parrots are considered a particularly vengeful species because individual parrots can develop hatreds for various categories of humans such as redheads or all adults.[1] In human beings, vengeance can motivate both aggression and competitiveness (one-upmanship).

The desire for revenge is aroused when people are frustrated, insulted, or threatened with an attack. When people are prevented from getting what they want, or when there is a delay, they all tend to feel some degree of frustration, irritation, and hostility. Depending on the strength of their desire for vengeance, people may seek vindication. Anger is a common response to insult. When somebody insults a person, their self-concept is threatened and they may experience a desire to retaliate.

Competition falls under the desire for vengeance. When an opponent goes one up, the desire for vengeance motivates some people to retaliate. Whether through sports, business, or sibling rivalry, competitiveness is a nonviolent way to exact revenge on another person. Basketball player Michael Jordan is a good example of someone who is highly competitive— he desired to win every time he played, and to keep on winning season after season. On the other hand, the character Brick in *Cat on a Hot Tin Roof* is a good example of someone who is noncompetitive.[2] Brick watched passively when his brother fought to inherit their dying father's business empire. He chose not to compete for his inheritance.

Vengeance has an important genetic basis. The groundbreaking study on this topic was conducted by University of Michigan psychologists Leonard Eron and Rowell Huesmann, who followed 632 third-graders until they reached the age of 40. They found that the aggressive children became aggressive adults, and that nonviolent children became nonviolent adults. Here is how they summarized their research findings:

> Aggression . . . has the hallmarks of a deeply ingrained personality trait. It is related to genetic and physiological factors; it emerges in early life but is influenced and shaped by a child's experiences; it is consistently associated with gender and is stable or predictable over time and across situations.[3]

Studies from other countries yielded similar results. Various groups of re-searchers followed people for 24 years in Great Britain, 11 years in Finland, and 18 years in Sweden. The results of all of these studies showed few changes in aggressive and violent behavior as people grew older.[4]

Vengeful attitudes can last a long time and be passed on from one generation to the next. The famous Hatfield–McCoy feud began in the 1860s in the aftermath of the Civil War, when there was little law enforce-ment in the mountain region of the Kentucky–West Virginia border, and it lasted until the 1890s. The feud involved both extended families and led to a number of incidents of stealing and killing. Today, we see the effects of long-lasting feuds in the Balkans. Many Serbs and Albanians hate each other, and each group is out for revenge, sometimes regardless of the per-sonal cost. The depth of the horror caused by this vengeance has been shocking even to those who do not hold a particularly romantic view of human nature.

People seek revenge for no apparent reason other than the satisfaction of getting even. If you doubt this, look at the words of Theodore Kaczynski, the "Unabomber," who moved to a remote area of Montana where he mailed bombs to university professors. Over a period of more than ten years, his bombs killed three people and injured 22 others. In an entry in his diary dated April 6, 1971, he wrote,

> My motive for doing what I am going to do is simply personal revenge. I do not expect to accomplish anything by it. . . . I act merely from a desire for revenge. Of course, I would like to get revenge on the whole scientific and bureaucratic establishment, not to mention the communists and others who threaten freedom, but, that being impossible, I have to content myself with just a little revenge.[5]

As we see in these words, revenge can be its own reward.

Our modern legal system provides people with a nonviolent means of satisfying a desire for revenge. Revenge can be seen to be justified, as this passage from the Bible illustrates:

> If men strive, and hurt a woman with child, so that her fruit depart from her, and yet no mischief follow: he shall be surely punished, according as the woman's husband will lay upon him; and he shall pay as the judges determine. And if any mischief follow, thou shalt give life for life, eye for eye, tooth for tooth, hand for hand, foot for foot, burning for burning, wound for wound, stripe for stripe.[6]

Today, people turn to civil courts when they seek justified revenge. Fred Goldman, for example, sought revenge against O. J. Simpson for the wrongful death of Goldman's son, Ron. After Simpson was acquitted in a criminal trial, Goldman filed and won a civil suit against Simpson and obtained possession of Simpson's Heisman trophy. When asked what he planned to do with the trophy, Goldman said, "I'd like to have it so I can pound the daylights out of it with a sledgehammer."[7]

The school shootings seen throughout America in recent years have sent people looking for the root cause of this violence. One frequently debated issue concerns the effects of television and video-game violence. Can watching violent television programs or playing video games that depict violence lead to violent behavior? Scientific evidence provides a somewhat mixed answer to this question. On the one hand, children who watch television violence behave more aggressively. On the other hand, the amount of increased aggression that has been observed in scientific studies is minor. Pointing to the evidence for a cause-and-effect relationship, some scientists have called for limits on violent television programming for children. Pointing to the fact that the increase in aggression that can be attributed to watching violent television is actually quite small, entertainment moguls have opposed any government regulation of the violent content of shows.

When people feel there is too much aggression, anger, or competitiveness in their lives, they try to balance things out with peacekeeping behavior and acts of kindness. Frans de Waal,[8] an evolutionary biologist, has observed peacekeeping behavior in the many primate species he has studied. We are born not only with the potential to desire vengeance, but also with the potential to manage this desire by engaging in compassionate behavior. We have fights, but we also make up with people after we fight. De Waal has written that strengthening peacekeeping behavior should be an important part of society's effort to control aggression. He bases his opinion partially on the belief that it will not be possible to eradicate aggression completely because vengeance is a genetic trait. Generally, Susan Havercamp's and my research is consistent with de Waal's viewpoint.

Rate your desire for vengeance as *very important* to you if any of the following statements is generally true:

1. You have trouble controlling your anger.

2. You are aggressive.

3. You love to compete.

4. You spend a lot of your time seeking revenge.

Rate your desire as *less important* to you if any of the following statements is generally true:

1. You are slow to feel anger compared to most people.

2. You often "look the other way" when insulted or offended.

3. You dislike competitive situations.

Rate your desire for vengeance as of *average importance* if you have not rated it as very important or less important, of if you have endorsed statements indicating that vengeance is both very and less important to you. After you have rated yourself, you may rate the other people in your family or life. Keep track of the ratings on page 261, and refer to them when you read Part II.

ROMANCE

The desire for sex and beauty, called *romance,* has its primal origins in mating instincts. In human beings, romantic desire is affected both by biological factors, such as genetics and hormones, and by psychological and cultural factors, such as the perception of beauty. When people seek to arouse a partner's desire, they do whatever they can to make themselves look beautiful, using clothes, makeup, jewelry, and so on. Courting rituals—such as dating, dancing, buying flowers, and buying gifts—also arouse desire. Other common means of arousing desire include fragrances (such as perfumes and cologne), music, art, and touching (including holding hands).

The appreciation of beauty—what is called aesthetics—falls under the desire for romance. This includes the desire for physical beauty, art, and music. Although Freud was among the earliest psychologists to call attention to the sexual aspects of art and music, the connection is obvious to anyone who watches MTV videos. The overwhelming majority of popular songs have romantic themes.

The psychological study of beauty has produced few significant findings. Psychologists have learned that the average visitor to a city spends little time at the local art museum, and that most people who look at a painting for the first time do so for only a few seconds. Apparently, the desire to look at beautiful art is fairly weak in many people. Psychologists have not yet determined why this is so, nor have they learned much about how people perceive beauty.[9] Many researchers have tried to analyze beauty in terms of its physical elements, such as complexity, balance, and color. Beauty appears to be an intrinsic whole that defies scientific reduction to simple physical elements.

Beauty is not essential for romantic love. This point was demonstrated by Casanova, who became famous for making love with all types of women—short, tall, thin, fat, beautiful, ugly. When asked about his lack of preference, he said they were all the same when the lamp was extinguished.[10] He climbed walls, dodged husbands, and swam moats to be with his lovers. Casanova shows us in a colorful way that high libido not only leads to frequent sex but also is associated with having many partners.

Aristotle offered a thoughtful analysis of romance. When we feel happy about a person's presence, he said, that is only goodwill.[11] True love is indicated when we long for somebody who is absent and desire that person's presence. Further, true love is manifested through both affection and intimacy, not through affection alone.

Romance is a psychologically significant desire. If you added up all the hours people spend making themselves attractive to the opposite sex, flirting, dating, courting, marrying, having sex, and dreaming about romance or sex, it would be a significant percentage of many people's lives. If you add listening to music, appreciating art, and appreciating beauty, the sum would be much greater.

Freud said that within each person is a beast consisting of animal-like urges for wanton sex. Chaos and social destruction would result if the beast within us were ever set free. Civilized life, said Freud, requires that we find socially acceptable ways of releasing our sexual urges. More recently, author Daniel Goleman has argued that the key to success in life is our "emotional IQ," or ability to control our emotions intelligently. His idea is that we cannot allow our desires for sex to control our lives, but instead we must use our intelligence to satisfy these desires in an appropriate manner.

Some people rarely have sex and do not fantasize much about romance. They do not attempt to make themselves physically attractive to the opposite sex. A woman in her forties once wrote to advice columnist Ann Landers that she had had little sexual desire for much of her life. The woman had never been interested in sex and only rarely fantasized about men. "Am I a freak of nature?" she wondered. Assuming that she had no medical condition to explain her lack of interest in sex, the answer was "No." The woman's lack of desire may reflect nothing more than the low end of the normal individual variation in sex desire seen throughout the human species. In contrast, other people, like Casanova, want so much romance that they think of little else.

Up to this point, we have seen how most people actually aim for a moderate experience of each basic desire. What do people do when they experience an overwhelming amount of beauty or too much sex? As some rock stars have learned, they must deny themselves some pleasure and beauty to create balance or they burn themselves out. When self-denial of beauty is carried to an extreme—which is rare—it is called asceticism. Ascetics reduce to a minimum their experience of beauty and sensual pleasures. They dress simply and live in the plainest possible surroundings, forcing themselves to endure hardship.

Rate your desire for romance as *very important* to you if any of the following statements is generally true:

1. You spend an unusual amount of time, compared to other people you know who are about the same age as you, in the pursuit of romance.

2. You have a long history of sex with many partners.

3. You have trouble controlling your sexual urges.

4. Compared to most people you know, you spend much more time appreciating beauty.

Rate your desire for romance as *less important* to you if any of the following statements is generally true:

1. You spend little time pursuing or thinking about sex.

2. You think that sex is disgusting.

Rate your desire for romance as of *average importance* if you have not rated it as very important nor less important to you, or if you have endorsed statements indicating that romance is both very and less important to you. After you have rated yourself, you may wish to rate the other people in your family or life. Keep track of the ratings on page 261 and refer to them when you read Part II.

EATING

If you add up all the hours people spend shopping for food, preparing meals, and dining, eating accounts for a significant percentage of people's daily lives. Eating, which is a self-rewarding activity, is one of the few biological needs that also has psychological significance. The Duchess of York is an example of someone who struggles to control her desire to eat. As she once explained,

> With every smell, I smell food. With every sight, I see food. I can almost hear food.[12]

On the other hand, Ralph is an example of someone who has little desire to eat. He has such a weak appetite that he sometimes forgets to eat lunch or dinner. He will sit at home, watching television and relaxing, right through the dinner hours, never thinking that he should eat. He does not experience hunger as often as most people do. When he first got married, his wife bought snack food, but since he never went looking for a snack, she no longer buys such food. Except for a very small number of foods he does not like, he says he does not care what is served for lunch or dinner. Further, he says he would be happy to eat the same meal every day. He has never complained about nor praised his wife's cooking. He cannot ever recall having a fantasy involving food, and so far he has never had a weight problem. When it comes to the desire for eating, Ralph and the Duchess of York are psychological opposites.

Although many people think of hunger as a biological state, psychological factors are significant in influencing how hungry we feel. An attractively prepared meal or scrumptious dessert can make us experience hunger regardless of when we last ate, whereas much of the cafeteria food at a typical high school can make even a voracious eater lose his or her appetite. Our emotions also affect our hunger: Many people seek to eat when they are excited, under stress, bored, or lonely.

Comparison of the eating habits of overweight and normal-weight people reveals some interesting differences. Overweight people eat faster and take bigger bites than do normal-weight people. Evidence from interviews suggests that obese people are more intensely preoccupied by thoughts of food than are thin or normal-weight people.

Many people who struggle to control their weight do so for their entire adult lives. Even celebrities whose weight is the subject of national gossip—people such as Rosie O'Donnell, Marlon Brando, and Oprah Winfrey—have not been able to keep their weight down.

Before Judith Rodin became President of the University of Pennsylvania, she wrote:

> Of all the human frailties, obesity is perhaps the most perverse. Its penalties are so severe, the gratification is so limited, and the remedy so simple that obesity should be the most trivial of aberrations to correct, yet it is the most recalcitrant. Almost any fat person can lose weight, few can keep it off. It is this fact that makes the study of obesity so intriguing.[13]

Jackie Gleason was an example of somebody who struggled with weight his entire adult life. He told his biographer that he fluctuated between 210 and 280 pounds, but some say that the real numbers were 50 pounds higher. Since Gleason was 6 feet tall, we can infer that he spent much of his adult life 100 pounds overweight. Although Gleason was plump as a child, he did not develop significant weight problems until young adulthood.

Gleason loved to eat. W. J. Weatherby, author of *Jackie Gleason: An Intimate Portrait of The Great One,* described a meal in which Gleason ate "a Porterhouse steak so large that it hung over the sides of the dinner plate".[14] Gleason went on many binge diets, only to gain back all the weight he had lost. He lost 50 pounds when he first arrived in Hollywood and 86 pounds when he dieted for the opening of his television show, *The Honeymooners.* His weight went up and down so often that he maintained three wardrobes: thin, fat, and very fat. He even dieted on one of his television shows, weighing himself each week before a national audience.

Gleason made many jokes about his obesity. "Fat is funny," he said.

RALPH KRAMDEN: This is probably the biggest thing I ever got into.

ALICE: The biggest thing you ever got into was your pants.

Since dieting does not alter a person's desire to eat, it is only a matter of time before the weight is regained after the diet is over. The National Institutes of Health has estimated that more than 90 percent of people who diet gain back the weight within two years. The various organized diet centers have failure rates of 90% or higher—people lose weight, but they do not keep it off.

Anorexia nervosa and bulimia are psychological extremes of the basic desire for eating. Dramatic weight loss occurs, often to the point where the person becomes dangerously frail.

Rate your desire for food as *very important* to you if either of the following statements is generally true:

1. You spend an unusual amount of time, relative to other people you know who are about the same age as you, eating.

2. You spend an unusual amount of time, relative to other people you know who are about the same age as you, dieting.

Rate your desire for food as *less important* if either of the following statements is generally true:

1. You have never had a weight problem.

2. You rarely eat more than you should.

Rate your desire for food as of average importance if you have rated it neither a very important nor less important desire, or if you have endorsed statements indicating that eating is both very and less important to you. After you have rated yourself, you may wish to rate the other people in your family or life. Keep track of the ratings on page 261, and refer to them when you read Part II.

PHYSICAL ACTIVITY

Because the human body is built for movement, many people enjoy sports, walking, jogging, or even physically demanding jobs or housework. Mark, for example, is a 34-year-old man who likes mountain running, obviously a highly vigorous form of exercise. Deanna likes to run with her dog, and has found that not only is she fit, but the dog is contented and better behaved. Michelle went for a run on New Year's Eve because she couldn't think of a better way to start 1999. I know of a man who mows lawns professionally. He's had other jobs with more pay and prestige, but he sticks with lawns because of the workout he gets. He considers physical activity its own reward.

When we play sports for fun—for no apparent purpose other than the intrinsic enjoyment of exercising—physical activity is an end goal. Here is how Walter Payton, the National Football League's great running back, expressed the intrinsic joy of athletics in the 1985 rap song, "The Super Bowl Shuffle":

> My name is Sweetness,
> And I like to dance.
> Runnin' the ball
> Is like makin' romance.

Athletics is so important to some people that it nearly dominates their lives. This is true of both men and women. When athletic-minded people are young, they spend a great deal of time working out and challenging themselves physically. They usually participate in more than one sport and feel a need for a lot of physical exercise. When these people become older, they often continue to stay fit, follow sports closely as fans, and may be attracted to coaching or to teaching sports to their children.

Vijay Singh, winner of the 1998 Master's golf tournament, has indicated that golf is one of the most important activities in his life.

> I have a family, but golf was always me and I was always golf. I could
> do nothing but play golf and that's the way I've been for the last 29

years. I wake up thinking about my game and I go to sleep thinking about it.[15]

Tara Lipinski, a 16-year-old Olympic women's champion in figure skating, began roller-skating at age 3 and ice-skating at age 6. "I can't say exactly how I felt the first time I ice-skated, but I know I loved it," Lipinski told a reporter for *International Figure Skating*.[16] She said she looked forward to skating every day and didn't miss any practices.

The desire for physical activity is not the same as athletic ability. Many people enjoy playing golf even though they are not good enough to win any tournaments; similarly, many people enjoy swimming even though they lack the ability to compete in that sport. Whether or not we intrinsically enjoy a physical activity depends on how that activity relates to our desire profile—especially how much we intrinsically enjoy physical exertion—much more than it depends on level of ability.

Individuals differ considerably in how much physical exercise they desire. In contrast to the athletic-minded person, some people carefully avoid physical exertion, or try hard to "pace themselves." They prefer to drive when they can walk, and to stay home when they have little or nothing to do. They may not go to the store to buy something they want simply because they do not want to expend the energy. People who consciously pace themselves plan significant rest periods between periods of activity.

Rate your desire for physical activity as *very important* to you if either of the following statements is generally true:

1. You have exercised regularly all your life.

2. Playing a sport is an important part of your life.

In contrast, rate your desire for physical activity as *less important* in your life if either of these statements is generally true:

1. You have a history of being physically lazy.

2. You have a sedentary lifestyle.

Rate physical activity as of *average importance* in your life if you have rated it neither a very nor less important desire, or if you have endorsed statements indicating that this desire is both very and less important. After you have rated yourself, you may wish to rate the other people in your family or life. Keep track of the ratings on page 261 and refer to them when you read Part II.

TRANQUILITY

Tranquility is a psychological state that is defined as the absence of disturbance and turmoil, or the absence of anxiety, stress, and fear. Its primal origins are in animal instincts to flee danger and seek safety. How strongly people desire tranquility depends on how motivated they are to live a stress-free life. Some people fall apart at the first signs of stress. These people have a strong need for a tranquil, or stress-free, lifestyle. Other people can tolerate stress reasonably well even though they do not enjoy it. These people have a low need for a tranquil lifestyle.

People with a strong desire for tranquility are motivated to make changes in their lives that significantly reduce stress. For example, some people have changed their careers or turned down promotions because they did not want the added stress of the new position. In contrast, people with a weak desire for tranquility can tolerate significant levels of stress. A good example is a thrill-seeker who likes to skydive or race cars for fun. Volunteer combat soldiers have a weak desire for tranquility. They show courage, not avoidance, in the face of fear.

Tranquility is a psychologically significant desire partially because people spend a considerable amount of time managing anxiety. Many people regularly consume tranquilizers to manage anxiety, and they take vacations seeking relaxation and escape from stressful jobs. Some social thinkers called the 1960s the "Age of Anxiety" because of the rapid rise in the use of tranquilizer medications.

A very strong desire for tranquility is seen in people who have spontaneous panic attacks.[17] These attacks seem to come from out of the blue and are not apparent reactions to any particular cue or situation. Sometimes the individual stays at home and is afraid to go outside at all. *Agoraphobia* is commonly known as the fear of the marketplace, but the term is a misnomer because what the person is really afraid of is having a panic attack outside the home. People with agoraphobia not only experience spontaneous panic attacks but also exhibit an extremely strong desire for tranquility.

Certain types of substance abuse are associated with a strong desire for tranquility. Because alcohol depresses bodily signs of stress, some drinking problems may be caused by a person's efforts to escape from stressful experiences.[18]

People who tolerate pain poorly show a strong desire for tranquility, while those who tolerate pain relatively well show a weak desire for tranquility. Some evidence suggests that the pain associated with various chronic medical conditions is more troublesome to patients with a strong desire for tranquility. The desire for tranquility is also associated with how many fears a person has. People who have many fears have a strong desire for tranquility, and those with relatively few fears have only a weak desire for tranquility.

Virtually all psychological theories imply that people are strongly motivated to avoid stress. In fact, psychologists have been so consistent in predicting that people avoid stress and anxiety that they cannot easily explain the fact that it is commonplace for some people to actively approach stressful situations. Although it's usually during a ballgame's most stressful moments that a relief pitcher is called to the mound, the pitcher is often still eager to come when the manager calls. If psychological theories of anxiety and stress were valid, the relief pitcher should run away from the mound when called upon in such a tense situation.

In 1977, Stanford University psychologist Albert Bandura put forth the idea of self-efficacy in part to explain why some people enter such situations rather than run away from them. Bandura's idea was that people enter such stressful situations primarily when they have self-confidence and think they can master the task at hand. Bandura said that relief pitchers enter ballgames during times of stress, for example, because they think they can pitch their teams out of a jam. Their self-confidence reduces their stress to tolerable levels.

In 1985, Harvard University psychologist Richard McNally and I put forth the idea of anxiety sensitivity to help explain why it is commonplace for people to approach stressful situations.[19] Our idea was that people differ in how they interpret stress. People who think that stress is unhealthy or embarrassing tend to avoid it at all costs. They show a strong desire for tranquility and have a propensity to develop anxiety problems, especially panic attacks. On the other hand, people who believe that stress is a temporary nuisance show a weak desire for tranquility. They tend to be courageous and fearless, and they function well under highly stressful conditions.

Anxiety sensitivity provides a simple explanation of how a pitcher can enter a ballgame at a stressful moment. Most relief pitchers consider stress to be a harmless nuisance that will dissipate soon after the game is over. Since they do not fear the experience of stress, they have little reason to refuse to come into the game when the manager calls. On the other hand, if a cardiologist were to tell a relief pitcher that he had a heart condition and should avoid stressful situations, the relief pitcher might choose to quit the team.

I first became intrigued by the idea of anxiety sensitivity back in 1978, when I interviewed a secretary who was thinking about not taking a promotion because it meant working on a higher floor in a 25-story building, and she was afraid of working on a higher floor. I kept asking her what she thought would happen if she went to that floor. Was she afraid of falling? "No," she said, "I know I will not fall." Did she worry that the elevator cables might break and cause a crash? How silly of me to ask such a question, she said.

I persisted. What will happen if you go to the top floor and look out? "I would faint," she finally said. I immediately realized that the secretary's reason for her fear was inconsistent with every idea of anxiety and stress in psychology. According to these ideas, she was supposed to think that heights are dangerous. What she actually thought, however, was that stress and anxiety are dangerous. Most people will go to the top floor of a skyscraper because they know that any anxiety they experience is harmless and temporary. In contrast, the secretary had a phobia of heights because she thought that her anxiety would escalate into a dangerous panic attack. She feared a possible heart attack, embarrassment, or the development of a mental illness.

One way to assess the desire for tranquility is to evaluate how much sensitivity a person has to anxiety. My colleagues and I developed a simple questionnaire for evaluating a person's anxiety sensitivity. This questionnaire, called the *Reiss–Peterson–Gursky Anxiety Sensitivity Index* (ASI), essentially asks people how harmful they think it would be if they experienced anxiety. Some of the items are as follows:

> It scares me when I feel "shaky" (trembling).
>
> It scares me when my heart beats rapidly.
>
> When I notice that my heart is beating rapidly, I worry that I might have a heart attack.
>
> It embarrasses me when my stomach growls.

Numerous studies have shown that the ASI can be used to help predict panic attacks before they occur. In fact, psychologist Wendy Silverman is trying to predict panic attacks at age 25 based on the presence of high anxiety sensitivity at age 10. Murray Stein, a professor of psychiatry at the University of California at San Diego, and his colleagues have obtained evidence that anxiety sensitivity is inherited. According to these researchers, the genes that create a propensity for anxiety sensitivity also might create a propensity for spontaneous panic attacks.

Ohio State University psychologist Norman Schmidt and his colleagues have demonstrated how well the ASI, which can be thought of as a measure of how strongly a person desires tranquility, can predict people's reactions to stress.[20] In each of two years, they tested the entire entering class of cadets at the U.S. Air Force Academy. Basic training at the Academy is designed to be highly stressful. The cadets are awakened in the middle of the night and sent on marches, they are yelled at, and they are not allowed to call home. Cadets who thought that stress is harmful, as measured by the ASI, experienced significantly more panic attacks during basic training than did all other cadets. The cadets with high anxiety sensitivity also showed other significant adjustment problems to basic training. Apparently, the ASI can help the military identify those soldiers who are most likely to panic during the stress of combat. By using this information, psychologists can counsel people on how to overcome the problem, significantly improving a soldier's tolerance for stress.

To sum up, the desire for tranquility is driven by an individual's tolerance of anxiety, stress, and pain. The key factor in such tolerance is how harmful the person thinks anxiety and stress are. When some people become anxious, they worry about possible embarrassment, mental illness, or heart attacks. These people show a strong desire for tranquility; they need a stress-free lifestyle. In contrast, people who view anxiety as a temporary nuisance have a weak need for tranquility and a high tolerance for stress and pain. Individual variations in the desire for tranquility have a genetic basis and play a role in some drinking problems, phobias, and chronic pain reactions.

Rate your desire for tranquility as *very important* to you if any of the following statements is generally true:

1. You strongly agree with at least two of the four ASI statements listed on page 81.

2. You have a history of recurring panic attacks.

3. You are generally fearful and timid.

Rate your desire for tranquility as *less important* if either of the following statements is generally true:

1. You are a brave person.

2. You have noticeably fewer fears than do your peers.

Rate tranquility as having an *average importance* if you have rated it as neither very important nor less important, or if you have endorsed statements indicating that it is both very important and less important. After you have rated yourself, you may wish to rate the other people in your family or life. Keep track of the ratings on page 261 and refer to them when you read Part II.

One Size Does Not Fit All

The relative importance we place on each of the 16 desires is what makes us individuals. In other words, every human being places a different level of importance on each desire. You may feel that status, family, and order are most important, and I may feel that idealism, power, and curiosity are most important. The way in which you prioritize these 16 desires is what makes you uniquely you.

What this means is that individuals differ to a greater extent than psychologists have previously realized. Largely because of genetic diversity, every person has a unique desire profile. Culture and experience also help to determine a person's desire profile, but probably to a lesser extent than genetics. Because individual variations occur in the genes that control each basic desire, some people experience a given desire more intensely and frequently than do others. Individual differences in the genes that make sex a pleasure, for example, cause some people to enjoy sex more than other people do. Similarly, individual variations in the genes that make anxiety a displeasure cause some people to avoid anxiety and stress at all costs while others are able to tolerate stressful experiences with relative ease.

What you have done in the last three chapters is figure out what's most important to you and to your significant others. This is called a *desire profile.* There are more than 43 million possible combinations of the 16 basic desires that can be produced by answering the questions in Chapters 2, 3, and 4. More than 2 trillion different profiles can be assessed by the *Reiss Profile*. As these numbers show, the system of 16 basic desires has the sensitivity needed to express the uniqueness of every person.

Your desire profile holds the secrets of who you are. It determines what you need to gain value-based happiness, or a sense that your life is meaningful. You did not choose your desire profile—you were largely born that way. Although you may not be conscious of your desire profile, you can discover it easily enough by using the information in this book. When you learn your desire profile, you gain insight into who you are and why you do what you do.

MOTIVATIONAL THEMES IN FOUR LIVES

To understand how to use desire profiles, it may help you to see the desire profiles of others. I have analyzed the desire profiles of four celebrities so that you can compare the profiles to learn how they express each person's individuality. What you will learn from this analysis is how desire profiles capture the essence of a person's life goals.[1]

When we analyze life histories in terms of the 16 basic desires, it becomes clear that different people prioritize these desires in their own unique fashion. The desires that are most important in understanding the life of one person can be relatively unimportant in understanding the life of another individual. Further, a person's desire profile gives rise to the striving and psychological themes in the individual's adult life.

HOWARD HUGHES[2]

STRONG (HIGH) DESIRES	AVERAGE DESIRES	WEAK (LOW) DESIRES
Power	Curiosity	Honor
Independence	Acceptance	Family
Order	Saving	Social Contact
Idealism	Vengeance	Status
Romance	Eating	
Tranquility	Physical Activity	

Howard Hughes (1905–1976) was a fascinating man because he was driven by very strong desires. His father became wealthy by developing the world's most successful oil-drilling tools. After his father's death, young Howard bought out his relatives and gained sole ownership of what was later called the Hughes Tool Company. But he was not satisfied with being a millionaire. Driven by a need to achieve and be even more successful than his father, Howard turned a big fortune into a much bigger one by being at the cutting edge of new developments in a number of fields, from aviation to movie making.

Katharine Hepburn once said that Hughes was driven by a "wild desire to be famous"[3] and by an addiction "to fame."[4] Although already famous because of his wealth, Hughes wanted to be admired for personal achievement (indicating a desire for power). He attacked his goal with the intensity of a man who craved success. He designed and manufactured planes, made movies about planes, bought Trans World Airlines, sold planes to the Air Force, and flew planes himself. He was a daredevil pilot who took "reckless chances." He won the 1937 Harmon International Trophy as an outstanding aviator, and he set transcontinental speed records, flying coast-to-coast in 7 hours and 28 minutes in 1937 and around the globe in 3 days, 19 hours, and 17 minutes in 1938. He conceived and manufactured the air-to-air missile, revolutionized the military helicopter, and was a pioneer in satellite technology.

Hughes was a fiercely independent person who more than once went his own way in the business world and came up a winner. He made a profit owning RKO Radio Pictures Inc. by making movies that pushed the limits with regard to sex. He built businesses that made him the largest defense contractor in the nation. When Hughes bought TWA, there was doubt that the airline industry would become profitable. When he started to buy Las Vegas hotels, at one point owning as much as 20 percent of the accommodations on the strip, Vegas was considered a financial risk. Hughes invested in a number of businesses years before others saw the commercial potential.

In addition to his desires for power and independence, Hughes was driven by a desire for romance. Blessed by good looks and wealth, he spent an extraordinary amount of time, energy, and money in the pursuit of women. After moving to Hollywood he seduced women with charm, movie contracts, gifts, and false promises of marriage. He dated scores of women, and maintained detailed logs of his sexual (or romantic) exploits.[5] He even employed teams of detectives with sophisticated electronic surveillance equipment to keep track of potential conquests. At one point in his life, he kept available as many as 167 women, receiving a report every day on each one. His efforts were so extensive that he became the first person ever to own 100 percent of a major Hollywood studio just to bed beautiful women. Hughes may have spent more money pursuing women than any other man in the world.

Hughes wasn't very keen on conventional ideas of loyalty and morality (indicating a low desire for honor). He treated people badly, especially yesterday's girlfriends, but also many of his employees. In order to smooth the way for his business interests, he made women and loans available to politicians.

Although Hughes was wealthy, he did not show even ordinary concern for what other people thought of him (indicating a low desire for status). Referring to his romance with Katharine Hepburn, biographers Brown and Broeske wrote, "Back in Hollywood, [Hughes and Hepburn] were oblivious to what anyone else thought."[6]

Hughes suffered from a mental illness called obsessive-compulsive disorder (OCD). His chief symptom was a morbid fear of germs and becoming ill. These fears began during childhood when "he became a uniquely talented hypochondriac."[7] His fears were encouraged by his mother, who reacted in overly protective ways that psychologist Raymond Fowler found "weren't normal."[8] To minimize the risk posed by germs, Hughes always carried with him a bar of surgical soap.

Hughes's OCD was driven by a strong desire for order, as was shown by his extreme concerns about cleanliness and cleaning rituals. Further, he may have suffered from panic attacks (indicating a high desire for tranquility). He once was quoted as saying, "I'm dying. I'm certain I've already suffered one heart attack and that the next one will finish me off."[9] In reality, however, he was just highly anxious.

Howard Hughes was a private person who bonded poorly with people (indicating a weak desire for social contact). Because he did not care about people, virtually everybody in his life eventually walked out on him. He spent the last years of his life as a recluse, apparently controlled by unscrupulous aides who kept him heavily medicated while they ran his business empire and rewarded themselves handsomely. When Hughes disappeared into hotel suites in his final years, there was no relative or close friend to come to his rescue. In the public memory, Howard Hughes's reputation as a daredevil millionaire aviator and business tycoon was superseded by the image of a bedridden, eccentric recluse who lived in hotel suites with the shades perpetually drawn.

SALVATORE GRAVANO [10]

STRONG (HIGH) DESIRES	AVERAGE DESIRES	WEAK (LOW) DESIRES
Power	Independence	Honor
Vengeance	Curiosity	Idealism
Physical Activity	Acceptance	Tranquility
	Order	
	Saving	
	Social Contact	
	Status	
	Romance	
	Eating	

Salvatore "Sammy the Bull" Gravano (1945–) sees himself in heroic terms: "I think I'm somebody with a very, very limited education and I fought and kicked and punched and did the best I could to get ahead. I dealt with the reality that someday I will probably be killed or go to fucking jail, and I lived with that reality all my life. That's the life I chose."[11] But "to get ahead," as he put it, he murdered 18 or 19 people. He also ran money-lending operations and multimillion-dollar rackets, and represented the mob in the New York construction industry. He became the highest-ranking Mafia figure ever to turn state witness. His testimony sent Mafia boss John Gotti to prison, along with a Mafia consigliere and three Mafia captains. When asked why he turned government witness, he said it was because the Mafia no longer lived by its own code of honor.

For much of his life, Gravano was driven by a desire for vengeance. In relating his life history to his biographer, Peter Maas, he spoke repeatedly of how he got even with this or that guy, which usually meant that he killed him. Time and again he went after people who crossed him, who showed him "no respect." Here is how he explained why he killed somebody: ". . . he was plotting to kill me. I felt the rage inside me."[12] Gravano prides himself on having "balls," or being "Sammy the Bull." He was fearless, ferocious, and streetwise. "So long as people are straight with me, everything is OK. But when they do things behind my back, when they betray me first, I can't stand that, I hate it."[13] When Sam hated something, he struck to even the score. I suspect that he turned state witness in part to get even with Gotti.

Today, Gravano thinks of himself as loyal to Mafia values. He once said, "All things I looked for in life was part of that [Mafia] oath."[14] Despite this statement, however, I do not think he places a high value on loyalty (indicating a low desire for honor). After all, he turned against two of his Mafia bosses (Gotti and Paul Castellano) and found reasons to violate various Mafia rules. When he took the Mafia oath, he pledged not to turn government witness, but he later found reason to change his mind. Although he thinks of himself as driven by honor and loyalty, I suspect that he's driven instead by vengeance.

Gravano experiences little guilt and is fearless, which means he has little desire for honor and for tranquility. An example of how little guilt he feels was his statement that he "slept like a rock"[15] after having just murdered somebody. Evidence of a low desire for tranquility is that he chose a dangerous career in the Mafia.

Gravano killed people in part because it gave him a feeling of power. Here is how he expressed his reactions to killing and dominating various people: "I was used to being in charge";[16] "I felt a surge of power";[17] and "I felt a tremendous surge of power and confidence."[18] His need for power is unusually high.

Gravano is driven by a need for physical activity. When he was in prison testifying against the Mafia, he risked his life by jogging outdoors, thereby exposing himself to other prisoners. Physical exertion is one of the greatest joys in his life. According to his biographer, he works out "religiously."[19]

On a personal level, Gravano is said to be a likeable guy. He is sensitive to the needs of others, and he inspired loyalty in those who worked for him.

He managed a number of Mafia businesses. All this suggests that he desired social contact to an average extent.

Gravano was probably happy in the Mafia. The Mafia lifestyle satisfied his need for revenge, power, physical exercise, and social contact. His fearlessness served him well, given his choice of career.

JACQUELINE KENNEDY ONASSIS[20]

STRONG (HIGH) DESIRES	AVERAGE DESIRES	WEAK (LOW) DESIRES
Saving	Power	Idealism
Family	Independence	Social Contact
Status	Curiosity	
	Acceptance	
	Order	
	Honor	
	Vengeance	
	Romance	
	Eating	
	Physical Activity	
	Tranquility	

Although Jacqueline Kennedy Onassis (1929–1995) was surrounded by great wealth, throughout her childhood and most of her adult life she herself was not wealthy. After her husband, President John F. Kennedy, was assassinated, she did not inherit enough money to make her wealthy by the standards of high society. Six years later she married Aristotle Onassis, one of the world's wealthiest men, and due to a transfer of funds, became wealthy on her own for the first time in her life.

In my opinion, Jackie Onassis was driven by a desire for status. She wanted to be admired as a person of great wealth and social standing. A recent biography reported the following comments about her at various points in her life:

> "She behaved like a social climber."[21]

> "She wanted the supposed glamour."[22]

> "Jackie was . . . aristocratic."[23]

> "She wanted to be noticed."[24]

All of these comments directly suggest a desire for status and for the notice that goes with status. Further, when Onassis was First Lady, she used her influence to support projects valued by high society, such as the restoration of the White House. She did not become interested in projects relating to social justice (indicating a low desire for idealism). Although her husband's work addressed the issues of civil rights and poverty, Onassis showed little personal interest in these issues. Her interests were directed much more at beautiful things and historic buildings, all of which were expensive and of interest to high society.

Jackie Onassis also was driven by a need for privacy. People who place a high value on privacy have a weak desire for social contact. Her aloofness functioned to satisfy her desire for privacy by holding casual acquaintances at bay. Happiness, fun, and joviality are not words that were associated with Onassis. Although she did accomplish her most important goals—wealth, children, and collections—she did not do so until late in life. Her marriages were not especially happy ones, and she had many challenges in her life, including the divorce of her parents and the early death of her first husband. Generally, the relatively low amount of fun in Onassis's life is consistent with her low desire for social contact (high need for privacy). Private people are rarely jovial and fun-loving.

Jackie Onassis enjoyed saving and collecting things. Although a bit of a spendthrift with Onassis's money, she was said to be thrifty with her own funds. She reportedly tried to get out of paying merchants, giving them a hard time when they came to collect on bills. According to her biographer, she charged expensive clothes to her husband's credit cards and then sold the clothes back to stores, crediting the proceeds to her own bank accounts. Money was not all that she enjoyed saving; she also saved beautiful things and clothes.

People might have found it difficult to understand why anybody would spend so much money to buy clothes in duplicate, triplicate, and in wholesale quantities. The overspending called attention to her wealth (status), which may be part of what motivated it. The shopping sprees also might have been motivated by a desire to collect clothes (indicating a strong desire to save).

Family is another desire that guided Onassis's behavior. She was a dedicated mother who was determined to protect her children from the constant media attention that surrounded her family. These efforts earned her worldwide admiration and respect.

Onassis did not change much during her adult years. Throughout her life, she was impressed by status, high society, wealth, glamour, privacy, and collections. As far as I know, she never showed much interest in social causes or power. She was always a dedicated mother. She will always be remembered as the First Lady who brought glamour and excitement to the White House.

HUMPHREY BOGART [25, 26]

STRONG (HIGH) DESIRES	AVERAGE DESIRES	WEAK (LOW) DESIRES
Independence	Power	Acceptance
Honor	Order	Curiosity
Idealism	Saving	Family
Romance	Social Contact	Status
	Vengeance	
	Eating	
	Physical Activity	
	Tranquility	

Humphrey Bogart (1899–1957) was perhaps the greatest actor of his era, starring in such classic films as *The Maltese Falcon* (1941), *Casablanca* (1942), and *The Treasure of the Sierra Madre* (1948). He was born into a well-to-do family, the oldest of three children and the only son. His father was a successful physician and his mother a nationally known illustrator. As a child, he attended private schools and spent his summers in Seneca Point, New York, with other children from well-to-do families. He was very handsome and modeled for his mother's illustrations. Although bright, he was unmotivated by school (indicating low curiosity).

When he became a senior in high school, his father enrolled him in the prestigious Philips Academy in Andover, Massachusetts, in preparation for a college career at Yale. However, he pursued girls and parties, did not strive academically, flunked out, and joined the Navy. He began his acting career at age 20 with help from the mother of a childhood friend. His good looks served him well in this endeavor, and he went to Hollywood in 1935 to work for Warner studios. His first important movies were in 1936 and after that 1941. In between he worked steadily, playing it safe, backing down in stormy contract disputes with Jack Warner. Of his four wives, Lauren Bacall was the last and was 20 years younger than he was. He died in 1957 of cancer.

Bogart was driven by a desire for romance, which was one of the joys in his life. Not only did he marry four times, but he took chances with his career in doing so. His marriage to Bacall posed risks to his career because it alienated a powerful director and because of her young age. Romance appears to have been the single greatest source of happiness in Bogart's life.

He also was driven by a desire for self-reliance (indicating a desire for independence). His main financial goal was to get enough money to support his lifestyle and to provide security. His early career strategy of playing it safe and not becoming excessively demanding with the studio company was consistent with this goal. He was more demanding later in his career after he had become established and had the money he needed to maintain his self-reliant lifestyle. Overall, he handled his money wisely.

Bogart was only moderately ambitious (indicating an average desire for power)—he worked hard, but he quit work on time each day. He enjoyed competition and interpersonal power games (indicating an at least average desire for vengeance). These interests affected his personal life, which was stormy, but did not seem to have much effect on his professional life. He apparently enjoyed leadership roles to some extent, but this desire was not extraordinary.

Bogart was loyal to his family, thus exhibiting a strong desire for honor. His mother was unaffectionate, and his father died a failure because of a bad investment decision. His sisters became mentally ill. Bogart brought his ailing mother and sisters to California and took care of them out of a strong sense of duty, not because he enjoyed their company and wanted to spend time with them. He had only a weak desire for a family of his own. He had to be talked into having children late in life.

Bogart had long bouts of drinking during which he could become sarcastic, angry, and verbally abusive. His drinking did not interfere with his career, although it did interfere with his personal relationships. He handled criticism and failure much better than do many people (indicating a low desire for acceptance), which is important given the amount of critical review in an actor's life. Especially in his early career, he had many setbacks. These did not result in withdrawal, quitting, resentment, or efforts to retaliate. Perhaps his good looks from childhood created an inner sense of confidence.

Later in his career Bogart led protests against the blacklisting of alleged communists in Hollywood (indicating a high desire for idealism). Prior to these activities, he did not show a strong interest in politics or social justice.

Born upper-class, Bogart developed a strong dislike for snobbery (weak desire for status). He did not buy a mansion until his fourth wife did it for him. He lived modestly, given his income, and did not seek attention. Even his acting style was known for its minimal use of attention-grabbing gestures. His lack of interest in social status may have been a factor that slowed his rise to stardom. He does not seem to have spent a great deal of time planning his career. He did not actively court the friendship of influential people, although he did court the friendship of writers and other people of ability. He enjoyed attention when it came in the form of appreciation of his work as an actor, not when it came in the form of respect for his money.

Happiness for Bogart meant a successful marriage, a successful career, and a significant amount of money to ensure his financial security.

AS SHOWN IN THESE BIOGRAPHIES, people value the 16 basic desires in their own individual ways. What one person must have, another person dislikes and avoids. Jackie Onassis, for example, spent her entire adult life seeking wealth and status, trying to impress high society with her beauty and class. She paid attention to her reputation and to other people's impressions of her. In contrast, Howard Hughes, who was fantastically wealthy, could not have cared less what high society thought of him. Onassis and Hughes behaved in very different ways because they had different desire profiles, and thus different goals.

The four celebrities differed regarding family values. Hughes lacked both loyalty to his relatives and an interest in raising children of his own (weak desires for honor and family); Bogart was loyal to his mother and sisters (strong desire for honor) but did not father a child until late in life (weak desire for family); Onassis was loyal to her parents and sister and strongly motivated to raise her children (average desire for honor and strong desire for family); and Gravano betrayed the Mafia and spent little time with his children (weak desire for honor and weak to average desire for family).

In reviewing the four desire profiles, we notice how unusually strong or weak desires can make people interesting. Howard Hughes seems the most engrossing character in the bunch because he had the most unusual passions. He showed ten unusual desires—very strong desires for power, independence, order, idealism, romance, and tranquility, and weak desires for honor, family, social contact, and status. Gravano, whom most people find to be the second most intriguing life history in the group, showed seven unusual desires—strong desires for power, vengeance, and physical exercise, and weak desires for honor, idealism, family, and tranquility. Onassis had a fascinating life, but her personality is not as interesting as you might have thought it would be. She showed only five unusual passions—strong desires for saving, status, and family, and weak desires for idealism and social contact. Bogart showed moderately strong passions for independence, honor, idealism, and romance, and moderately weak passions for curiosity, family, and status. Although he was a great actor, he is not very captivating as a psychological subject because he had no very strong or weak passions. Different people will be attentive to different aspects of each person's life. But generally unusually strong or weak desires make people interesting.

Unusual desires also create adjustment issues. When a person is as independent as Howard Hughes, he or she cannot easily satisfy that desire. Hughes went to extreme lengths to gratify his need for independence, in fact, he distanced himself from nearly everyone and was left with no friends, relatives, or partners at the end of his life. Gravano became a murderer to satisfy his overwhelmingly strong desire for vengeance, and he had trouble adjusting to prison life because he could not satisfy his desire for physical exercise without risking his safety. Onassis's passionate pursuit of wealth (status) earned her a reputation for snobbery. Lacking unusually strong or weak passions, Bogart adjusted reasonably well to life.

HOW AGING AFFECTS OUR DESIRES

How do basic desires change as people grow older? Will a curious adolescent still be curious at age 30, 50, or 70? Do shy children grow out of their shyness and become more sociable? Do aggressive adolescents mellow when they become middle-aged? How does aging affect our individuality?

Relative to same-aged peers, our basic desires show significant stability after about age 14. For example, an adolescent girl who is more athletic than her sister probably remains that way throughout life. When one sister loses some interest in physical activity as she grows older, so does the other sister, so that little *relative* change occurs. I suspect that this principle of little relative change is generally true of all 16 basic desires. Compared to same-aged peers, aggressive children become aggressive adults; sociable teenagers become sociable adults.

In contrast, our desires can change significantly on an absolute basis. By looking at the Reiss Profile scores for people in various age groups, I have tried to get a handle on how our basic desires change as people grow older. Although we observed considerable individual variation in how aging affects our desires, the results of our research suggest that many people change their priorities after about the age of 40. As young adults, the biological desires (eating, physical exercise, romance, and vengeance) are stronger in intensity than are many of the psychological desires. With advancing age, however, the biological desires decline in intensity beginning around age 30. People become less vengeful after about age 21, and they continue to show increasingly less interest in vengeance throughout their adult years. The desires for romance and physical exercise also decline significantly, especially after about age 35 to 40. Further, we found large decreases in the intensity of the desires for power and status after ages 35 to 40. This suggests that many people become less interested in their careers as they grow older.

On the other hand, the intensity of certain psychological desires (family, honor, and idealism) increase in strength with advancing age. As people become older, they become more family-oriented, as indicated by an increase in both the desire for honor (which connects us to our parents) and the desire for family (which connects us to our children). The desire for idealism (which connects us to society) also increases with advancing age.

An intriguing result of our research was that the desire for tranquility increased in people over the age of 56. The finding suggests that many people may be prone to become increasingly fearful as they approach old age and possible death.

These considerations underscore the importance of comparing ourselves to same-aged peers when we determine our desire profile. A person who is 45 should not think, "I'm less romantic than I used to be, so I'll rate myself as below-average for romance." The fact is that most people above the age of 40 are less romantic than they used to be. To be below-average for romance, you have to be significantly less interested in romance than other people your age. Otherwise, you are at least average for romance.

Clearly, there is considerable individual variation in how age affects our desires. As noted in Chapter 2, for example, Ben Franklin was still writing articles on his ideas right up to the weeks immediately prior to his death at an advanced age. We have had active presidents of the United States and of major corporations in their sixties and even seventies. John Glenn went into space at age 77.

MASLOW'S HIERARCHY OF SELF-ACTUALIZATION

A different theory of how basic desires change with advancing age was put forth by psychologist Abraham Maslow.[27] This theory essentially says that with advancing age, human growth occurs sequentially through five stages of development. During the first stage, people satisfy their biological needs—such as the needs for food, sex, and shelter—before all others. When a biological need is unsatisfied, people stop everything else they might be doing and direct all of their attention and energy to satisfying that need. When a person at work becomes hungry, for example, the person stops work in order to eat. When a child is playing outdoors and feels cold, the child stops playing long enough to come inside and dress warmly. Observations such as these convinced Maslow that people satisfy biological needs before they gratify any other kind of need.

When the biological needs are more or less met, the person places the highest possible value on the need to feel safe. (Maslow's need for safety is roughly equivalent to the basic desires for tranquility and order.) The biological needs, now satisfied, are pushed into the background, and safety becomes the individual's most important concern.

Maslow thought that our third-highest priority is to satisfy our belonging or social needs. At this time, "the person will feel keenly, as never before, the absence of friends, or a sweetheart, or a wife, or children. He will hunger for affectionate relations with people in general, namely, for a place in his group, and he will strive with great intensity to achieve this goal. He will want to attain such a place more than anything else in the world and may even forget that once, while he was hungry, he sneered at love."[28]

Maslow's fourth priority is the need for esteem and status. Gratification of these needs leads to feelings of self-confidence, worth, and capability, but people have feelings of inferiority and helplessness when these needs are thwarted.

If all of the needs discussed thus far are satisfied, Maslow believed a new restlessness sometimes occurs. It is the need for self-fulfillment, to become everything that one is capable of becoming. It is at this stage that our individuality is most fully developed. A musician must make music, an artist must paint, a poet must write, if the person is to be ultimately happy. "What a man can be, he must be,"[29] asserted Maslow.

Maslow thought that young people cannot self-actualize. His views gave emphasis to the development of wisdom and maturity as preconditions for self-actualization. He saw aging as a personal growth experience and not necessarily as inevitable decline.

Although this brief treatment of Maslow's theory does not do justice to its complexity, I hope it is sufficient to support some general points of comparison with the theory of the 16 basic desires. The main point of similarity is that I follow Maslow in looking at behavior as essentially an effort to satisfy our needs and basic desires. Another point of similarity is that Maslow discussed the importance of individuality and that I embrace what might be called radical individualism.

Generally, our results are consistent with Maslow's hypothesis that self-actualization (or human growth) occurs with advancing age. We found a decline in the intensity of biological motives and an increase in the intensity of "self-actualization" motives. However, our results are not entirely consistent with all of the details of Maslow's hierarchy of motives. For example, Maslow wrote that the desire for order falls under the need for safety. His theory predicts a decline in the intensity of safety needs in the later stages of life. The results of our research showed no such tendency. Although Maslow appears to have been correct in analyzing how motives change generally with advancing age, not surprisingly he did not guess correctly in regard to all specific predictions.

However, my work departs from Maslow's in two important respects. First, my theory is based on scientific research and, thus, has a significant and growing factual basis to it. I developed the Reiss Profile as an objective basis for determining a person's desire profile, and my colleagues and I have studied more than six thousand people. In contrast, Maslow's theory has no factual basis: Maslow conducted no scientific research to test his theory, and he offered no evidence to support it. Maslow himself wrote in 1970 that he had tried to think of a way to test his theory scientifically but was unable to do so.[30] Maslow based his theory on his personal opinions about the people he knew and on reading biographies of famous people.

Second, I favor the idea of an individual desire profile over Maslow's idea of a hierarchy of human needs. In my opinion, each individual's growth as a person is best measured against that person's desire profile, rather than some common metric such as Maslow's hierarchy. An hierarchy applicable to all people lends itself to misuse. Under Maslow's hierarchy, for example, a person who is focused on achievement has reached a higher stage of development than a person who is focused on being loved. The implication is that the former individual is a more "perfect specimen"[31]—as Maslow once put it—of the human species. I feel that this viewpoint can be misunderstood as implying that achievers are more important people than are those seeking love or that achievement is a higher value than romantic love. Therefore, I prefer the idea of an individual desire profile in which self-actualization is measured individually, by the extent to which each person has fulfilled his or her unique desire profile.

I Don't Get It,
and Neither Do You

Your desire profile affects how you communicate with other people. You may find that you communicate instinctively and fluidly with people whose desire profiles are similar to yours. But your desires can also create an invisible wall that leads to miscommunication between you and those with desire profiles similar to your own. There are two main types of miscommunication, *ineffective communication* and *not getting it*. Ineffective communication occurs when a person does not know another person's viewpoint; for example, a spouse who is having a bad day becomes angry when asked to wait for dinner. The anger is confusing to the partner, who has not seen all of the frustrations that led up to it. When this is later explained, the partner has a better understanding of why the spouse became angry, even when the partner does not approve of the outburst. In contrast, "not getting it" is the result of everyone having such unique desires that we literally cannot always understand each other. More information does not solve this problem—it only sharpens the differences.

An example of "not getting it" occurs between people who do and do not value curiosity. The intellectual looks at the non-intellectual and wonders why he or she has not discovered the joy of learning. The non-intellectual looks back at the intellectual and wonders why he or she is such a nerd.

No amount of explanation can help them appreciate their differences—both are baffled as to how the other can want what they themselves cannot stand.

The best description I have read of "not getting it" was written in 1842 by a British philosopher named George Ramsay. He wrote,

> The same difference of feeling and dullness of imagination in men explain what has often been observed, that one half of mankind pass their lives in wondering at the pursuits of the other. Not being able either to feel or to fancy the pleasure derived from the other sources than their own, they consider the rest of the world as little better than fools, who follow empty baubles. They hug themselves as the only wise, while in truth they are only narrow-minded.[1]

"Not getting it" occurs when people hold conflicting opinions or desires regarding the same value. It has three elements: misunderstanding, self-hugging, and everyday tyranny.

1. *Misunderstanding* refers to the confusion people experience when they try to understand how another person experiences, likes, or dislikes something much different than they do themselves. For example, some people have a hard time understanding why a workaholic spends so much time on the job.

2. *Self-hugging* refers to people's automatic assumption that their goals and values are best, not just for themselves, but also for other people as well. A good example of this is the heterosexual parent who keeps encouraging a homosexual son to date women.

3. *Everyday tyranny* refers to the use of pressure tactics to try to get someone to change his or her basic goals, values, or lifestyle. One example is a parent who refuses to pay for college for a child who chooses a career against the parent's wishes.

The Greek movie *Never on Sunday* provided a humorous look at "not getting it." The movie tells the story of two people, Homer and Ilya, who have opposite desires. Homer is a philosopher pursuing an intellectual lifestyle (indicating high curiosity), and Ilya is a fun-loving prostitute pursuing a sensual lifestyle (indicating high romance and high social contact). Ilya takes off every Sunday to watch Greek tragedies and imagines that the endings are happy. Since she confuses fantasy with reality, she could not be more different from Homer, who believes that facing reality is essential for "true" happiness. Although Ilya seems happy, Homer thinks that deep down she is not "really" happy. He tries to change her into an intellectual, educating her about books, art, morality, and classical music. At first, she changes in response to his efforts, but by the end of the movie she reverts back to her old ways.

In *Never on Sunday,* all three elements of "not getting it" occur. The misunderstanding is that Homer, an intellectual, cannot comprehend how Ilya could possibly be happy with her sensual lifestyle. Self-hugging is shown by Homer's presumption that an intellectual lifestyle potentially leads to deeper or superior satisfactions, not just for himself, but for Ilya as well. Everyday tyranny is involved in Homer's efforts to intimidate Ilya into changing her lifestyle.

"Not getting it" can be difficult to recognize in everyday life. Let's take a closer look at self-hugging and everyday tyranny to deepen our understanding of how these communication problems manifest and why they may never really get resolved.

SELF-HUGGING

People who self-hug think that what is best for themselves is best for everyone else as well. They think that we have the potential to enjoy their lifestyle. When Aristotle thought that philosophy led to the greatest possible happiness in life, for example, he was self-hugging. Philosophy was the greatest pleasure in *his* life, but it is not the greatest possible pleasure in the lives of all people. When the Big Daddy character in *Cat on a Hot Tin Roof* thinks that the key to happiness is success, he is self-hugging.[2] Ambition is the greatest desire in his life, but it is not the greatest possible desire in everybody's life. When a football coach says that winning is everything, he is self-hugging. Competition may be the greatest pleasure in the coach's life, but it is not the greatest possible pleasure in everybody's life.

We all self-hug, and we do it often. It is only human nature to presume that other people can learn to enjoy what we enjoy. The sociable partner tries to teach his or her spouse to be more fun-loving. The saver advises his or her partner that, in the long run, they will be better off if they postpone buying the new car and save money instead. The timid parent teaches his or her child the virtues of caution. Moral people argue that a person's character and strict adherence to principles are the hallmarks of a successful life.

What is striking in all of these examples is the absence of any concept of individuality. The values are "one size fits all." Having discovered the values that are best for themselves, self-huggers are ready to improve us by advocating that we become more like they are. Yet the only way we can be happy is if we become who we are, not who somebody else would like us to be.

Self-hugging leads directly to miscommunication because self-huggers misread what other people want from life. They never get it—other people pursue different goals in life, not because they have settled for inferior pleasures, but because they have different natures.

EVERYDAY TYRANNY

Everyday tyrants also think that if only we would give their way of doing things a real try, we would learn its superior satisfactions and change our behavior for good. They use a variety of tactics to induce us to try things their way, such as intimidation, criticism, quarreling, guilt, incentives, and punishment. They do not realize that others may never learn the "superior" satisfactions of their lifestyle because they have a different nature. Individuality can create a wall between people, and everyday tyrants cannot see how things appear on our side of the wall, only on their side.

The paradox of everyday tyranny is that although it doesn't work, people keep using it as their primary method of changing others. Spouses try every day to make their partners more like they are. They may never quit, despite a lack of success. They tell their children and partners to be neater, more ambitious, more principled, more sociable, or more active. Why haven't they realized that we are not going to change because we do not enjoy the changes they want us to make?

Everyday tyranny produces only temporary changes in behavior. It does not work over the long haul because people cannot change their basic natures. People can pressure their partners or children into complying with their wishes for short periods of time, but sooner or later their efforts fail because the individual reverts back to his or her basic values and ways of behaving. Everyday tyranny ruins relationships. It can lead to resentment, divorce, children leaving home and not coming back, and even mental illness.

As portrayed in the motion picture *Titanic,* Rose DeWitt Bukater has to choose between two men, one offering wealth and social standing, the other offering romance and love. Does she marry ruthless Cal Hockley, one of America's richest men, or run off with artist Jack Dawson, who made her feel happy? Although she considers the prospects of marrying Cal Hockley akin to death, she has already consented to do so. Jack Dawson is exciting, but is poor and unable to support her; he could not even afford passage on the *Titanic* until he won the money at poker. While Rose considers her options, her mother decides to pressure Rose to stay loyal to Hockley. If Rose does not marry him, Rose's mother says, the family will fall into disgrace because it no longer has any money. "Do you want me to be a seamstress?" her mother asks Rose. Although Rose listens to her mother at first, she runs to her true lover hours before the *Titanic* goes down.

Many parents use everyday tyranny to pressure their children to make certain career choices, but the tactics rarely work. Robert Darwin, for example, fought with his son, Charles, to become a physician.[3] But it wasn't in Charles's nature to become a doctor—Charles had little interest and was too squeamish. It took his father a while to realize that Charles would never take the career path envisioned for him, but at least he backed off from his demand and their relationship was not ruined.

WHY ROCK 'N' ROLL WAS SEEN AS THE DOWNFALL OF SOCIETY

"Not getting it" can occur between generations as well as people. Music (which is part of the basic desire for romance) is a good case in point. When

I was a kid in the 1960s, my parents could not understand how I could like rock 'n' roll. They thought it was noise and did not let me play it when they were home. Some said it was the music of the devil, or at least the communists, but the communists argued that rock 'n' roll music was a certain sign that western civilization was crumbling under the weight of capitalism. Like most parents, mine dismissed the hours I spent listening to rock 'n' roll as the behavior of a foolish teenager. When I got to college, however, I dated a number of women who thought I was some kind of cultural lowlife for liking rock music. In their opinion, people who liked classical music had reached a higher level of consciousness than had rockers. The general principle was, "If you like music X, and I like music Y, it is because I am superior to you, and Y is the music of superior people."

One young lady asked me, "How could a smart person like you be such a cultural imbecile?" Being a curious person, I have spent many hours pondering that very same question. I never came up with an answer, but now that I have developed my idea of "not getting it," I no longer need feel shame for my interest in rock 'n' roll.

The great debate between rockers and classical music enthusiasts has never been resolved. At one time, the world was divided by what type of music people liked—the under-30 group versus the over-30 group—rather than by nationality, race, or political ideology. Rock music eventually became part of mainstream culture, not because people actually changed their minds about it, but because the young people of the 1950s and 1960s became the adults of the 1980s and 1990s. My parents died disliking rock 'n' roll music, and I will die liking it.

THE 16 ODD COUPLES

In the following charts, you'll see how people who strongly value each of the 16 basic desires can miscommunicate with people who do not feel strongly about the same intrinsic value, and vice versa. (As the title of this chapter suggests, this type of miscommunication is always a two-way street.) All three elements of "not getting it" occur between people holding the opposite values shown in these charts. They misunderstand each other, self-hug, and either dismiss each other or use everyday tyranny.

POWER	WHAT PERSON THINKS OF SELF	WHAT PERSON THINKS OF OTHER
Strong Desire: Ambitious	leader, hard-working, strong, success-oriented, dominant, powerful, achiever	lazy, weak, unsuccessful
Weak Desire: Unambitious	people-oriented, submissive, follower	workaholic, driven, bossy, dominant, annoying, controlling, single-minded

"Not getting it" can occur between ambitious and unambitious people, who experience the basic desire of power at very different intensities. *Misunderstanding* occurs because ambitious and unambitious people view themselves differently from how they view each other. Ambitious people think of themselves as being success-oriented, strong, and powerful, but unambitious people criticize them for being bossy, controlling, or single-minded. Unambitious people think of themselves as being people-oriented, but ambitious people criticize them as being unsuccessful or lazy. *Self-hugging* occurs when, for example, unambitious people tell ambitious people that they would be happier if they didn't work so much and instead stopped to smell the roses. They do not realize that ambitious people enjoy what they are doing. As Pablo Picasso put it, "When I work, I relax. Doing nothing makes me tired."

Everyday tyranny occurs when, for example, ambitious people encourage unambitious people to work harder. I once tried to help out an employee who was getting off to a slow start. I introduced her to influential people, one of whom was willing to giver her significant career assistance. Although I thought I had helped the employee and expected appreciation, what I found instead was resentment. I was pressuring her to be more successful than she wanted to be. I am ambitious and oriented toward success and achievement, but this woman was unambitious and more interested in pacing herself and not becoming overworked. From my perspective, I was helping the employee become a success; from the employee's perspective, I was trying to get her to work harder for the same pay. I had erroneously assumed that the employee's goals were similar to mine.

INDEPENDENCE	WHAT PERSON THINKS OF SELF	WHAT PERSON THINKS OF OTHER
Strong Desire: Independent Person	self-reliant, autonomous, free	immature, weak
Weak Desire: Interdependent Person	loving, needing love, trusting, devoted, attached	uncompromising, stubborn, prideful

"Not getting it" can occur between independent and interdependent people, who experience the basic desire of independence at very different intensities. *Misunderstanding* occurs because independent and interdependent people view themselves differently from how they view each other. Independent people, who like to control their own fate, think of themselves as self-reliant and free, but interdependent people criticize them as prideful, uncompromising, and stubborn. In contrast, interdependent people, who enjoy being in need of others, think of themselves as loving and trusting people, but independent people criticize them as being immature and weak.

Self-hugging occurs when independent and interdependent people tout the superiority of their values. Self-reliant people tout the virtues of auton-

CURIOSITY	WHAT PERSON THINKS OF SELF	WHAT PERSON THINKS OF OTHER
Strong Desire: Intellectuals	smart, interesting, mindful, scholarly	boring, ignorant, superficial, mindless, dumb, emotional, provincial
Weak Desire: Non-Intellectuals	practical, down-to-earth, street-smart	boring, egghead, nerds, arrogant, highbrow, overly analytical, cold, lacking in common sense, impractical, cerebral

omy and entrepreneurship, whereas interdependent people tout the virtues of teamwork and love of others. *Everyday tyranny* occurs when interdependent people put pressure on independent people to be less self-serving and better team players. Coaches will bench a child if he is too much of a "hot dog" and has not learned to be a team player. On the other hand, independent people often push interdependent people to be more self-reliant.

"Not getting it" can occur between intellectual and non-intellectual people, who experience the basic desire for curiosity at very different intensities. *Misunderstanding* occurs because intellectuals and non-intellectuals view themselves differently from how they view each other. Intellectuals think of themselves as being smart and interesting people, but non-intellectuals think of them as arrogant, boring, impractical, or coldly analytical. Non-intellectuals think of themselves as being practical and down-to-earth, but intellectuals think of them as being boring and superficial. *Self-hugging* is evident when intellectuals argue that learning is life's greatest joy or value, or when non-intellectuals argue that eggheads miss out on all the fun. Everyday tyranny is evident when the two groups criticize or ridicule each other. For example, the movie *Of Human Bondage* tells the story of Philip Carey, a medical student, and Mildred Rogers, a waitress. Philip likes to read, but Mildred has no interest in books. At one point, she shows irritation at his intellectualism by commenting, "For a gentleman of brains, you do not use them."

ACCEPTANCE	WHAT PERSON THINKS OF SELF	WHAT PERSON THINKS OF OTHER
Strong Desire: Insecure	nonassertive, insecure, lacking in confidence	conceited, overly confident, slick
Weak Desire: Self-Confident	assertive, confident, self-assured, positive self-image	needy, quitter, crybaby, immature, overly sensitive

"Not getting it" can occur between insecure and self-confident people, who experience at different intensities the basic desire of acceptance. *Misunderstanding* occurs because insecure and self-confident people view themselves differently than they view each other. Insecure people, who have a high sensitivity to rejection, criticism, and failure, admit to being nonassertive, insecure, or lacking in self-confidence, whereas self-confident people criticize them as being needy, quitters, or crybabies. Self-confident people, who have a low sensitivity to rejection, criticism, and failure, think of themselves as being assertive and self-assured, but insecure people criticize them as being conceited or slick. *Self-hugging* occurs when self-confident people try to talk insecure people into having more confidence. Insecure people may not show self-hugging—they may be the exceptions to the rule, the one group so lacking in self-confidence they do not self-hug much. *Everyday tyranny* occurs when confident people try to pressure insecure people out of quitting or into being more confident.

ORDER	WHAT PERSON THINKS OF SELF	WHAT PERSON THINKS OF OTHER
Strong Desire: Organized People	neat, organized, in control, socialized	sloppy, dirty, out of control, disorganized, unkempt, unsanitary
Weak Desire: Flexible People	flexible, spontaneous	too perfect, controlling of others, concerned with trivia, rigid

"Not getting it" can occur between organized and flexible people who experience the basic desire of order at very different intensities. *Misunderstanding* occurs because organized and flexible people view themselves differently from the way in which they view each other. Organized people think of themselves as organized and neat, but flexible people criticize them for being too perfect and concerned with trivial matters. Flexible people think of themselves as being flexible and spontaneous, but organized people criticize them as sloppy, out of control, or disorganized.

When living together, each person thinks that his or her lifestyle is best (*self-hugging*) and tries to change the other (*everyday tyranny*). The organized person is after the flexible person to be more neat in appearance and to keep rooms neat, while the flexible person complains about rigid schedules and unnecessary rules. Organized parents may teach messy kids to keep their rooms clean and to live by schedules and rules. Flexible parents may teach their kids to show greater flexibility and spontaneity and to not follow rules mindlessly.

SAVING	WHAT PERSON THINKS OF SELF	WHAT PERSON THINKS OF OTHER
Strong Desire: Saver	frugal, thrifty, planning ahead	irresponsible, imprudent, foolhardy, living for today, wasteful
Weak Desire: Spender	enjoying life, deserving	miser, money-grubber, cheap, self-denying

"Not getting it" may occur between savers and spenders, who experience the basic desire of saving at very different intensities. *Misunderstanding* occurs because savers and spenders view themselves differently from how they view each other. Savers think of themselves as frugal, but spenders criticize them as being tightwads. In contrast, spenders think of themselves as being deserving of good things, but savers criticize them as irresponsible and wasteful.

Self-hugging occurs when savers and spenders think that their way of living is best. For example, commercials for major investment firms tout the values of saving as the best way for a happy retirement. The underlying message is that everybody is better off as a saver, not just those who enjoy it.

Everyday tyranny occurs when partners fight over how much money they are saving or spending. One partner wants to spend more, and the other wants to save more. Conflicts may arise when one partner wants to take a vacation while the other would rather bank the money. Couples who fight over how much money to spend may never fully resolve the issue, because it concerns a basic psychological desire.

"Not getting it" may occur between principled and expedient people, who experience the basic desire of honor at very different intensities. *Misunderstanding* occurs because principled and expedient people view themselves differently from how they view each other. Principled people think of themselves as having character, but expedient people criticize them as self-

HONOR	WHAT PERSON THINKS OF SELF	WHAT PERSON THINKS OF OTHER
Strong Desire: Principled People	responsible, moral, loyal, principled, having character, conscientious, dutiful	unprincipled, disloyal, dishonorable, self-serving, uncaring, lacking character
Weak Desire: Expedient People	practical, opportune, like everybody else	self-righteous, preachy, sanctimonious, holier-than-thou

righteous and preachy. In contrast, expedient people think of themselves as pragmatic, realistic, and no different from anybody else, but principled people criticize them as self-serving and lacking in character.

Self-hugging is evident in political debates on the importance of "character," in which each side of the debate views itself as superior to the other side. In the impeachment of President Clinton, for example, people with high value for honor complained that Clinton was an arrogant person who thought of himself as superior to others and above the law. On the other hand, expedient people complained that President's Clinton's accusers were self-righteous and hypocritical individuals who considered themselves morally superior to everyone else. *Everyday tyranny* was apparent in all the mudslinging, ridicule, and criticism each side of the Clinton controversy directed toward the other. The two groups debated the issue for months with little change in positions.

In my opinion, the reason positions changed so little throughout the impeachment process is that the underlying debate concerned a basic psychological desire that is not easily changed. People agreed on the facts of what President Clinton had done, but they disagreed on the significance of his mistakes and what should be done about it. Communication and debate did not lessen the disagreement; they only sharpened it. The problem was not a lack of communication, but rather that each side did not get it when it came to understanding the other side's position.

IDEALISM	WHAT PERSON THINKS OF SELF	WHAT PERSON THINKS OF OTHER
Strong Desire: Idealistic People	caring, compassionate, visionary, just, humane	heartless, insensitive, unfeeling, self-centered, cynical
Weak Desire: Realistic People	realistic, pragmatic, looking out for number one	dreamer, meddlesome, unrealistic

"Not getting it" may occur between idealistic and realistic people, who experience the basic desire of idealism at very different intensities. *Misunderstanding* occurs because idealistic and realistic people view themselves in different ways than they view each other. Idealistic people have a strong sense of fairness or social justice and are interested in what is happening in the society as a whole. They think of themselves as being compassionate, visionary, or caring, but realistic people criticize them as being dreamers. In contrast, realistic people pay little attention to what is going on in society and think of themselves as smart not to worry about things they cannot control. However, idealistic people criticize realistic people as heartless, cynical, and uncaring.

Self-hugging occurs when idealistic people encourage realistic people to become more involved in a cause or when realistic people tell idealistic people that their efforts are futile. *Everyday tyranny* occurs when arguments break out on the importance of idealism. During the 1960s, for example, the question of idealism versus realism became a major issue dividing generations of Americans. Generally speaking, "adults," defined in those days as people over the age of 30, took a "realistic" view of communism, advocating that it must be stopped in southeast Asia or it would dominate the world. "Kids," defined as people under the age of 30, generally took an idealized view of things, imagining a world filled with peace and love, and without war. Each side thought its viewpoint was valid, and people did what they could to force their views on the other side.

SOCIAL CONTACT	WHAT PERSON THINKS OF SELF	WHAT PERSON THINKS OF OTHER
Strong Desire: Sociable	friendly, congenial, fun-loving, outgoing, lively	stuffed-shirt, serious, unhappy, withdrawn, unsociable, lonely
Weak Desire: Private	private, serious, shy	superficial, shallow, boisterous

"Not getting it" may occur between sociable people and private people, who experience the basic desire of social contact at significantly different intensities. *Misunderstanding* occurs because sociable and private people view themselves in different ways from how they view each other. Sociable people think of themselves as being friendly, lively, and fun-loving, but private people criticize them as being superficial and boisterous. Private people think of themselves as serious or shy people, but sociable people criticize them for being stuffed shirts, withdrawn, and unsociable.

Self-hugging occurs when sociable people advise loners to let their emotions go and to live it up. Do you remember the lyrics to the song "Cabaret?" They say that it is better to go out and listen to music than to waste time sitting alone in one's room. The lyrics suggest that this is what life is all about, having a good time. Well, it's a nice song, but from a psychological perspective, it is self-hugging and touts the values of sociability above the values of privacy. Private people probably will not be happy going to cabarets—they will not discover the great joys of being sociable, but instead will feel uncomfortable.

Everyday tyranny occurs when a social and a private partner fight over their social life. One spouse wants to party and have fun, while the other prefers to spend quiet evenings at home.

"Not getting it" may occur between family-oriented and non-family-oriented people, who experience the basic desire for family (parenthood) at different intensities. Family-oriented people enjoy raising children, but-non-family-oriented people experience parenthood as more of a burden

FAMILY	WHAT PERSON THINKS OF SELF	WHAT PERSON THINKS OF OTHER
Strong Desire: Family People	nurturing, responsible, domestic	selfish, irresponsible, will grow old alone
Weak Desire: Non-Family People	independent, free	burdened, foolish, domestic, tied down

than a joy. *Misunderstanding* occurs because family-oriented and non-family-oriented people view each other very differently than they view themselves. Family-oriented people think of themselves as nurturing and domestic, and they think of non-family-oriented people as selfish and irresponsible. Non-family-oriented people see themselves as independent or free, and they wonder why family-oriented people have chosen a lifestyle filled with domestic burdens and responsibilities. When family-oriented and non-family-oriented people live together as a couple, they argue over having children (everyday tyranny).

Family-oriented and non-family-oriented people do not appreciate each other. The disagreement has spilled into the political arena where "family values" have been debated. Each side in this debate tries to change public policy to reward people who share their values. The debate is heated at times because it concerns a basic psychological desire.

Self-hugging is evident when family-oriented people argue over whether one parent should stay at home rather than pursue a career. In a recent letter to the *Columbus Dispatch,* for example, a family-oriented person complained that women who send their kids to day-care are not "true mothers." Some career women who would prefer not to have to work need to do so to help support their families. On the other hand, some women want to have both children and a career. They feel that both their needs and those of their children can be adequately fulfilled if they pursue both a career and motherhood. Still others want only a career.

Our metropolitan newspaper reported the story of a man who gave up his career as a chef in order to raise his three children. The newspaper dubbed him "the man who traded career for family wealth." "I would like to make a lot of money," he said. "But I'm wealthy now."[4] While he stayed home and took care of children aged 2, 4, and 6, his wife pursued a career with a large national bank. His wife praised his efforts, but his friend reportedly thought he was "nuts," using ridicule, a form of *everyday tyranny*, to devalue his lifestyle. He became the subject of "Mr. Mom" jokes to the point where even he began to wonder if he was doing the right thing. Although the people who laughed at him understood that he was doing something he enjoyed, they just did not understand how any man could possibly want to be a househusband and thought him a fool for this desire (misunderstanding).

STATUS	WHAT PERSON THINKS OF SELF	WHAT PERSON THINKS OF OTHER
Strong Desire: Elitist	important, prominent, prestigious, renowned, eminent	unimportant, insignificant, misfit, trash, low-class, poor taste
Weak Desire: Egalitarian	democratic, equitable, libertarian, fair-minded	snob, arrogant, aloof, show-off

"Not getting it" may occur between elitists and egalitarian people, who experience the basic desire of status at very different intensities. *Misunderstanding* occurs because elitists and egalitarian people view themselves in different ways from how they view each other. Elitists, who take pride in status, place a high value on things that are prestigious. They like to think of themselves as important people, but egalitarian people criticize them as snobs. Egalitarian people place a high value on treating each person as a center of worth. They like to think of themselves as fair-minded and democratic, but elitists dismiss them as unimportant and low-class.

Self-hugging occurs when elitists assume that they are above the rules and are more important than everyone else. It also occurs when egalitarian people pat themselves on the back for being democratic. *Everyday tyranny* occurs when a parent argues with a teenage child to pay more attention to what the neighbors might think, to dress nicely, or to pay greater attention to the prestige value of purchases. For example, a student had been living on a modest stipend for over a year when her wealthy mother visited. Looking at the wardrobe the student had acquired, the mother was appalled that the clothes were second-hand. She tried to buy her daughter expensive clothes and also wanted to refurnish her dormitory room. The daughter refused and the two fought over the issue.

Differences in the desire for status can be a source of conflict in marriages. The partner who "marries up" as part of his need for high status may feel a need to prove himself—for example, the husband of a wealthy wife may feel pressure to prove he can earn his own fortune. The partner who "marries down" but has a high desire for status may resent the loss of status associated with his or her spouse and worry about the wisdom of the decision. "You just married me for my money," thinks the wealthy spouse.

VENGEANCE	WHAT PERSON THINKS OF SELF	WHAT PERSON THINKS OF OTHERS
Strong Desire: Competitive People	winner, competitive, aggressive	loser, nonassertive, passive
Weak Desire: Cooperative People	conflict-avoidant, kind, forgiving, cooperative	aggressive, competitive, angry, always wants to win

"Not getting it" may occur between competitive and cooperative people, who experience the basic desire for vengeance at very different intensities. *Misunderstanding* occurs because competitive and cooperative people view themselves in different ways from how they view each other. Competitive people think of themselves as winners, but cooperative people think of them as aggressive. *Self-hugging* is evident when cooperative people tell competitive people that they should become less aggressive, and when competitive people tell cooperative people that they need to stand up for their rights because "it's a dog-eat-dog world."

Everyday tyranny occurs, for example, when cooperative people tout the value of collaboration. A good case in point is author Alfie Kohn's argument that schools should embrace the values of cooperative learning. "American schools offer two basic modes of instruction," wrote Kohn.[5] One mode has children competing for "artificial" grades and prizes, and the other has them working together in small teams in what is called "collaborative learning." Kohn claimed "rigorous" scientific support for his position favoring collaboration. But he was actually engaged in self-hugging, ignoring individual differences and presuming that his values should be imposed on everybody.

ROMANCE	WHAT PERSON THINKS OF SELF	WHAT PERSON THINKS OF OTHER
Strong Desire: Sensualists	romantic, sensitive, virile, exciting, high sex drive, lover	self-denying, prudish, hung-up, frigid/impotent
Weak Desire: Ascetics	virtuous, saintly, self-controlled	beast, lacking in control, hedonistic, superficial

"Not getting it" may occur between sensualists and ascetics, who experience the basic desire for romance at very different intensities. Sensualists are driven to experience as much pleasure as they can find, but ascetics are motivated to deny themselves any pleasure. *Misunderstanding* occurs because sensualists and ascetics view themselves in different ways from how they view each other. Sensualists think that ascetics are mentally unbalanced or hung-up over sex, whereas ascetics dismiss sensualists as hedonistic people who pursue superficial pleasures.

Self-hugging and *everyday tyranny* are evident in moral debates in which sensualists and ascetics criticize each other's values while championing their own. Plato was a good example of someone whose attacked the values of sensualism. Even before religion had declared sex to be a sin, Plato complained that it distracted his students from philosophy; apparently, he did not appreciate the fact that his students preferred sex to his lectures. He wrote,

> [Those] who spend their whole time in feasting and self-indulgence are all their lives, as it were, fluctuating downwards. . . .

Never really satisfied with real nourishment, the pleasure they taste is uncertain and impure. . . . They grow fat and breed, and in their greedy struggle kick and butt one another to death . . . because they can never satisfy. . . . Does it not follow that the pleasures of such a life are illusory phantoms of real pleasure?[6]

Hugh Hefner is a good example of a sensualist. Hefner has been concerned that if people thought of sex as downward drift, they would not buy his magazine. So he invented the "*Playboy* philosophy," which essentially holds that sex is good. The debate between sensualists and ascetics has been going on for centuries and will never be resolved because it concerns differences in how people value a basic psychological desire.

EATING	WHAT PERSON THINKS OF SELF	WHAT PERSON THINKS OF OTHER
Strong Desire: Hearty Eaters	happy, sensual, hedonistic, gourmand	self-denying, unhealthy
Weak Desire: Light Eaters	slender, healthy, strong-willed, sensible	lacking self-control or willpower, unhealthy, pleasure-seeking, glutton

"Not getting it" can occur between hearty and light eaters, who experience the basic desire for food at very different intensities. *Misunderstanding* occurs because hearty and light eaters view themselves in different ways than they view each other. Hearty eaters think of themselves as happy and sensual people, and they think of light eaters as people living in self-denial. Light eaters think of themselves as strong-willed, slender, and healthy, and they criticize hearty eaters as gluttons who lack willpower. The differences reflect cultural attitudes toward fat and thin people. Both *self-hugging* and *everyday tyranny* are apparent in the negative attitudes to fat people in American society. A good case in point was the joking over President Clinton's fondness for McDonald's hamburgers. Thin people may make fun of President Clinton for his eating habits because they think it signals a lack of control.

PHYSICAL ACTIVITY	WHAT PERSON THINKS OF SELF	WHAT PERSON THINKS OF OTHER
Strong Desire: Active People	energetic, vigorous, fit, athletic, strong, muscular	lazy, listless, slow, sedentary, weak, frail, sluggish, tired, couch potato
Weak Desire: Inactive People	self-paced, easy-going, low-key	jocks, physical, exhausting, fast-paced

"Not getting it" can occur between active and inactive people, who experience the basic desire for physical exercise at very different intensities. *Misunderstanding* occurs because active and inactive people view themselves in different ways than they view each other. Active people, who enjoy working out, think of themselves as athletic, strong, and healthy, but inactive people think of them as "jocks." Inactive people, who don't like to exert too much energy, think of themselves as self-paced, but active people think of them as lazy.

Athletic people sometimes form their own subculture within schools and perhaps within society. For example, a few years back at a major university a basketball player with a troubled history was charged with theft. The athletic director, who saw this incident as the final straw, immediately announced the player's dismissal from school. That prompted a query from the faculty, who wondered what authority the athletic director had to dismiss students from the university. The debate arose over the presumption that the student somehow "belonged" to the athletic department.

Self-hugging is evident when active people believe that their lifestyle leads to the greatest happiness. You will often see *everyday tyranny* occurring when active people lecture inactive people about the importance of regular physical exercise and the dangers of inactivity. Active people often feel that if only an inactive person tried exercise, he'd love it, and they can't understand how anybody can enjoy "lying around." In his book *Keep the Connection*, Bob Greene attacks physical inactivity, calling it "laziness" and a "sin."

TRANQUILITY	WHAT PERSON THINKS OF SELF	WHAT PERSON THINKS OF OTHER
Strong Desire: Timid People	cautious, prudent, careful, mindful	reckless, foolhardy, mindless, unaware, daredevil, rash, fearless
Weak Desire: Brave People	courageous, daring, bold, confident, valiant, stalwart	cowardly, neurotic, fearful, worrier, overprotective

"Not getting it" can occur between timid and brave people, who experience the basic desire of tranquility at very different intensities. *Misunderstanding* occurs because timid and brave people view themselves in different ways than they view each other. Timid people think of themselves as being cautious and prudent, whereas brave people consider them cowardly. Brave people think of themselves as courageous and daring, but timid people criticize them as reckless daredevils who expose themselves to unnecessary danger.

People who invest in the stock market provide many examples of self-hugging. Timid investors have a saying, "If you can stay calm in the stock market while everybody else is experiencing panic and selling, maybe you do not understand the situation." As the phrase suggests, timid people see wisdom in being mindful of risks. Believing that timidity can be a virtue, such investors are easily frightened about their stock market positions and may sell too early. Because they are risk-averse, they prefer only the safest investments. "The better part of valour is discretion," wrote Shakespeare.[7] In contrast, brave investors have sayings of their own: "Markets climb a wall of worries," and "No pain, no gain." Because they are thrill-seekers, brave investors see wisdom in "going for it." They can hold risky positions, sometimes winning or losing a lot of money.

Everyday tyranny occurs when brave people shame timid people into being courageous. A famous example of this occurred during World War II when General George Patton visited a hospital and became enraged at a soldier who had a psychiatric disorder but no apparent physical illness. Patton slapped the soldier, called him a coward in front of others, and made him leave the hospital and rejoin his fighting unit. (Patton was later disciplined by the U.S. command for confusing a psychiatric disorder with cowardice.) The system of 16 basic desires implies that Patton's negative attitude toward timid people was a specific example of the more general tendency of people at opposite ends of a basic desire to disrespect (or at least not appreciate) each other's values.

"NOT GETTING IT" is part of our everyday lives. Although some examples are amusing, "not getting it" can be serious business. Every so often it breaks out into a cultural war, but even when that does not happen, it is a major factor in what people do not like about each other. It is so basic to human thinking that people do not realize when it is occurring, and how it biases their attitude toward other people.

Interestingly, "not getting it" primarily occurs when people have significantly different desire profiles (motives, pleasures, and values). It usually does not occur between people who have different abilities, opinions, personalities, or habits. People can learn to appreciate others who are different from them in many regards; it is only when it comes to pleasures, values, and desires that "not getting it" is seen.

What you have learned about "not getting it" can help you understand how other people—such as your spouse, boss, parents, or children—perceive you and why you perceive them in certain ways. In Part II, we will learn how this information can help you improve your romantic relationships (Chapter 8), your relationships at work (Chapter 9), and your family relationships (Chapter 10).

PART

II

HOW
THE BASIC
DESIRES
ARE
SATISFIED

Value-Based Happiness

Your desire profile shows the priorities you may follow in order to find long-lasting, deep happiness and fulfillment. Satisfying your most important desires can help you experience life as meaningful, bringing a sense of deep satisfaction that is beyond pleasure and pain. Even when you do not reach your most important goals in life, the act of striving can make your life meaningful and satisfying. On the other hand, you may experience life as meaningless if you do not strive to satisfy your most important basic desires.

TWO KINDS OF HAPPINESS

There are two different kinds of happiness, *feel-good happiness* and *value-based happiness.* Feel-good happiness refers to pleasant sensations and sensual feelings. When people are having a good time, eating something they like, or getting a massage, they experience feel-good happiness. The positive sensations make them feel good but may not satisfy their inner need for meaning. In contrast, value-based happiness refers to the general feeling of well-being that people experience when their lives are meaningful. When people give blood to help out a loved one, for example, they feel good about themselves even though the actual sensations of giving blood are unpleasant. Giving blood leads to value-based happiness but not to feel-good happiness.

The two types of happiness differ greatly in how long they last. Generally, feel-good happiness lasts no more than a few hours. The pleasure people feel while watching a good movie or attending a party does not last very long. Because feel-good happiness is short-lasting, people who want their lives to be filled with feel-good pleasures are frequently looking for thrills and excitement. Some even turn to drinking or drugs to get high. Since feel-good happiness obeys the law of diminishing returns, kicks keep getting harder to find, and a life of excessive pleasure-seeking can easily degenerate into nothingness and despair.

In contrast, value-based happiness can last for years. It does not obey the law of diminishing returns—there is no limit to how meaningful a person's life can be. Value-based happiness is enduring. People who experience value-based happiness do not need a steady stream of pleasurable sensations because they have a basic sense that their lives are meaningful. They can savor simple pleasures such as the everyday beauty of a sunrise, the joy of being in love, or the pleasure of watching their children grow older.

Value-based happiness is enduring partially because it can be experienced again and again through recollection and contemplation. For example, at any time she wishes, Se Pak Re can recall her victory in the 1998 Ladies' Professional Golf Association championship. When she focuses on this fact, she will experience anew the deep satisfaction of the achievement. Similarly, people in love need only contemplate the strength of their relationship to experience value-based happiness. Parents can experience value-based happiness merely by recollecting experiences they had while raising their children.

Value-based happiness is meaningful even in the absence of feel-good happiness. Parents who make sacrifices for their children can have a satisfying life even if it is marked by moments of anguish and self-denial. The soldier who sacrifices his life for his country has found meaning even though the cost is life itself. In the final analysis, human beings must find a lifestyle that affirms their personal values, or they cannot be truly happy. True happiness comes from meaning, and meaning comes from basic desires and values. Pleasurable sensations are not enough.

The story of Daisy Buchanan, the fictional literary character in F. Scott Fitzgerald's *The Great Gatsby*, provides an excellent example of someone who sought feel-good happiness rather than value-based happiness.[1] Daisy was one of the "careless" people, the fantastically wealthy individuals who smash things up and then retreat back into their wealth, leaving others to clean up the mess. Daisy lived a mostly superficial, meaningless life, with nothing much to look forward to except vacations, flirtations, parties, and affairs. Ultimately, her character shows readers how a life aimed at the pursuit of feel-good happiness is empty and superficial.

In contrast, actor Christopher Reeve provides an excellent example of a person who knows value-based happiness.[2] Reeve gained international fame for his portrayal of Superman in the motion-picture series that began in 1978. At age 42, he was thrown from his horse and damaged his spinal cord. The accident made him a quadriplegic who is dependent on machines for basic life support. In a short period of time, the physical world went from a source of significant pleasure in his life to a source of significant displeasure. He cannot feed himself, he has to wait for others to bring him water when he is thirsty, and he cannot hug his children or make love to his wife. However, he still enjoys a purposeful and meaningful life. He and his wife have a close relationship, and together they are raising their three children. He continues to work as an actor and director. He has become an inspiration to millions of people with disabilities and a national leader in the fight to increase funding for spinal cord research. Are his days filled with laugher and fun? Of course not. Is his life meaningful? More than most! He does not get to experience much feel-good happiness, but he still has valued-based happiness.

Because Daisy Buchanan's life has little in it that is meaningful to her, she experiences excruciating boredom and emptiness between her nights of pleasure, and as she ages, she will have less to look forward to with every new wrinkle that nature leaves on her face. In contrast, Christopher Reeve experiences some discomfort nearly every minute of his life. He lives in fear that the machines supporting his life will fail him, or that a spasm will embarrass him in front of an audience. Yet in between the moments of discomfort, Reeve's life is filled with the happiness that comes from a loving family, the support of his fans, and the significance of his work.

Although value-based happiness (meaning) is much more valuable than feel-good happiness (pleasure), there is nothing wrong in pursuing feel-good happiness in moderation. Feel-good happiness adds significantly to the quality of life when it is experienced by people who also have value-based happiness. Because of bad fortune, however, some people are at a significant disadvantage in experiencing feel-good happiness. A person in a hospice dying of cancer may be in pain and unable to experience feel-good happiness. The harsh reality is that millions of people with a disability have a disadvantage in gaining feel-good happiness. Very poor people and members of minority groups also are at a significant disadvantage in finding feel-good happiness.

The good news is that everyone can find value-based happiness. Even people in a hospice can contemplate the meaning in their lives. When it comes to value-based happiness, people with a disability do not have a disability. The poor may not have the opportunity to enjoy the finer things in life, but the very best things really *are* free. Don't get me wrong—I'm not saying that poor people or people with disabilities should not pursue feel-good happiness. Instead, my point is that value-based happiness is more deeply rewarding than feel-good happiness and that all people are fairly equal in their ability to pursue value-based happiness.

Some special education teachers have dedicated a portion of their careers to working with people with mental retardation. Sometimes these teachers wonder why they should bother to educate a child with mental retardation, since he or she cannot use the knowledge in a significant way. In response, we can argue that desire, not ability, is what justifies education. Because curiosity is a basic desire, learning is an integral part of what life is about. People with mental retardation are not smart, but they have curiosity. If teachers do not educate them, they take away from them an important aspect of their humanity.

One of the oldest questions in philosophy is whether or not people can find happiness while being tortured on the rack[3]—in other words, can we be happy while living under objectively miserable conditions? Can people living in poverty be happy? Can people living with terminal illness be happy? I say it is often possible to find meaning (value-based happiness) in such situations but not pleasure (feel-good happiness). Consider the case of a soldier who refuses to give his captors military information, despite being tortured or sent to live in a squalid POW camp. Although the soldier experiences pain and anxiety, his suffering is meaningful because he is withholding information his torturers need. Consequently, the soldier can experience value-based happiness, or the sense that his life has a purpose.

Value-based happiness is the great equalizer in human life. All you need to do in order to experience it is to become clear on who you are and what you value, and then to live your life accordingly. You can achieve the greatest satisfaction possible in your life if you live in accordance with your own unique profile of basic desires and values. You can have those things that are of much greater value than pleasure, such as family, reputation, justice, knowledge, friendship, acceptance, security, order, honor, romantic love, involvement, achievement, independence, fitness, tranquility, and devotion. By identifying which goals are most important to you, you identify the most important psychological values that make your life meaningful.

FEEL-GOOD HAPPINESS

You have learned that feel-good happiness comes from maximizing sensual pleasure and from minimizing sensations of physical pain. Although nearly everybody seeks some degree of feel-good happiness, problems can arise when people go to extremes to find it. In order to understand how this happens, let's take a look at hedonism, which is a philosophy that advises us to make the pursuit of feel-good happiness our greatest life goal.

Hedonism can be pursued by two different lifestyles, which I will call self-indulgence and self-denial. The goal of a self-indulgent lifestyle is to maximize the experience of sensual pleasures. The pleasure-seeking hedonist experiences life as one party after another, seeking out feasts, uninhibited sex, and thrills. Because of the law of diminishing returns, however, the person has to go to further and further extremes for a thrill. Drug addiction is a common risk with the self-indulgent (pleasure seeking) lifestyle. When there is little left that is still experienced as exciting, an individual may feel as if there is nothing left to make life worth living.

In contrast, the goal of a lifestyle of self-denial is to minimize the experience of physical pain and discomfort, including the avoidance of anxiety and stress. For example, some hedonists deny themselves romance in order to avoid any possibility of experiencing the pain of being rejected. They avoid drinking alcohol because they do not want to experience hangovers. They even avoid buying expensive cars because they do not want to suffer the agony of having an expensive car stolen or damaged. Their overarching goal is to keep life as simple and tranquil as possible.

If your goal is to maximize feel-good happiness, you have to choose between a self-indulgent lifestyle aimed at maximizing your experiences of sensual pleasures and a self-denying lifestyle aimed at minimizing your experience of physical pain, anxiety, and stress. It is impossible to pursue both goals simultaneously because self-indulgence and self-denial are contradictory goals. Historically, nearly all influential hedonists advocated a lifestyle of self-denial. In a world filled with war, famine, and epidemics, philosophers who promised an end of suffering were more popular than those who promised never-ending sensual pleasures.

Epicurus (341 B.C.–270 B.C.) is perhaps history's most influential advocate of hedonism.[4] People think he advocated the philosophy of "eat, drink, and be merry, for tomorrow we die." Like most great philosophical hedonists, however, Epicurus advocated a lifestyle of self-denial, the exact opposite of what people think he favored. He cautioned people to eat little lest they experience indigestion, drink infrequently lest they experience hangover, and avoid merriment lest they become exhausted.

Some of Epicurus's most important contributions to humanity concerned his practical advice for controlling worry and stress. According to Epicurus, you can reduce the amount of worrying you do simply by changing both your expectations and your interpretations of things. Epicurus taught people to expect the worst so they would never be disappointed. He also taught people to overcome their fear of death by focusing on the fact that dead people do not experience pain or stress. Furthermore, he was among the first to tout the advantages of positive thinking, advising people that they would worry less if they focused more on the positive aspects of a situation.

Epicurus's idea that people can control their feelings by controlling their thoughts is the premise of modern-day cognitive therapy. Epicurus's philosophy can work fairly well in reducing your worry and stress. If you are significantly unhappy, depressed, or anxious, you may be able to regain feel-good happiness by using Epicurus's philosophy.

Epicurus's ideas thrived for 700 years and were immensely popular among Greeks, Syrians, Jews, Egyptians, Romans, Africans, and Gauls. The word *epicure,* meaning a connoisseur of food and drink, was coined in his honor, even though his favorite meal consisted of barley and water.

BEYOND PLEASURE AND PAIN[5]

When pursued to an extreme, hedonism can lead to a downward spiral of depression, despair, and self-destruction. This is because pleasure and pain are not enough to give life purpose, and a life without purpose may not be worth the pain of existence.

Malcolm X is a good example of somebody who had lost his way until he found the meaning in his life.[6] His father, the Reverend Earl Little, was a Baptist minister and dedicated organizer for the Universal Negro Improvement Association. Malcolm was proud of his father's activities, but his family paid a heavy price when their house in Omaha, Nebraska, was burned by the Klu Klux Klan. Later his father was murdered and the family moved to Lansing, Michigan. As a lad, Malcolm did well in school, even becoming class president one year, but he became discouraged when a teacher told him that a black man could not hope to become a lawyer. With his ambition thwarted by racism, Malcolm's life started to lose its meaning. He moved to Boston to live with an older sister, and he pursued a life of pleasure-seeking.

Still in his teens, country-boy Malcolm Little was fascinated by the ways of Boston. His main goals in life were having fun, gaining prestige among his peer group, and romance. In Boston, he went to dance halls in his zoot suit and did the lindy hop. He also "conked" his hair in a painful process that straightened out the curls and made his hair shiny. He eventually turned to selling drugs. By age 21 he was addicted to cocaine and sent to jail for burglary.

In prison Malcolm had to decide if he wanted to overcome his drug addiction and survive, or just die and end his suffering. When his brother encouraged him to become a follower of Elijah Muhammad and the Nation of Islam, Malcolm found a new lifestyle that satisfied his basic desires and made his life meaningful. He gave up partying and embraced the basic values of honor, leadership, and social justice (idealism). He became a devout Muslim and he quickly rose to a position of leadership within the Nation of Islam.

Malcolm X, as he became known after he converted to Islam, had undergone a dramatic change. He went from street hustler to religious leader; from drug addiction to strict adherence to the laws of Islam; from a life of irresponsibility to one of social concern for his people. However, the seeds of this change were in Malcolm X from childhood. He had always been proud of his heritage and concerned about social justice for African-Americans. When the Nation of Islam provided an opportunity for him to satisfy these deep desires, Malcolm X found the meaning in his life.

Malcolm X's life story teaches us the difference between feel-good and value-based happiness. When he pursued feel-good happiness, his life was meaningless, and he was in a downward spiral that led to much more misery than happiness. When he pursued value-based happiness, he redeemed himself and regained his sense of purpose and general sense of well-being.

THE WILL TO LIVE

Some people disagree with the idea that value-based happiness is so important that it is essentially the reason for living. They say that life is a self-sustaining goal. In other words, they believe that the will to survive, not psychological or social goals, is ultimately what drives human life. The following e-mail, was sent to me from a person in Australia who'd read of my research.

> I read your theory of basic desires in our local newspaper. You obviously do not know anything at all. You left out the will to survive, which is the greatest of all motives. This motive guides the behavior of all animals and people. It led to natural selection and evolution of the human being. How could you be so ignorant?

What is the fundamental purpose of human life? Is it life itself, as the e-mailer asserted, or is it value-based happiness, a position advocated in this book? Do we seek spirituality because (as some say) it makes us healthier, or because it is an essential means of experiencing value-based happiness? In regard to biological life versus psychological life, which is the means and which is the end purpose?

The will to live, I believe, is best considered as a means for experiencing the end goal of value-based happiness. Life itself is not the *purpose* of our existence. When life is meaningless or holds no hope of value-based happiness, we experience despair and no longer care if we live. For example, imagine that a long time from now you developed a rare disease that would cause you to lose consciousness. You would survive, but only in a coma from which there is absolutely no hope of recovery. Would you wish to live as long as possible in the coma, or would you just as soon die? If your end goal is to maintain biological functions—to keep the cellular activity going for as long as possible—you should value living in a coma when there is no hope of regaining consciousness. If your end goal is to experience value-based happiness, you should not value life in a coma because it cannot lead to value-based happiness. The results of this thought experiment are obvious: We prefer a life with consciousness to a meaningless life in a coma.

When I analyze my own life, I conclude that I want to live so I can experience value-based happiness. That is, I want to experience beauty, watch my children grow, do my work, and enjoy thinking about things. Without life, I could not do any of these things. Although life is an essential means for pursuing what it is I really want, life itself is not what I want.

When I was lying in a hospital bed diagnosed with a life-threatening illness, I faced the question of how badly I really wanted to live. Preparing for death was the easy choice—every morning I could hear the patients who had had operations on their GI tracts wake up screaming with pain, and in that context, dying seemed like the wiser alternative. But when I understood more fully the meaning in my life, dying was no longer an option. I chose to survive because I had things I still wanted to see and do. Survival was a choice, not a biological imperative dictated by the laws of natural selection.

HOW VALUE-BASED HAPPINESS LEADS TO THE WILL TO LIVE

If you still doubt my position that value-based happiness gives rise to the will to live, please read Viktor E. Frankl's moving account of life inside Nazi concentration camps.[7] Frankl was a psychiatrist who had been trained in the psychoanalytic school of thought. As a Jew living in Vienna when World War II broke out, he was rounded up by Hitler's SS and sent to a concentration camp.

If anybody deserves to be considered a survivor, it is Frankl. His father, mother, brother, and wife died in camps. When he first arrived at Auschwitz, a Nazi officer divided his group into the 90 percent who would be sent immediately to the gas ovens versus the 10 percent who would be assigned to forced labor. Poorly fed, poorly clothed, and beaten by sadistic guards, Frankl managed to survive the epidemics that ran through the camps. He did not know his family's fate—were they alive or dead? He worked in snow with shoes that had holes in them and endured frostbite. He watched people in the camps waste away until they died of exhaustion, beatings, torture, famine, or disease. At one point, he observed cannibalism.

If there is a biological instinct for survival, surely it would be felt strongly in a person who had survived the horrors of the Nazi camps. If survival is the overriding goal of human existence, surely it would have been the subject of Frankl's book. Yet Frankl did not write about the will to live; instead, he wrote about how striving for meaning can give rise to a will to live so strong that it can help a person survive enormous adversity.

Frankl concluded that the search for meaning is the key to survival. In the Nazi camps, the people who survived were those who had hope, who had found inner meaning in their suffering, or who looked forward to some future goal. People survived the camps by striving toward a goal that gave their suffering a purpose. In the camps, the people who had no goals lost all inner strength, gave up, and died.

What were the goals that kept people alive inside the camps? According to Frankl, there was no single goal; different goals made life meaningful for different people. The principle of individuality held true even for prisoners living under inhumane conditions. Some felt a duty to help others, as Frankl himself did when he counselled people who were suicidal. Others were kept going by the hope of seeing their children after liberation. For some professionals it was the goal of getting back to their scientific work and writing the important research paper or book that they had been working on prior to the Holocaust. Some people could appreciate beauty even while living as prisoners in a concentration camp.

How can striving or desire affect survival? Some physicians think that a person's inner strength has implications for the human immune system. When people still want to live, the immune system somehow responds and does its job. When they no longer care, it is believed, the immune system no longer seems to work very well. Frankl observed people in the camps who did not succumb to disease until after they had given up all hope and had stopped caring about anything.

Frankl's experiences teach us that our goals make our lives meaningful. By embracing the 16 basic desires, we experience a general feeling that life has purpose. The more passionately we embrace the 16 desires, the more purposeful our lives become, and the more we desire to live. Desire, purpose, and goals are the main differences between life as biological mass and life as a human being. Human life is more than the "stuff" of the universe—it can have purpose, which is what distinguishes us from biological "stuff."

THE REALITY OF VALUE-BASED HAPPINESS

Since "meaning," "purpose," and "goals" do not exist in time and space—they are not physical things we can observe directly—some philosophers have said that they do not exist at all. Value-based happiness is a romantic myth, they say, created by the human mind in order to make us feel self-important. How can there be such a thing as "meaning" when this word does not refer to anything physical? Given that human beings are biological machines—we are part of the physical world—how can our behavior be driven by goals, purpose, or meaning, which are not physical entities? Scientists say that biological events have no goals and purposes. There are no life spirits, biologists reason. The universe has no purpose, physicists say. If there are no purposes to biological and physical things—and if we are ultimately reducible to our biological and physical natures—then it would seem that we, too, cannot have any goals or purposes.

Although this philosophy—known as *naturalism*—is a formidable theory, it is based on selective evidence. When we look at all of the evidence, we see that human beings have a dual nature. Scholars who say that human beings are more than just biological entities use words like "spirit," "mind," and "goal-oriented" to express the non-physical aspects of human nature. Although nobody really knows how it is possible, the fact is that human beings have a dual nature. We seek feel-good happiness because we are biological beings and value-based happiness because we are spiritual beings.

There is substantial evidence of the non-physical aspects of human life. Through consciousness we can transcend the physical-biological world, and through self-consciousness we can become individuals and transcend social groups. By recording human history, people transcend their existence in the here-and-now of the physical world. We can think about the past and be influenced by people who died a long time ago. We also can transcend our physical nature by anticipating the future. Even though the past and the future do not "exist" in the physical world, both are "real" events that affect our lives. Further, we can experience, behold, or understand mathematics, which is not part of the physical world that exists at a particular moment in time.

Self-consciousness is another indicator of our transcendent nature. By treating ourselves as an object—as an "I"—we can transcend our existence in the here-and-now of the physical world. Similarly, people can transcend the world by becoming aware of it and by treating it as an object.

So what should we say to those who argue that human life has no meaning beyond its biological functions? How should we reply to those who think that value-based happiness is a romantic idea with no real-world relevance? We can point to the objective evidence indicating that human beings have a dual nature, so that all is not understandable in terms of physics or biology.[8]

FINDING VALUE-BASED HAPPINESS

While a person can aim for feel-good happiness by going out and having a good time, value-based happiness cannot be sought by directly aiming for it. In order to find value-based happiness, you have to aim for fulfillment of your most important basic desires, and let value-based happiness come to you in passing, as an unintended consequence of your pursuits. As philosopher John Stuart Mill (1806–1873) taught,

> Those only are happy (I thought) who have their minds fixed on some object other than their own happiness; on the happiness of others, on the improvement of mankind, even on some art or pursuit, followed not as a means, but as itself an ideal end. Aiming thus at something else, they find happiness by the way.[9]

The pace at which we satisfy our desires can be crucial. If we live in the fast lane, we risk feeling overly stimulated; if we live in the slow lane, we risk feeling bored. In regard to most goals we might have, moderation is desirable. Thus, we need to avoid the twin problems of excess and deficiency.

Aristotle (384 B.C.–322 B.C.) was one of history's earliest and most articulate advocates of moderation,[10] arguing that moderation is a virtue and extremism is a vice. He published a table of 12 virtues and 24 vices in his book *The Nicomachean Ethics*. His ideas still have practical value for people aiming for value-based happiness.

According to Aristotle, each person has to learn how his individual nature tugs him toward certain extreme tendencies that get him into trouble. Some people have difficulty controlling their temper, others struggle to control their appetite, and still others have problems controlling their spending. Some people tend to be too selfish, whereas others tend to be too independent or stubborn. Aristotle argued that value-based happiness usually requires that we learn how to control our extreme tendencies.

Suzanne Somers's experience provides an example of the importance of moderation in gaining value-based happiness.[11] A poor child of an alcoholic father, Somers set out to prove herself. Her ambition paid off during the 1970s when her television show, *Three's Company*, was rated number one in the nation. Yet she kept pushing the envelope, pressing for careers in film and nightclubs, while continuing her television work. Although she was fulfilling her ambitions, she was living life in the fast lane and was not very happy. After she lost her show over a contract dispute, her career went downhill for about six years. During that time, she learned to take life at a slower pace and found meaning by spending more time with her family and by writing a book about alcoholism. When she regained success in her acting career, she did not resume a super-fast pace of life. Instead, she set aside time for family, romance, and vacation. She was still a highly ambitious person devoted to her career, but now her life also had family and social purpose (educating the public about alcoholism). In her book *After the Fall*, she wrote, "Now I am happier than I have ever been in my life."[12]

How can you analyze your current degree of value-based happiness? First, look at those of the 16 basic desires that are most meaningful to you and estimate generally whether or not you are satisfied with that aspect of your life. If you are dissatisfied, determine if the problem is one of excess or insufficiency, and then develop a practical plan for improvement. Would more or fewer friends make you happier? Would more or less challenge in your life make you happier? By asking yourself questions such as these, you can set goals to improve your value-based happiness. Let's look at how satisfaction of each of the 16 desires can lead to value-based happiness.

Power. Achievement and leadership lead to value-based happiness by satisfying the basic desire for power. If you are looking for a more meaningful life, and you have always enjoyed the experience of mastery, maybe you need to challenge yourself. You may try to do so by setting higher career goals, seeking a leadership role in an organization, finishing a marathon, earning "master points" in bridge, or training prizewinning dogs or horses. On the other hand, you may be unhappy because you have become more achievement-oriented than you really want to be. In that case, you need to spend less time working and more time satisfying other desires. It is okay to be a workaholic if the lifestyle makes you happy, but when you find yourself working more than you want to work, it may be time to try to cut back.

Independence. If you are not as happy as you think you should be, maybe you are not as free as your nature requires. Freedom leads to value-based happiness by satisfying the basic desire for independence. If you live with roommates or parents, you may be happier finding a place of your own. You may also be able to increase your happiness by learning skills that make you less dependent on others or by gaining financial self-reliance. Examples of common activities that increase self-reliance include learning how to fix your own car, make repairs in your home, or sew your own clothes. On the other hand, you may not be as happy as you would like because too much independence is being demanded of you. This can be the source of a great deal of stress in a person's life. In that case, you need to increase the support you receive from other people. A spouse who is experiencing great stress raising the kids or managing the finances often can reduce stress by receiving more emotional support from the other spouse. Support also can be obtained from close friends.

Curiosity. Wisdom and knowledge lead to value-based happiness by satisfying the basic desire of curiosity. You may be able to increase your value-based happiness by engaging in activities that expand your knowledge.

Common examples include traveling, taking a course at a community college, or setting aside time for reading. Perhaps you would enjoy finding friends with whom you can have intellectual conversations. On the other hand, some people are unhappy because their lives are more intellectual than they want them to be. Common examples are a student who doesn't like school and an engineer who would prefer a less intellectually demanding job. It is important to recognize that too much intellectual stimulation is unpleasant—not unlike what happens when we eat too much—and that long-term happiness for some people can require a rebalancing of their daily schedule to include less time spent on intellectually demanding activities.

Acceptance. Being accepted leads to self-esteem and a sense of self-worth. Sometimes we can gain value-based happiness by improving or expanding our relationships with our parents, a partner, or close friends. Meaningful roles within a club or other group also can satisfy the desire for acceptance.

Unhappiness results both from being overly sensitive and focused on criticism and from being so insensitive to criticism that we do not pay adequate attention to constructive feedback from others. Generally, such problems are associated with a lack of self-confidence and a strong desire for acceptance. Professional counseling can help people gain greater self-confidence and acceptance.

Order. When our lives have the amount of order our nature requires, we feel secure because events are experienced as being under control. Common ways of satisfying the desire for order include rituals, routines, and planning of activities. Getting organized, planning a vacation, or cleaning up the house all are enjoyable activities for people with a strong desire for order. On the other hand, some people may be unhappy because they feel that their lives are overly organized and controlled. They need greater spontaneity and more uncertainty in their lives.

Saving. Collecting leads to value-based happiness because it satisfies the intrinsic desire to save. For example, some people collect stamps, military insignias, or rare books. Finding a hobby and starting a collection can bring real happiness. On the other hand, you may be spending so much time collecting things that it has become a problem in your life. The most common example of this occurs when a person saves so much money that he or she lives a lifestyle of self-denial.

Honor. Loyalty leads to value-based happiness because it satisfies the desire for honor. Common examples include respecting one's parents, participating in patriotic activities (e.g., singing of the national anthem, participating in Fourth of July celebrations), and becoming active in culture groups or causes (e.g., the National Association for the Advancement of Colored People, the Anti-Defamation League). If you are not as happy as you would like to be, maybe you need to rediscover your ethnic roots or heritage or change your lifestyle to show more loyalty to your origins. On the other hand, some people are unhappy either because they are overly concerned with morality or because they are loyal to people who do not deserve it.

Idealism. This desire is most commonly satisfied by becoming involved in social causes, charity, or politics. For example, people with a strong desire for idealism may find value-based happiness by volunteering for the Peace Corps, working with the elderly at a hospital or nursing home, or becoming social activists. If your life is not as meaningful as you would as, maybe you need to devote some time to a cause you think is worthwhile. Give something of yourself to make your community a better place and, as J. S. Mill advised, value-based happiness may come to you in passing. On the other hand, some people spend more time pursuing idealistic goals than they really want to spend. These people might be happier if they reorganized their activities and devoted less time to community work or social causes.

Social Contact. Social contact can be superficial or substantial. Superficial social contact, which leads to feel-good happiness, occurs when we spend time with casual acquaintances or attend parties or social functions. In contrast, value-based happiness comes from long-term friendships, which require substantial contact with people whom we truly care about. Such friendships can be formed through participating in a group activity, such as acting in a community play or joining a community or church social group. On the other hand, private people can be unhappy if their daily schedule brings them into contact with more social situations than they desire. These people should be able to increase their happiness by spending more time alone.

Family. Raising children leads to value-based happiness because it satisfies the basic desire for family. The lives of millions of parents are centered around their children, and many experience a profound loss when their children move on and they become "empty-nesters." If you are in this situation, you may be able to increase your happiness by inviting exchange students or a relative to live with you.

Status. A common way of satisfying this desire is to move to a neighborhood that has the level of status with which you are most comfortable. Similarly, the desire for status can be satisfied by buying impressive cars or clothes. Some people can gain value-based happiness by taking actions that will improve the reputations of their families. For example, the son of Sam Sheppard, the physician whose life story became the basis of the motion picture *The Fugitive,* has pursued legal action to recognize his father's innocence and restore his good name. Why does he spend so much money and energy on the effort so many years after the fact? Because status is meaningful to him.

Vengeance. Value-based happiness is usually enhanced when you experience a degree of competition in your daily life that is consistent with your desires. A common way of managing how much competition you experience is controlling how often you participate in various contests, such as sporting events or dance or band competitions. Your happiness can also depend on your being comfortable with the degree of competitiveness at the workplace. If you experience the workplace as too much of a "dog-eat-dog" situation, you are probably experiencing it as more competitive than you would like it to be. Alternatively, you may be experiencing the job as less competitive than you would like. Regardless, you may be able to improve your happiness by changing jobs to one that is better matched to your desires.

Romance. The desire for romance can be considered from the perspectives of both feel-good and value-based happiness. Feel-good happiness results when a romantic experience involves sexual gratification and other sensual experience. On the other hand, value-based happiness arises when a relationship leads to the deep bonds of romantic love. When on a date or a one-night stand, a person usually experiences feel-good happiness. Value-based happiness can be experienced only through a more meaningful relationship in which love is experienced. Even when all else is going wrong in our lives, romantic love can be a source of value-based happiness.

The desire for romance also can be satisfied through art and music. Happiness can be deepened through visiting art museums, enjoying the beauty of the outdoors, and listening to beautiful music. On the other hand, some people are unhappy because they spend so much time pursuing romance that it interferes with their other goals. This problem is common among those adolescents and young adults who organize their lives to find romance.

Eating. Because eating is sensation-based and yet a powerful symbol, it is a desire that is relevant to both feel-good and value-based happiness. Feel-good happiness occurs when we eat a good meal, whereas value-based happiness occurs when eating has taken on a deeper significance in our lives. Some people, for example, can find value-based happiness by developing an interest in cooking or by joining a gourmet club.

Eating has implications for our self-concept. Unhappiness occurs when people do not like their weight and think of themselves as too thin or too fat. The results of some studies show that our image of our weight does not change easily, even after our weight has changed. An overweight person who loses a lot of weight still tends to think of himself or herself as overweight. People who experience significant unhappiness need to focus less on their weight when they evaluate their worth. Counselors can help those who are experiencing significant unhappiness related to these concerns.

Physical Activity. Adults who become fit after a period of inactivity often comment on how much better their mood is. Because exercise is a basic desire, fitness creates a sense of deep satisfaction. This desire is most commonly satisfied through a physically demanding job, playing sports, or participation in exercise programs. Jogging, walking, bowling, and golf all are common ways by which adults satisfy their need for physical activity. Although much less common, some people are unhappy because their job or daily schedule is too physically demanding. The obvious solution in such a situation is to find another job if at all possible, convince your boss to reassign you to less physically demanding work, or change your schedule.

Tranquility. If you are experiencing too much stress, you can increase your value-based happiness by gaining a greater degree of tranquility. Learn to relax—find a recreational activity that takes your mind off your troubles. Common examples include walking, fishing, and reading. Psychological training in stress management can be helpful. On the other hand, you may be bored because your life is too peaceful. You can address this problem by seeking a more exciting job or hobby.

THE 16 BASIC DESIRES OF HUMAN LIFE

Power	Order	Social Contact	Romance
Independence	Saving	Family	Eating
Curiosity	Honor	Status	Physical Activity
Acceptance	Idealism	Vengeance	Tranquility

AND HOW WE SATISFY THEM

Happiness	Relationships	Work
Family	Sports	Spirituality

IN THE REMAINING CHAPTERS, you will learn new ideas for finding value-based happiness. You will discover how your most important desires are satisfied through relationships, work, family, sports, and spirituality. By improving the extent to which these areas of life satisfy your basic desires, you can attain a greater level of value-based happiness.

How Relationships Grow

A male colleague of mine has been married and divorced five times. When I asked him why this is so, he said, "I haven't found the right woman." I still marvel that the first four divorces did not discourage him from marrying a fifth time. Although he knew that compatibility is the key to a successful marriage, he did not know how to evaluate compatibility and find the right woman for him.

The idea that compatibility is the key to a successful relationship is an old, established principle of marriage counseling.[1] What is new is how the system of 16 basic desires can be used to assess compatibility. In the past, compatibility was evaluated in terms of a couple's intelligence, personalities, abilities, and backgrounds. In contrast, the system of 16 basic desires makes it possible for us to assess compatibility in terms of a couple's desire profiles.

Can a relationship succeed if one partner is much smarter than the other? According to the theory of 16 basic desires, the success of a relationship depends more on how curious the partners are than on how smart they happen to be. When both partners are curious, they can enjoy intellectual conversations and activities together, even if one partner is notably smarter than the other. When they are both non-curious, neither partner will want to spend much time in intellectual activities, so that the difference in intelligence may not matter much. If one partner is curious and the other is non-curious, however, they are incompatible even if they are both very smart. The curious partner will want to have intellectual conversations much more often than will the non-curious partner, who will tend to find such conversations boring.

The general rule of compatibility of desire profiles is that like-mindedness attracts and opposites repel. The following two principles express this rule and are demonstrated throughout this chapter:

> *Principle of Bonding:* Couples bond when their desire profiles are similar.

> *Principle of Separation:* Couples grow apart when their desire profiles are dissimilar.

When used as long-term indicators, these principles can help identify couples who are likely to grow together versus those who are likely to grow apart. However, they do not tell us much about short-term relationships. Two people with incompatible desire profiles can be physically attracted to each other, so that it is only after the sexual interest loses its novelty that the basic incompatibility drives them apart.

Sometimes it appears that opposites attract, as in the example of a shy man who is attracted to a fun-loving woman. In books and movies, we often see a female character who is vivacious and a male character who is socially inhibited. The inhibited male falls in love with the vivacious female, and in the process loses many of his inhibitions. Is this realistic or just Hollywood? Generally, it depends on how satisfied the man is with his shyness. Many shy people do not value shyness and wish they were more sociable. A shy man who feels that way will be of a like mind with a sociable woman, rather than in opposition, because both place a high value on social contact. Although the man is shy and the woman is vivacious, he admires her ability to have fun with people and wishes he could be more like her. On the other hand, if a shy man wants to remain shy, he and a fun-loving woman would be mismatched on the basic desire for social contact. They will quarrel with each other repeatedly—he will complain that she spends too much time with her friends, and she will complain that he spends too much time alone.

Because there are 16 basic desires, it is likely that partners will be matched on some of them and mismatched on others. How similar must the desire profiles be for a couple to be considered compatible? There isn't really any objective way of determining this because each couple must decide for themselves whether the positive factors in their relationship outweigh the negative, or vice versa. One way to look at a relationship is to focus on just the five or six basic desires that are most important to you. You will probably experience meaningful problems concerning incompatibility with any partner who is *significantly* different than you are on two or more of them.

Let's take a look at how compatibilities and incompatibilities determine whether or not a couple can use their relationship to satisfy their basic desires.

POWER

Many people think that two powerful people are incompatible, expecting that they would fight over who will be boss. Isn't compatibility much greater between a powerful and a submissive person—the powerful person leads, and the submissive person follows? Actually, two powerful people are compatible with each other (like-mindedness attracts). In order to understand how this can be, we need to recall that the desire for power is defined in this book relative to the average person. Two people can both be powerful relative to the average person, but with respect to each other, one can be more powerful than the other. In a marriage of two powerful people, the more powerful partner becomes the leader and the less powerful partner becomes the follower. Further, the partners can both satisfy their desires for power by taking charge of different areas of the household—for example, one can take charge of handling finances, while the other handles social arrangements and entertainment.

In a marriage of two powerful people, both partners are ambitious. They can pursue their dreams together, supporting each other in their career goals. Both are prepared to make sacrifices to get ahead, including working long hours. Both President Bill Clinton and Hillary Rodham Clinton are ambitious attorneys. He ran for public office with her loyal support; she became a successful attorney in her own right and is campaigning for a seat in the United States Senate in 2000. The First Lady is obviously very proud of the President's accomplishments, and the President is obviously very proud of his wife's success. Their shared ambition has been one of the forces widely credited as holding them together up to this point.

Couples also bond when neither is ambitious (like-mindedness attracts). For example, both Sherry and Saul enjoy an easy, non-pressured lifestyle. They have moved to a remote town where the pace of life is slow and to their liking. The fact that neither partner pushes the other toward greater success in a career is one of the key factors supporting the relationship and allowing them to enjoy a simple lifestyle together.

When an ambitious person (indicating a strong desire for power) marries a significantly less ambitious person (indicating a weak desire for power), they tend to quarrel over how much time the ambitious partner spends at work (opposites grow apart). The ambitious partner feels misunderstood, and the non-ambitious partner feels neglected. A good example of this is the marriage of Kathy and Bill. Although Kathy enjoyed her job, she left her work at the office and looked forward to spending quiet evenings with her husband. But Bill, highly ambitious and hardworking, was always thinking about his job. When he began staying late at the office and coming home too tired to spend time with his wife, she felt neglected and resentful.

INDEPENDENCE

A marriage between two independent-minded people can work out if each respects and understands the other's need for freedom (like-mindedness attracts). For example, Bill and Susan are independent-minded physicians who work in different cities 500 miles apart. During the week they each live near their jobs, but they get together every weekend. They have a successful marriage in part because each offers the other a large measure of freedom.

Two interdependent people are compatible because each wants to become as close as possible to the other (like-mindedness attracts). A well-known example of this is ex-Beatle Paul McCartney, who insisted that his wife, Linda, become a member of his rock band, *Wings*. They were devoted to each other. Up until her untimely death from cancer, they were rarely apart even though he was an international celebrity.

In contrast, independent and interdependent partners are incompatible (opposites grow apart). The independent partner, who wants more freedom than the interdependent partner is prepared to give, must go outside the relationship to feel free. When this happens, the interdependent partner will not have his or her needs satisfied. They will likely quarrel repeatedly over the situation. For example, Sam wants to spend every weekend with his wife, Audrey, but she wants some weekends to herself to visit her family and travel. This difference has been a source of quarreling in their relationship for many years. When she takes off to visit her family in another state, he pouts and feels that he cannot trust her to fulfill his needs.

ACCEPTANCE[2]

We have the potential to use relationships to satisfy our need for acceptance. For example, partners who are deeply in love can share with each other their most intimate thoughts and feelings without fear of criticism. Such intimacy creates a deep sense that each partner is accepted for who he or she is. Acceptance at this level draws the partners closer to each other and strengthens the relationship.

Problems can arise in a relationship when one or both partners has a very strong need for acceptance. Generally, a strong desire for acceptance is associated with negative self-esteem, or what is commonly called "needy" behavior, which can lead to adjustment problems.[3]

The desire for acceptance is an exception to the general rule that like-mindedness attracts and opposites grow apart. Generally, a low need for acceptance increases compatibility with most partners, whereas a very high need for acceptance decreases compatibility with many partners. People with a very high need for acceptance can benefit from psychological counseling, especially when they experience significant relationship problems arising from their "needy" behavior.

Insecure people are highly sensitive to rejection and criticism. They can be self-critical and judgmental toward others. They criticize their partners frequently, partially to discourage the partner from criticizing them.[4] Some worry that their partner will reject and abandon them, and they seek frequent reassurances that this will not happen. Their need for reassurance can be burdensome to the partner and even lead to a loss of respect.

There can be balance, however, in a relationship when one partner enjoys being supportive of the other. What can be damaging in relationships is the *extreme* of the desire for acceptance. On the other end of the spectrum, those with an average desire for acceptance can have difficulty understanding a partner who has a low desire and therefore seems overly confident.

ORDER

Organized partners are compatible because they can use their relationship to satisfy their desire for order (like-mindedness attracts). For example, each partner will appreciate the fact that the other is clean and neat. Further, they can enjoy planning together their vacations or getaways, and they will develop and take pride in their family rituals such as always sitting in the same places at the dinner table.

Flexible partners, such as Ken and Jeanne, are also compatible because both have a low desire for order (like-mindedness attracts). When you visit their house, newspapers, books, papers, and clothes usually are lying around the floor. The grass is not edged, the shrubs are not trimmed, and burned-out lightbulbs have not been replaced. Since both prefer to live this way, they are compatible and have had a strong marriage for more than 15 years.

When a sloppy person lives alone, there is no problem, but problems arise when he or she moves in with a neat person (opposites grow apart). Although the neat person hates the mess created by the sloppy person, the sloppy person may not even notice that there is a mess. For example, the sloppy person may think that leaving dishes in the sink is only a trifle at most, not realizing that it can be truly upsetting to the neat person. On the other hand, the neat person may be too perfect in cleaning the house or in enforcing household rules. Generally, couples who differ in the desire for order have to learn to make compromises to keep their differences from getting out of hand.

SAVING

Many couples enjoy saving memorabilia of their marriage. The wedding album, for example, is commonly saved, as are reminders of special romantic occasions, such as the plane-ticket stubs of a romantic getaway to Hawaii.

Generally, though, saving in a relationship, especially in a marriage, is about attitudes toward money. Couples with a strong desire for saving enjoy building their nest egg (like-mindedness attracts). For example, Sandy and John live on a strict budget and spend much less than their income. Their home is sparsely furnished, and their car is ten years old. Although they could easily afford it, they have not bought a nicer home. They rarely return calls, waiting for others to call them back so they can save the dollar. To save money, they take their lunches to work, keep their gasoline bills down, and watch the heat in the winter. They owe nothing and enjoy excellent finances. Although many would hate their lifestyle of self-denial, it works for them. They are both savers and have a great relationship.

Two spenders are compatible in marriage (like-mindedness attracts). Cheryl and Ben, for example, spend more money than they make, and borrow the difference. They have been in debt their entire married lives. No matter how much their income has increased over the years, they have managed to increase their spending even more. They are distressed by their lack of savings for retirement and their inability to travel as much as they would like. However, these problems have not had a negative impact on their marriage. Although they are going broke, they are doing so together, which is one reason why they have such a strong marriage.

When two people first start to date, they both have their own incomes and/or families to support them, so that differences in attitudes toward money are not necessarily a source of quarrels. After marriage, each partner's desire to save or spend significantly affects what the other can do. The first signs of trouble usually emerge when one partner sets a budget that the other ignores. Usually the spender does not even know how much money he or she is spending and may buy things without first checking to see if the money is there to pay the bills. A young husband I know came home one day to find a crew ripping up the lawn to his home and laying down sod. When he asked his wife how much this was going to cost, she said that she had bought the sod without asking the price. When he asked her how they were going to afford the bill, she had no idea.

Conflict arises when one partner wants to save and the other wants to spend (opposites grow apart). "Keisha and Anthony are fighting over money," said a local television news reporter. "Keisha is the saver. She is trying to scrape together some money to invest for the future. Anthony is the spender."

"I believe you can't take it with you," Anthony explained.

"Keisha has inherited some money," the reporter continued. "She wants to save it, but Anthony wants a new car. They have been fighting so badly that sometimes they do not talk to each other all day."

Some marriage counselors think that quarrels over money are really about some other problem in the relationship. One idea, for example, is that couples who quarrel over money are really arguing about power. Yet our research suggests that saving and power are separate basic desires. When people quarrel about money, one partner may have a much stronger genetic disposition to hoard than does the other partner.

If a couple is fighting repeatedly over money, some accommodation must be made. I suggest they separate the family finances to as great an extent as possible. In this way, the spender can spend, and the saver can save, so that each partner's basic desire is satisfied.

HONOR

Since honor is the desire to be loyal to our heritage, people can satisfy this desire by marrying someone with the same religious and ethnic background (like-mindedness attracts). This allows each partner to experience loyalty each time they practice their faith or the traditions of their ethnic group. For example, Karen and David are religious Jews who raise their children in a traditional, kosher home. They both share a need to strictly follow the Jewish traditions. They attend synagogue together, celebrate all Jewish holidays, and enjoy reading books on their Jewish heritage. By keeping the old traditions alive in their home, together they honor their parents and ethnic group.

Unprincipled people are potentially compatible with each other (like-mindedness attracts). Bonnie Parker and Clyde Barrow provide a famous example of such a couple. In Depression-era America, their idea of a good time was to rob a bank and make a fast getaway. The FBI eventually caught up with them, and they died prematurely in a shootout.

A partner with a strong desire for honor is incompatible with an unprincipled partner (opposites grow apart). Nelson and Winnie Mandela provide an example of such a couple. He is world-renowned as a man of principle, but she was accused of conspiracy to murder a young lover she took while he was in jail as a political prisoner. The marriage ended in divorce.

IDEALISM

Couples who share a strong desire for idealism can satisfy this need through such common activities as discussing current affairs, working together for a charity, or participating together in a local service organization (like-mindedness attracts). Politics provides many examples of husband-and-wife teams, such as Bob and Elizabeth Dole. Another example is a former employee of our research center at the university who married a fellow she met through a local service organization.

Problems can arise when one partner is idealistic and the other is not (opposites grow apart). The idealistic partner is interested in current affairs, but the non-idealistic partner finds such activities a waste of time or boring. For example, Marge had a much stronger desire for idealism than did her husband, Dan. She read the newspaper regularly, watched all the television talk shows on current affairs, and always wanted to talk about politics, poverty programs, and various injustices that were in the news at the time. Dan, who was not interested in these matters to anywhere near the extent that Marge was, ignored her quite a bit and increasingly spent his free time alone. The difference became one of the forces that drove them apart.

SOCIAL CONTACT

Couples can satisfy their desire for social contact by joining clubs, taking vacations with other couples, or having parties (like-mindedness attracts). When both partners have a strong desire for social contact, they tend to be adventurous and fun-loving. For example, Betty and Steve met at a social club sponsored by their local church. They have maintained their friendships with the members of that club for more than 20 years. They have very active social lives—they go out several times per week and take about six vacations together a year.

Isabel and Ramon, on the other hand, are both private people (like-mindedness attracts). Although they have a good income, they stay home nearly every weekend and rarely go to movies or restaurants. They are not trying to save money—they spend their money on other things and actually save very little—they just enjoy quiet evenings at home. Since they are matched in this regard, they have had a successful marriage. When both partners have a low desire for social contact, their shared desire to spend time in home-based pursuits can bring them both satisfaction and happiness.

A partner with a strong desire for social contact is incompatible with a partner who has a weak desire for social contact (opposites grow apart). The sociable partner wants to be around other people, but the private partner wants to spend time as just a couple. Alan and Kim, for example, have been fighting for years over how many people visit the house. She likes to have a lot of company, and he hates it. Socializing is fun for her but a burden for him. Kim does not even realize how often people are over at the house and is confused as to why her husband gets upset by it. Alan does not understand her insensitivity and gets annoyed by what he sees as the constant parade of people in the home. The difference even surfaced when they went shopping for a home. Alan preferred a home that featured privacy, but Kim preferred one that was on a block with a lot of other families.

FAMILY

One reason people marry is because they want to raise a family (like-mindedness attracts). When a couple raises children to respect each parent, love grows between the partners.[5] Many couples have strengthened their relationships by raising a family.

In contrast, couples have a significant problem when one partner wants children and the other does not (opposites grow apart). People sometimes underestimate just how significant this problem can be. Sociologist Robert Blood reported the following case:

> Shelly flatly told Sam that she would never under any circumstances have children and that if he would be unhappy without them, the wedding would be cancelled. They have been married six years, but to his great unhappiness she has not changed her feelings.[6]

Some couples fight over how much time one of them spends with the children. When a couple gets married, the partners can give each other their undivided attention. Things may change, though, when children arrive. Raising kids requires so much effort that it affects how much attention each partner can pay to the other. As marriage counselor Robert A. Harper observed, happy couples who do not prepare themselves seriously and well for the hard work and real sacrifices of parenthood are often in grave danger of having their previously sound marriages undermined by the arrival of children and the accompanying increase in life's stresses. Couples . . . not infrequently mention that their troubles either began with, or were markedly increased by, the arrival of children.[7]

Problems sometimes arise when one partner takes primary responsibility for raising the children. For example, a stay-at-home wife may resent her husband's freedom to pursue a career, travel, and spend time out of the home. Further, she may resent it if her husband does not help when he is home from work or if he spends time after work with friends instead of coming home. On the other hand, the husband may resent his wife's greater opportunity to be close to the kids and watch them grow. If these issues become significant concerns in a marriage, the couple needs to find some compromise to improve the situation. Sharing the duties of parenthood more completely is one possible compromise, while planning more frequent family activities is another.

STATUS

Marrying for wealth and social standing is quite common. People who place a high value on social class may try to use relationships to move up in status. A good example is the relatively young partner who marries an elderly partner who is wealthy but too old for a satisfactory sexual relationship. Another example is the person who seeks to marry into wealth to show off impressive homes, clothes, or furniture. Sarah is a good example of such a person. When she was a high school student in Denver, she only dated popular boys. She joined all the "right" clubs and was impressed with wealth. After majoring in the arts in college, she married a well-to-do man 20 years her senior. At the time, he was a successful corporate officer, and she was a middle-class secretary. Her second marriage was to a very wealthy individual from the upper class of Los Angeles society. They bought a showcase home in Beverly Hills that has been featured in the local newspapers. Sarah enjoys being able to use her relationships to draw attention to herself as a person of high social standing and some importance.

When both partners place a high value on social class, they can use their relationship to satisfy this desire (like-mindedness attracts). Both will seek to live in the most expensive neighborhood they can afford, dress in the nicest possible clothes, and drive the most prestigious car. The marriage of Leona and Harry Hemsley is a good example of how some couples use their relationship to satisfy their desire for status. He enjoyed giving her the great wealth she had always wanted, elevating her from real-estate agent to the status of a wealthy real-estate investor.

When people have a low desire for status, neither is impressed with wealth or social standing (like-mindedness attracts). They live a much more modest lifestyle than they can afford. A good example is Chris and Jackie, who are wealthy but live in a middle-class suburb of Denver. Although they could easily afford a Mercedes, they drive a Chevrolet. They dress nicely but not extravagantly. Because they both have low desire for status, this aspect of their relationship has been a source of strength.

Couples can grow apart when one seeks a much higher level of status than the other. Larry is much more status-oriented than his former wife, Joan. He wanted to live in a more prestigious neighborhood, drive a luxury car, and take expensive vacations. He borrowed money to get what he wanted, going so deeply into debt that at one point he had to use money from his children's savings accounts just to keep the family afloat. Their marriage lasted about ten years.

VENGEANCE

Some couples use their relationship to satisfy their desire for vengeance by competing together as a team (like-mindedness attracts). They compete in bridge, bowling, tennis, dance contests, and so on. The shared experience strengthens the relationship when each partner places a high value on competition.

When both partners have a weak desire for vengeance, they are motivated to treat each other with kindness (like-mindedness attracts). Tyrone and Jo Ellen are good examples. They are both non-aggressive, kind people who have been married for twenty years thus far and have had few quarrels.

Quarrels are the most common way in which partners use relationships to satisfy their desire for vengeance (opposites grow apart). When a partner has a need to express anger, to compete, or to vanquish, he or she starts a quarrel. An argumentative partner, for example, looks for opportunities to quarrel simply because he or she has a need to compete. The person may criticize the partner, not because he dislikes the partner, but as a means of experiencing intrinsically valued, competitive feelings.

Marriage counselors say that a key factor behind the breakups of many couples is that one partner has become vengeful toward the other. A good example of this is the failed marriage of Ike and Tina Turner. Ike was a young musician who needed to team up with a great singer to make it to the big time. He and Tina formed a successful act, and also fell in love and married. Ike started to feel competitive with Tina, however, and became jealous when the crowds overlooked him but applauded her. After he physically abused her for years, she eventually left him to establish a successful career on her own. Even though Ike's abuse of Tina jeopardized his own career and livelihood, he kept at it because vengeance is its own reward.

The case of Ron and Amy Shanabarger provides an example of how vengeance can be so strongly desired it can motivate extreme actions.[8] Ron never forgave Amy for refusing to cut short an ocean cruise to come home and comfort him when his father died. To get even, he married her, planning to have a child and then kill the baby. He did just that, even waiting seven months for Amy to bond with their baby boy, Tyler. He then killed Tyler on Father's Day, and left him in the crib so Amy would be the one to discover his body. "Now we're even," he told her.[9]

ROMANCE

When a couple starts dating, everything is new and exciting, including sex. Once a couple starts to have sex, they may have a lot of it, especially during the "honeymoon" period of their relationship. The shared sexual experience becomes a major source of bonding in the relationship. As time passes, some couples continue to have a high sex drive (like-mindedness attracts), but often this is not the case (opposites grow apart). Problems occur when one person desires sex, for example, almost every day and the other desires it once a week or so. The person who wants less frequent sex may think of the partner as having a one-track mind or even as a pervert. The person who wants frequent sex often thinks of the other as cold. It can even affect the way the two look at their relationship. The person who wants infrequent sex may feel that since so much is hanging on this issue, the relationship was only sex and is therefore not a good relationship. The person who wants frequent sex may take it personally ("He/she does not find me sexy anymore") or may develop negative feelings toward the partner ("This is not the guy/girl I fell in love with"). In either case, the relationship is in jeopardy.

Couples who have significant differences in libido need to find a compromise each partner can accept. This is a long-term problem that is difficult to solve and will not go away on its own. A marriage counselor may help them work through the problem. A variation may be found that will increase the desire of the partner with lower libido. It is also possible that the partner with lower libido is angry or depressed and might develop greater interest if the underlying emotional problem is resolved. Alternative shared activities, such as golf or cooking a meal together, might satisfy the desire for intimacy of the person with the higher libido.

EATING [10]

Romantic dinners are a common means of combining the desires for eating and romance. Nearly all couples who get along try to eat together on a regular basis. Going out to a restaurant is a common romantic experience. Eating with someone is seen as a bonding experience in nearly all cultures.

Problems can arise in relationships when couples differ significantly in appetite (opposites grow apart). Serious problems can occur when a person becomes overweight to the other partner's dissatisfaction. When the thin partner regards the overweight partner as lacking in control or not caring enough about the relationship to stay thin, the couple has a problem they need to work on together and solve.

TRANQUILITY

We have the potential to satisfy our desire for tranquility through relationships. When a couple is together, the partners are less frightened by danger than when they are apart. In a good relationship, a couple support each other in facing the uncertainties of the future.

When a timid person is attracted to a brave person, it may seem as if opposites have bonded, but that is usually not the case. If the timid person wishes he or she were more brave, then both partners are actually like-minded in valuing bravery. They should bond. In contrast, a partner who believes in discretion will not appreciate a partner who seeks out danger. Barbara Bush reportedly is not pleased that her husband, ex-President George Bush, has taken to skydiving every so often.

Problems arise in a relationship when one person is much more anxiety-ridden than the other (opposites grow apart). Woody Allen often portrays anxiety-ridden males who drive away more tranquil females. Generally, anxiety-ridden partners are burdensome to tranquil partners.

YOUR PARTNER AND YOU: SHARED AND COMPETING GOALS

The system of 16 desires can help you evaluate the areas in which you and your partner are alike or dissimilar.

Using the relationship worksheet below, enter the 16 desire ratings for each partner.

For every question you/your partner answered with:	*Please enter below:*
Very Important	+
Average Importance	0
Less Important	−

Under the column called "Goal," write an S for "shared" next to each pair of desires rated either (+, +) or (−, −). Write a C for "competing" next to each pair of desires marked either (+, =) or (−, +). Write an N for "not a major factor" next to each remaining pair of desires. These will be pairs with a + or − from one partner and no rating from the other.

Relationship Worksheet

	Example: Joe and Linda			*Your Ratings*		
	Joe	*Linda*	*Goal*	*You*	*Your Partner*	*Goal*
Power	+	+	S			
Independence	0	0	N			
Curiosity	0	0	N			

Relationship Worksheet (continued)

	Example: Joe and Linda			*Your Ratings*		
	Joe	*Linda*	*Goal*	*You*	*Your Partner*	*Goal*
Acceptance	0	0	N	___	___	___
Order	0	0	N	___	___	___
Saving	–	–	S	___	___	___
Honor	–	0	N	___	___	___
Idealism	0	0	N	___	___	___
Social Contact	+	–	C	___	___	___
Family	+	0	N	___	___	___
Status	+	+	S	___	___	___
Vengeance	0	0	N	___	___	___
Romance	0	0	N	___	___	___
Eating	–	0	N	___	___	___
Physical Activity	0	+	N	___	___	___
Tranquility	0	0	N	___	___	___

Finally, graph your answers on page 158. For each S desire, place a dot at the level indicated by "shared goals." For each C desire, place a dot at the level indicated by "competing goals." For all other desires, place a dot at the middle level labeled "not a factor."

HOW TO INTERPRET THE GRAPH

An "S" indicates that you and your partner share similar goals with regard to the particular desire. This is a source of mutual attraction in your relationship. A "C" indicates that you and your partner have significantly different goals with regard to a particular desire. This is a potential source of repeated quarreling in your relationship. An "N" indicates that a particular desire is probably not an important psychological factor in your relationship.

Example

Power, saving, and status represent shared goals in Joe and Linda's relationship. They are both ambitious (indicating a desire for power), they both like to spend money, and they would both like to live in prestigious

JOE AND LINDA'S RELATIONSHIP GRAPH

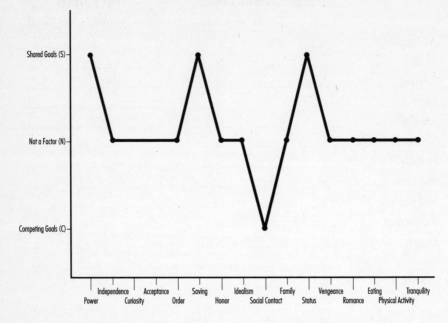

MY RELATIONSHIP GRAPH

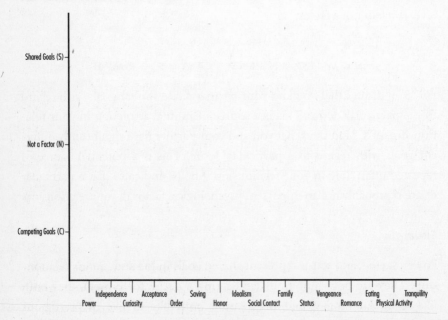

neighborhoods and buy expensive cars. Social contact is a source of competing goals in Joe and Linda's relationship. Joe likes to go out and socialize, but Linda prefers quiet evenings at home. In Joe and Linda's relationship, the desires for independence, curiosity, acceptance, order, honor, idealism, family, vengeance, romance, eating, physical activity, and tranquility represent neither shared nor competing goals.

STRENGTHENING RELATIONSHIPS

We have seen how relationships are strengthened when couples are matched for basic desire (Principle of Bonding), and how problems may arise when they are mismatched (Principle of Separation). The only important exceptions to these general principles concern people with very strong desires for acceptance or vengeance, who are mismatched to many partners.

People sometimes marry for the wrong reasons, such as sex. Although romance can hold a marriage together during the first few years, eventually the compatibility of other desires becomes more important. When sex is primarily what a couple has in common, it is only a matter of time before the relationship becomes unsatisfying for each partner. Lasting relationships are built on a compatibility of each partner's most important basic desires.

Although improved communication can help solve some of the problems discussed in this chapter, it may not always be enough. When desires are significantly mismatched, the more the partners communicate their true feelings, the more apparent are their differences. The main problem is not that they misunderstand each other, but rather that one enjoys a lifestyle that the other dislikes. What makes one partner happy makes the other uncomfortable, and vice versa. Improved communication can help a couple understand that the situation exists, but it does not directly lead to any solutions.

People cannot solve these problems by exerting pressure on their partners to give in to their demands or to do things their way. The partner may submit temporarily to the demands, but he or she cannot be happy doing so. It is only a matter of time before the problem reemerges.

Assuming both partners want to stay in the relationship, the first step toward improvement is to become clear on the intrinsic values that are holding the partners together. A quick way to do this is to use the Relationship Worksheet described in the preceding pages to analyze the couple's compatibility of basic desires. In doing this exercise, an "S" or shared goal indicates a basic desire that is bonding the couple together, and a "C" or competing goal indicates a force that is driving them apart. The basic strategy for increasing satisfaction in a relationship is to readjust the couple's everyday schedule or priorities to give greater significance to the shared goals than to the competing goals. How well this exercise works, of course, depends on how accurately each partner rates his or her basic desires.

Many marriages can be improved by finding workable compromises in regard to the issues that divide the couple. Essentially, compromises fall into one of three categories: 1) separating activities, 2) one partner giving in on one issue and the other giving in on a different issue, and 3) splitting the differences.

1. The partners can separate certain areas of their life to minimize conflict. If one person is a spender and the other is a saver, for example, they can separate their finances into funds to pay for common expenses, the wife's money, and the husband's money. In this way, they minimize the problem of one partner's financial habits affecting the other's. If one partner is very neat and the other is sloppy, they can agree that the common areas of the house will be neat but each partner will have a work room that can be neat or sloppy.

2. One partner gives in on some issues and the other gives in on other issues. For example, if one partner is intellectual and the other is highly motivated by the desire for physical activity, they can alternate Friday nights between playing bridge and working out at the gym.

3. They can split the differences between them. For example, if a wife is spending every night with the kids while her husband is coming home late, the husband can agree to give his wife time off every Wednesday night and every Saturday afternoon. If one partner wants to have friends in the house all the time and the other wants the house to be more private, they can agree that on certain days nobody will be invited to the house.

The easiest and quickest way to improve a marriage is to readjust the couple's schedules to spend more time on activities they both enjoy and less time on activities only one of them enjoys. This allows them to appreciate their relationship more without having to change each other. A plan in which the wife does something the husband likes, followed by the husband doing something the wife likes, is less desirable because little time is spent together on activities they both like. The basic principles in readjusting schedules are as follows:

- Increase the time spent on activities both partners enjoy.

- Decrease the time spent on activities one partner does not enjoy but engages in only to please the other partner.

- Perform separately essential chores that lead to arguments and fights.

Here are two sample solutions:

- A husband and wife have been spending less time together since the kids were born. They plan to go out together at least once a week and take regular vacations, just the two of them.

- The couple makes a list of activities they can both do together— play golf, hike, join a bridge club, go to movies, eat out, and so on. They then schedule these activities and stick to the schedule. Even though this may cost more, it is cheaper than a divorce.

DIFFERENCES BETWEEN MEN AND WOMEN

Up to this point, we have focused on analyzing how each partner's individual desire profile affects the quality of a relationship. We have found that partners bond when they have more or less the same desires but may grow apart when they have significantly different desires. We now look at how general differences between the sexes can affect the quality of a relationship.

Do men and women look for different things in a relationship? Well, I can tell you that they certainly differ in regard to some of the 16 basic desires, all of which play out in relationships. We have to keep in mind, however, that these differences refer to average tendencies and that many individual exceptions can be found for any general rule. We do not want to stereotype people on the basis of gender.

In general, there is a tendency for men to be more vengeful and competitive than women. They place a higher value on aggressive behavior and on getting even with those who offend them. Thus, men may be more likely to become competitive with their partners; they probably have a higher need to win arguments. Women may be more likely to avoid conflict.

According to the desire profiles of the people we studied, men are more interested than women in the sexual aspects of a relationship. The males in our surveys reported significantly higher levels of libido, or sexual desire. This does not mean that women are uninterested in sex or that sex is not important to them; the results suggested that women are very much sexually-minded, only less so than are men. Further, this is an average difference to which many individual exceptions occur.

In the profiles, men were more independent-minded than women, who were more interdependent. The men placed a greater value than did the women on becoming self-reliant. The women were more likely than men to enjoy interdependence. According to some theories of romantic love, our results suggest that women may have a higher capacity for romantic love than do men. The fact that women are, on average, more interdependent also may explain why they are, on average, more religious. (See Chapter 12.)

Interestingly, we found that the sexes are more or less equal in the desire to have a family. Men enjoy fatherhood as much as women enjoy motherhood. The maternal instinct can be very strong, but the same is true of the paternal instinct.

Further, women are more stress-avoidant than are men. According to Dalhousie University psychologist Sherry L. Stewart, women are more likely than men to turn to alcohol to cope with stress. Stewart has reported pioneering research showing a connection between the desire for tranquility and women's drinking problems.[11] In our surveys, the women seemed to be a bit more fearful than were the men. They are more likely than men to develop various types of anxiety disorders. What was learned from these surveys is that, while every individual has a unique desire profile, which may or may not be compatible with the profile of another individual, there are certain tendencies that seem to run consistently through the profiles of men and women.

Turning Work Into Play

We can satisfy our desires at work in two different ways. First, we can use our relationships with people at work—such as bosses, subordinates, or co-workers—to satisfy our desires. Second, we can use the work itself to satisfy our desires. Let's take a look at how all this happens.

HOW DESIRES AFFECT RELATIONSHIPS AT WORK

Your desire profile affects how you relate to people at work. If you have a significantly different desire profile than your boss, for example, your boss will tend to misunderstand you, and you will tend to misunderstand your boss. On the other hand, your boss will tend to appreciate you if your desire profiles are similar. The general principles in analyzing your relationship with your boss are that like-mindedness attracts, opposites repel, and the longer in time the relationship continues, the more powerful is the influence of compatibility of desire profile.

A good example of how desire profiles can affect the relationship between a boss and an employee is the misunderstanding that can occur between a highly organized assistant and a disorganized boss. The assistant has a low tolerance for chaos, but the boss has a low tolerance for being organized. As an organized person, the assistant tends to take pride in an ability to impose order where chaos rules. The organized assistant expects the disorganized boss to appreciate the scheduling, tidiness, and overall orderliness brought to the functioning of the boss's office. Up to a point, the boss is likely to be appreciative of such efforts, because the boss probably recognizes a need to be more orderly. But the assistant can easily push for a degree of order that is far beyond anything the boss is likely to appreciate. When this happens, the boss sees the assistant's efforts as inflexible, controlling, and largely unnecessary. The assistant may be confused as to why the efforts are unappreciated. Some type of compromise is required to resolve the problem, or perhaps the assistant should be reassigned to work with a boss who is more likely to appreciate a super-organized person.

Kyle and his boss provide another example of how incompatible desire profiles can lead to misunderstandings at work. Kyle is a psychologist working for a university hospital. He has excellent people skills, which he tries to use to his advantage. However, Kyle's boss is a private person who has no respect for people who try to get ahead by getting others to like them rather than by doing a good job. Kyle is very unhappy with his boss, who he thinks does not take enough interest in the people he supervises. Since Kyle and his boss have very different desire profiles, they do not get along, and the problem has only become worse with time.

Another common source of misunderstanding between bosses and subordinates can arise from a discrepancy in how much they value social status. Judy, the head of a university research center, is much more status-conscious than the average person. She does not realize the extent to which the people she supervises think she is pompous. When she gave a talk at a recent retirement party, she began by questioning whether or not it was appropriate for a person in authority to speak at such a festive occasion. Judy feared that her presence at the party might give the wrong impression—that it was okay for her employees to view her as an equal. The audience groaned, and Judy had no idea why her comments were not well received.

On the other hand, André cares so little about social status that he does not know the names of expensive fashion designers, luxury-car makers, or hot vacation spots. He frequently omits people's job titles when writing letters to them, in part because he presumes that titles are only a trifle and that nobody will really care much if he forgets what their exact title was. André's colleagues often become irritated by his behavior, interpreting it as a lack of respect. André knows that people become upset with him at times, but he has no idea what he has done to cause such reactions. Because social status is much less important to him than to the average person, he does not realize the extent to which he annoys other people by not paying proper respect to their status.

Our desire profile also influences how we relate to co-workers. We tend to appreciate co-workers who have desire profiles similar to our own. For example, Ursula and Alice were the two most ambitious young teachers in a group of six hired at a high school. They took a quick liking to each other, partially because they both wanted to talk about their jobs a lot, whereas the other young teachers preferred to talk about their social or family lives. By the end of the school year, other co-workers tended to avoid Ursula and Alice because frequent talk about getting ahead at work made them feel uneasy and nervous about their own careers.

As these examples suggest, we tend to get along with people at work who have similar desire profiles, but we often misunderstand those who have dissimilar profiles. In fact, we may not even realize that some of the problems we have with people at work are related to differences in how strongly we value a basic desire.

You can significantly enhance your understanding of people at work by comparing your desire profile with theirs. The following three steps provide guidelines for doing this. First, either recover a copy of your own desire profile or construct one anew based on how you answer the questions in the Appendix. Second, estimate the desire profile of supervisors, subordinates, or co-workers by rating them carefully on each of the 16 basic desires. Of course, you need to know the people at work reasonably well for your ratings of them to be valid. Third, use the charts in Chapter 6 to compare your own desire profile to those of each person at work with whom you have a relationship. Although the charts suggest specific misunderstandings that can arise, these suggestions are best regarded as hypotheses requiring further confirmation, not as inevitable outcomes. Only when you can confirm the suggestion with independent evidence (such as the opinion of others) can you assume that the suggested misunderstanding is likely to exist.

HOW JOBS SATISFY BASIC DESIRES

Your desire profile affects not only how you react to the people at work but also how you react to the work itself. Certain types of work are well-suited to satisfying your basic desires, whereas other types of work are poorly suited and may even interfere with your efforts to satisfy your desires. When you have a job that satisfies your desires, you tend to feel fulfilled by your work. When you have a job that interferes with your desires, you may feel trapped by your job and may even hate going to work every day.

Let's take a look at how people use their jobs to satisfy their motivational needs.

Power. When we achieve in our jobs or careers, we satisfy the desire to feel power (influence). Typically, people with a strong desire for power are ambitious and set challenging goals for themselves. For example, a young ballet dancer might dream of becoming a famous performer, a young entrepreneur might dream of becoming a millionaire by age 40, and a young farmer might dream of developing innovative techniques for harvesting crops. Merely working toward, and thinking about, such ambitious career goals can temporarily satisfy a person's desire for power; of course, the actual achievement of the goal produces much more lasting satisfaction.

In contrast, people with a weak desire for power do not want to feel influential. Their happiness is consistent with work that poses few challenges. They prefer to be followers rather than leaders, and they seek no particular glory. For example, a waiter might have the limited aim of holding on to his current job and keeping his customers happy—no dreams of owning his own restaurant. A trucker with a low desire for power might have few ambitions beyond that of providing a good income for her family, and an actor with a low desire for power might be content with minor roles in the theater. A significantly greater level of success could be experienced as stressful, possibly causing unhappiness.

Another common way of using work to satisfy the desire for power is to supervise other people. People with a high need for power like supervisory roles but tend to dislike the role of subordinate and may even find it stressful. In contrast, people with a low need for power react in the opposite manner—they are most comfortable being a follower at work and actually may even find it stressful to be a supervisor.

Independence. People vary greatly in how much independence versus help they want when they work at their jobs. When a job provides the right amount of assistance—not so much that you feel frustrated and not so little that you feel anxious—your desire for independence is temporarily satisfied. On such a job, you will experience a satisfying balance between support and freedom.

Independent workers like to do things without help from others. In contrast, interdependent people enjoy being able to rely on others for help in getting a job done. They prefer to work in teams or with colleagues who provide plenty of support and guidance.

Independent people generally are well matched to entrepreneurial jobs, owning small businesses, and some professional positions, but they are mismatched to civil service positions, positions in large corporations, or military positions. In contrast, interdependent people generally are well matched to careers in the clergy, or positions on corporate teams, but they are mismatched to entrepreneurial positions.

Entrepreneurs are self-starters who are driven by the basic desires of independence and power. They like to make their own decisions, go their own way, and ignore conventional wisdom. They hate it when anybody interferes with their freedom, which is why they do not appreciate bureaucrats.

The entrepreneurial spirit can lead to great success when a person's abilities match his or her ambitions. Sally, who is fiercely independent, has a long history of doing things at work her way. When she was young, she would meet with her supervisor, agree to a plan, and then ignore the plan and do what she wanted to do. Even after heart-to-heart talks in which Sally promised to accept a greater degree of supervision, nothing really changed. Sally likes other people and has a high need for social contact, but she needs to make her own decisions at work.

Sally is a very smart person who was determined to become wealthy. She used to play around with stock options and lose whatever money she had. When she first became a professional stock trader, she lost all of her funds in only a few weeks. Undaunted, Sally borrowed money and tried again, and once again she lost it all. It was not until the third try that Sally finally figured out how the game is played. She is now a reasonably wealthy person who consistently makes a lot of money every year by trading stocks.

Stock traders are among the most independent people in the world. They play with their own money and function as their own bosses. The ingredients of Sally's success were her desires for independence and power coupled with her intelligence. Her independence drove her into stock trading, and her achievement-orientation (desire for power) motivated her to stay with trading until she finally figured out how the game is played. Further, her intelligence gave her the ability to learn what was needed to be successful.

In contrast, Mike is an independent-minded person whose career has fallen far short of his goals, which is upsetting to him and a surprise to people who know him. Mike is a remarkably creative person who comes up with many important business ideas. However, he lacks important skills needed to start or operate a business. What he needs to do is to team up with people who have the skills that complement his own. Mike's friends do not understand why he does not do this. They keep thinking that someday Mike will realize that he needs help, get it, and become a big success. Yet year after year Mike continues to try to make a go of it by himself.

Although Mike knows that other people can help him, he is highly independent and hates having to accept assistance from others. He cares more about satisfying his desire for independence than he does about being successful (which would satisfy his desire for power). Because he has such a strong need to be independent, he would rather fail by himself than succeed as an idea person who is dependent for success on a business team that can implement his ideas. He is an excellent example of how a strong desire for independence can keep someone from being successful at work.

Curiosity. This basic desire creates a periodic need to learn. Some of the common ways of using a job to learn are traveling to new places, acquiring new skills, and collecting and analyzing information. Newspaper reporters, for example, must learn about one topic, place, or event after another. One day they are doing a story on a local fire, the next day they are covering a scandal at the mayor's office. Only a very curious person could do such a job well, because it requires learning about an event every day.

PHILOSOPHY STUDENTS

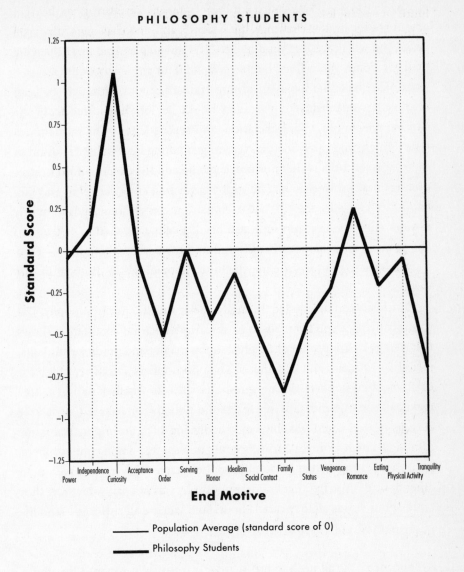

—————— Population Average (standard score of 0)

—————— Philosophy Students

Other jobs that can satisfy a high degree of curiosity include educational and professional positions such as teaching, dentistry, law, medicine, computer science, and nursing. In all of these jobs, people must keep up with the rapid pace of developments in their field.

Non-curious people should be happiest with jobs that require little learning, such as those in which the work is repetitive. Common examples of this include assembly-line worker, athlete, and security guard. Before you take a job, you should ask yourself if the job you are considering has the right amount of intellectual challenge. If it is significantly less challenging than you desire, you will be wasting your intellect. If it is significantly more challenging than you desire, you will not be able to stand it for any length of time.

Colette hates her job as an administrative assistant. Although she is an intelligent woman who enjoys reading books, her job consists mostly of answering telephones, taking dictation, and typing letters. The job requires little thought and rarely involves learning anything new. Colette is afraid to change careers because her position is secure and she cannot afford to start over again at a lower salary. She is slowly wasting away her mind and life, hoping every day for the 4:30 bell to ring so she can go home, only to return to work early the next morning and begin looking forward to 4:30 again. She needs to take charge of her life and find more stimulating work—even if she makes less money, she may be much happier with a different line of work.

Curiosity can be fulfilled through a career in academic philosophy. The accompanying graph from Susan Havercamp's doctoral dissertation shows the average desire profile of 52 philosophy majors and graduate students, including 29 males and 23 females. The philosophers scored very high for curiosity. Philosophers debate questions such as whether or not a tree makes a sound when it falls in a forest and nobody can hear it. Only a very curious person could possibly enjoy analyzing such an impractical issue. Although a high score for curiosity could be expected among philosophers, what's surprising is that these philosophers scored low or average on all other basic desires. In other words, philosophy was not just something they cared about, it was *all* they cared about. So if you are all curiosity—and little else—maybe philosophy is just what you need.

Acceptance. We all need to feel that we are basically accepted by others. We can satisfy this need at work by gaining the respect of our boss, co-workers, or colleagues.

How strongly we desire acceptance influences how much criticism we can handle on the job without becoming morose or feeling devastated. People with a high need for acceptance tend to be intolerant of even constructive criticism, whereas those with a low need for acceptance can cope with a great deal of criticism without becoming unduly nervous or unhappy.

In order to be happy in our jobs, it is important that the amount of criticism we experience is consistent with how strongly we need to be accepted by others. Some jobs can involve a great deal of criticism. Criticism is especially common in creative fields—such as literary work, art, and science—and in jobs that take place before an audience or within public view—such as acting, music, and politics. Imagine writing a play, watching it open on Broadway, and then reading newspaper reviews that say the play has no merit. Many people would find such public criticism so devastating they might never again write a play. To be successful as a playwright, you have to be able to withstand severe criticism and frequent rejection.

Wolfgang Amadeus Mozart is a good example of a person whose job as a composer was mismatched to his need for acceptance. Mozart had a very high need to be accepted as the musical genius that he was. When a duke suggested that his work could be improved, Mozart's need for acceptance was frustrated, and he became arrogant and obnoxious.[1] How could a genius like Mozart show such poor judgment by attacking the very patron he needed to support his work financially? Because his arrogance gratified a greater need than it frustrated—although it annoyed other people, his attitude also made them wary of criticizing his music. He was arrogant, not because he lacked "emotional intelligence," but because that was his best strategy for minimizing criticism while still allowing some chance of eventual glory.

When a boss has a high need for acceptance, his efforts to satisfy that need can lead to rough times for subordinates. A good case in point was a professor named Randall, who served as dean at a large university on the west coast. He was so afraid that his writings might be criticized that he stopped writing any original manuscripts by age 35. Ashamed of his lack of scholarly productivity, Randall started to criticize subordinates for not writing manuscripts, which intimidated them from looking too closely at his own record. He became exceptionally skilled in his ability to intimidate people. Like the meek Wizard of Oz who hid behind a curtain while projecting a frightful image of himself on a large screen, Professor Randall was a man who had a severe case of writer's block and yet terrorized his subordinates into thinking they could never write or publish enough to impress him. He pretended to be somebody he was not because he feared being criticized for who he was.

People who have a strong desire for acceptance need jobs that expose them to relatively few evaluations and little criticism. Examples include working for oneself (e.g., owning or operating a store), working as part of a team that is friendly and supportive (e.g., working for a church, in a police force, or as a firefighter), and working alone (e.g., as a night watchman or movie projectionist).

Order. This desire creates a periodic need to feel that things are predictable and under control. It can be satisfied by work that requires organizing, planning, scheduling, attention to detail, enforcement of rules, and ritualistic behavior. For example, a corporate employee can satisfy this desire by developing organizational schemes and procedure manuals. An editor can satisfy this desire by imposing organization on an author's article or book manuscript. Since neatness falls under this desire, working in a clean and neat office also creates a feeling of order and predictability.

People with a strong need for order match well with jobs that give emphasis to organizational skills—such as civil service positions and secretarial positions—but they match poorly with jobs that have a high degree of unpredictability. The opposite is true for people with a weak need for order.

Blair, a financial officer for a medium-size company, has a high need for order. He satisfies this desire at work by matching expenditures with appropriate accounts, seeing to it that the financial paperwork is in order, and tracking the payment of invoices. He has a very good eye for detail, leaving no bill or invoice without the proper documentation. He has such a high need for order that he sometimes stays late at work just to be sure that everything is in its proper place in the company's books. His boss and subordinates appreciate his efforts, although sometimes they complain that he is too inflexible and seems to spend more time keeping the finances tidy than may be absolutely necessary. Generally, Blair enjoys his work in part because it satisfies his need to organize.

Saving. This desire creates a need to collect, hoard, or own. Only a few jobs seem to be well-suited to satisfying this need—they include mutual fund manager, museum work, librarian, manager of Fort Knox or other caches of gold, and operator of a business that sells to stamp collectors. Examples of jobs that are poorly suited to satisfying this desire are any position in which money is spent freely.

Scrooge, the character in Dickens's *A Christmas Carol,* used his work to satisfy his high need for saving. He took special delight in counting his money at the end of each day and was such a tightwad that he didn't even give his employees unpaid leave to celebrate Christmas. All that changed, of course, when he was visited by the ghosts of Christmas. If your boss is a tightwad, maybe you need to expose him to a ghost or two to get a salary raise.

In contrast, Patrick was a business consultant who enjoyed spending money (indicating a low desire for saving.) Patrick's philosophy was to do things in the most expensive way that was readily available to him. He once checked into a San Francisco hotel, taking the presidential suite Richard Nixon had stayed in, at a cost of about $2,000 a night. He charged the expense to a publisher. When it came time to return to the airport, Patrick walked past colleagues waiting for a $5 bus at a corner and took a $40 cab ride instead. He bought first-class plane tickets when he could have saved money with business or economy class tickets. If clients wanted to hire Patrick, they had little choice but to pick up his tabs.

Honor. This desire, which creates a periodic need to experience feelings of loyalty, can be satisfied through work. Perhaps the most common examples are loyal employees of various companies. Honest and hardworking policemen who risk their lives to protect others bring honor to the force, their parents, and their heritage. Professional soldiers can satisfy the desire for honor through patriotism and conduct consistent with military honor codes. Businesspeople who take pride in following codes of ethics are satisfying their desire for honor.

Steven Spielberg has used his skills as a movie director to honor both his Jewish and American heritages.[2] His *Schindler's List* is a widely acclaimed movie that tells the story of the Holocaust in a way it had never before been told, and *Saving Private Ryan* honors the soldiers in World War II who courageously fought their way beyond the beaches of Normandy on D-Day. These movies provide Spielberg with feelings of loyalty to his heritage, and they are excellent examples of how work can be used to satisfy the basic desire for honor.

Idealism. This desire, which creates a periodic need to experience social justice, can be satisfied with work that contributes to the public good. Examples include charitable work, the clergy, medical research, health, law, teaching, newspaper reporting, and social work.

Since altruism falls under the desire for idealism, any work performed to benefit somebody else can satisfy the desire for idealism. Examples include a nurse, a lawyer who represents poor people, and the civil servant who is truly helpful. For example, Joe worked as a psychologist serving people with mental retardation. He took such an interest in the people he met that many of them considered him their personal friend. One former therapy patient visited him every April for help filing tax forms. Another former patient who did not like being transferred to a new group home gathered all his belongings and brought them to the university where he asked his friend/psychologist if he could move in with him. The psychologist helped him find a suitable place to live. Because Joe performed these acts selflessly, they satisfied his need for idealism.

Social Contact. Because jobs provide opportunities for co-workers to get to know one another, work can satisfy the basic desire for social contact. People with a strong desire for social contact are best suited for jobs in which there are frequent interactions with others. Sales, corporate positions, receptionist positions, barbering, and high school teaching all match well to the needs of sociable people. On the other hand, jobs that match poorly include night watchmen, and engineers assigned to remote places (e.g., an Antarctica research station). Sociable people who work from their homes tend to find the job less enjoyable than they had anticipated—although they avoid commuting, they also have far fewer opportunities to interact with others.

The desire for social contact can have significant impact on an employee's job performance. People with a strong desire for social contact tend to socialize more than the boss thinks appropriate. They may talk too long on the phone, and frequently leave their posts to make small talk with co-workers. On the other hand, people with a weak desire for social contact may avoid socializing even to the point of giving an impression of unfriendliness. They can be abrupt with clients, co-workers, or subordinates, and their need for privacy can be misinterpreted as a lack of interest in others.

Although people skills and the desire for social contact are not the same thing, they are usually related. People who have a strong need for social contact are motivated to improve their people skills as a means of making themselves liked by others, which is important to fulfilling their need for an active social life. In contrast, private people tend to lack the motivation to develop good people skills because they do not need a lot of people to like them.

It is important to find a job that matches well to your level of people skills and desire for social contact. When people lose their jobs or are passed over for promotion, it is sometimes because of poor people skills or a lack of interest in other people. Maybe the person offended a boss or found it hard to interact with co-workers.

Mary loves to interact with others. She started her own hairdressing parlor and loves to gab with clients, who take a quick liking to her. Her business has grown into a big success.

Tom, who had chosen the clergy as a career, did well in seminary school. He was too much of a private person to be successful and fulfilled as a minister, however. His nature was to spend a lot of time by himself; he did not really enjoy being with others, and it showed when he tried to minister to people. After graduating from the seminary, he decided to go back to school to become an accountant.

Family. This desire creates a periodic need to experience the love a parent has for a child. Generally, work interferes with our opportunity to satisfy this desire, so that people have to decide how much time they want to devote to family versus career. Public-school teaching jobs are popular in part because they are family-friendly positions—they provide generous vacation time that can be spent with one's children. Part-time work is another alternative for family-oriented people.

Although work usually limits how much time people can spend with their own families, there are some jobs that focus on the needs of other people's families. Common examples include social work, social research, clergy, family medical practice, and to a lesser extent, jobs that require frequent contact with children, such as elementary school teaching, youth activity coordinating, and pediatric work. These jobs may provide some measure of satisfaction of the employee's desire for family.

Sometimes a person with a low need for family simply does not like being around children. Employees need to know themselves enough not to sign on for work that involves frequent contact with children, such as working in a day care center. For such people, frequent contact with children can lead to frustration and stress.

Status. This desire creates a periodic need to experience a sense of self-importance. Since work gives people the potential of feeling self-important, it is a common way we have of satisfying our desire for status. We need a career, job, and job title that match the level of prestige we desire. The job title "IBM Senior Vice-President for Public Responsibility" scores high on the prestige factor because the computer industry has glamour, IBM is a premier corporation, and "Senior Vice-President" sounds very important. Because the prestige factor of this position is quite high, the job has the potential to satisfy a person's desire for status. A person who occupies this position needs only to think of what an impressive job title he or she has in order to feel a certain degree of self-importance.

Generally, prestigious jobs include physician, lawyer, dentist, positions in high-technology industries, executive, successful business owner, and any job that conveys a sense of wealth or pays a very high salary. Banking is an example of an industry where status is recognized as being so desirable that it is used to reward people. The title of vice-president of a bank sounds much more impressive than it really is. Large banks have a great number of vice-presidents, most of whom are in middle management positions and have little authority.

Vengeance. This desire creates a periodic need to experience competition or vindication. Attorney and prosecutor are ideal jobs for satisfying this basic desire. People who hold these jobs help their clients—attorneys assist individuals and prosecutors assist the state—get even with people who have injured or caused damage to individual(s) or society. Strictly speaking, it is the client who is seeking vengeance, but the attorney is so closely involved in the fight that he or she also experiences aggressive or competitive feelings.

Since the need for competition falls under the desire for vengeance, any job that involves a fair amount of competition can satisfy this desire. Common examples include entrepreneurial jobs, some sales positions, and professional athlete. Jobs that provide opportunities for physical aggression also satisfy this need. Examples include soldier, policeman, bouncer, and boxer. In contrast, examples of jobs where aggressive desires get people into trouble are those involving contact with young children (e.g., preschool teacher, pediatric nurse) and any job in which pleasing others is important (e.g., sales, negotiating). These latter careers are best suited for people with weak desires for vengeance and competition.

Romance. People with a strong desire for romance match well to jobs that give emphasis to aesthetic experiences, such as actor, artist, commercial artist, dancer, decorator, graphic designer, and musician.

Eating. Jobs in the restaurant industry—such as cook and waiter—provide workers with frequent opportunities to eat and enjoy the pleasure of being around food. Since overeating is one of the potential hazards of working in the restaurant industry, people struggling to control their weight may need other employment.

Physical Activity. Many jobs can satisfy this desire, including athletics, construction, farming, moving, military service, police work, shipping, and restaurant waiter or waitress. Before taking a job, consider the physical demands of the work. Are you comfortable with the level of physical activity expected of you? Is the job too strenuous? Is there too much inactivity or desk work involved?

Tranquility. People with a strong desire for tranquility require a job that is relatively free of stress. The person also is poorly suited for high-stress jobs such as athlete, senior corporate executive, stock or commodity trader, surgeon, air traffic controller, taxicab driver, or public relations specialist. Other examples of stressful jobs include those with deadlines (e.g., newspaper reporter) and those with uncertain outcomes (e.g., real-estate agent, financial trader). They will probably dislike a position that involves exposure to danger, such as test pilot, soldier, firefighter, security officer, or policeman. Relatively low-stress jobs include those that pose little danger and have few deadlines, such as florist, office worker, librarian, janitor, and dental assistant.

ROTC CADETS

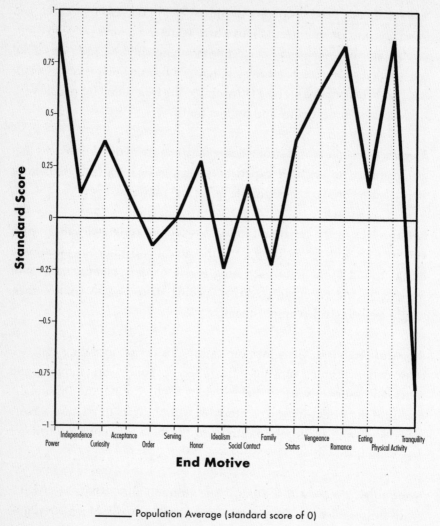

_____ Population Average (standard score of 0)

▬▬▬ ROTC Cadets

Grace is a West Coast pediatrician with an extremely high need for tranquility. She has difficulty handling the stress of deadlines, to the point that she is not able to get her medical reports written on time. Although she does a fine job examining her patients, she experiences writer's block when it comes time to write the reports. Parents become angry at Grace when the reports on their children are not ready when they are supposed to be.

The problem has only gotten worse as time passed. Grace has lost a number of jobs because of her inability to deal with her panic attacks under deadline.

Numerous research studies have shown that people with a weak desire for tranquility tend to be fearless. These people are psychologically suited to jobs that involve exposure to danger, such as firefighter or military positions. There is a strong tendency for military officers to have a low desire for tranquility.

A low desire for tranquility (indicating high potential for bravery) can be fulfilled through a military career. The accompanying graph from Susan Havercamp's doctoral dissertation shows the average desire profile of 65 ROTC students training to become military officers. The group included 54 men and 11 women. The students scored very low for tranquility. They also scored high for power (probably expressing the military value of leadership), physical exercise (probably expressing the military value of physical strength), and vengeance (probably expressing the military desire to fight). In all of the remaining desires, they were about average.

IS CHANGING JOBS WORTH THE RISKS?

If you have a job that does not fulfill your needs, there is a limit to how much you can improve the situation without changing jobs. You may be able to change your duties somewhat, but few employers permit their workers to significantly readjust job duties to match their desire profile. For this reason, you may want to give serious consideration to changing your job or career. Either you need different job responsibilities, a different supervisor, or a career change. It can be frightening to change jobs, especially when you need the income and are uncertain about your ability to replace your current salary. However, boldness is sometimes what is called for, because happiness is often worth the risk of changing careers or jobs.

Many people are reluctant to change jobs in search of a more enjoyable one. They figure that because work is generally unenjoyable, they probably will not like their new job much more than their old one. After all, isn't that why employers pay us to do it? Since work is about doing what our employers want, and play is about doing what we want, we expect that work should have unpleasant or boring aspects to it. We usually do not think of work as an opportunity to fulfill our basic desires and gain value-based happiness.

Many people work 40 hours or more a week, about 46 weeks a year. The weeks pass into months, the months pass into years, and the years pass into a lifetime. You should enjoy something quite a bit if you will be spending that much time doing it. Otherwise, you will spend a large percentage of your life doing something you dislike. Life is too short to waste so much of it on a job you do not value.

In deciding whether or not to make a change, you also need to consider how a growing unhappiness with your current job can eventually affect your performance and limit your future pay raises. When people hold on to jobs that are incompatible with their desire profiles, sooner or later their performance tends to suffer. The problem is that their desires prod them to do things that interfere with their work. Maybe they end up socializing too much, or perhaps they become bored because their intellect is not being challenged. Russ, for example, is a very curious person. No matter what job he is supposed to be doing, it is only a matter of time before he starts thinking about things deeply even if it means doing his job poorly. Sooner or later, Russ will be Russ. When he was a student at college working on a cafeteria food line, he used to wonder about the food—where do peas come from, why are there so many different shapes, and so on. All this thinking distracted him from the job at hand. He got by working in the cafeteria, but he did not do a mindful job. Throughout his life, Russ did poorly in any job that did not challenge him intellectually—his need to use his mind was so great that he had difficulty paying attention to mindless work.

I hope these considerations encourage some readers to take risks and change jobs if they are unhappy now. If you are one of the readers who plan to change jobs, or if you are a new worker planning a career, you can use your knowledge of your desire profile to choose a career that is likely to be fulfilling. Let's see how you might do this.

HOW TO CHOOSE A FULFILLING CAREER

Generally, we feel fulfilled in our work when we hold a job that satisfies our most important basic desires. Of course, we need to be able to perform the job reasonably well, but we are unlikely to find fulfilling work simply by choosing the job we can do best. We also are unlikely to find a fulfilling job if we choose primarily on the basis of salary. Step-by-step, here are my suggestions on how to choose a career or job that fulfills your basic desires.

Step 1. If you have not already done so, identify which of the 16 basic desires are most and least important to you by answering the questions in the Appendix. Your ratings will be more accurate if you first read Chapters 2, 3, and 4.

Step 2. Make a list of possible jobs you are considering. Your local library should have a book listing different occupations; if not, a nearby college library probably will. There are a lot of different kinds of jobs out there, so starting with a long list may be worthwhile if you want to find the one that is best for you.

Step 3. Now ask yourself the following questions about each prospective job.

    A. Does the career or job have the potential to satisfy your ambitions? (Relevant only if you rated yourself high on the desire for power.)

    B. Are you comfortable with the supervision? (Relevant only if you rated yourself high or low on the desire for power.)

    C. Are you comfortable with the number of hours of work that will be expected?

    D. Are you comfortable with how much work is performed independently versus as a team member? (Relevant only if you rated yourself high or low on the desire for independence.)

    E. Are you satisfied with the intellectual level of the work? (Relevant only if you rated yourself high or low on the desire for curiosity.)

    F. Are you comfortable with the amount of flexibility that comes with the job in terms of schedule and rules? (Relevant only if you rated yourself high or low on the desire for order.)

G. Are you comfortable with how much loyalty to the company or product will be expected of you? (Relevant only if you rated yourself high or low on the desire for honor.)

H. Are you satisfied with the ethical aspects of the job? (Relevant only if you rated yourself high on the desire for honor.)

I. Are you comfortable with the extent to which the work contributes to the betterment of society? (Relevant only if you rated yourself high or low on the desire for idealism.)

J. Are you satisfied with the opportunities to socialize and get to know your co-workers? (Relevant only if you rated yourself high or low on the desire for social contact.)

K. Is the career or job consistent with your plans for a family? (Relevant only if you rated yourself high or low on the desire for family.)

L. Are you satisfied with the prestige factor of the job, job title, and firm? (Relevant only if you rated yourself high or low on the desire for status.)

M. Are you comfortable with the degree of aggressiveness and competitiveness that will be expected of you? (Relevant only if you rated yourself high or low on the desire for vengeance.)

O. Are you comfortable with the degree of physical labor that will be expected? (Relevant only if you rated yourself high or low on the desire for physical activity.)

P. Can you easily handle the amount of stress associated with the job? (Relevant only if you rated yourself high or low on the desire for tranquility.)

After answering these questions in regard to each career or job you are seriously considering, you can make a list of careers or jobs that best satisfy your most important basic desires. Be sure that each career you consider satisfies not just one of the basic desires important to you, but all of them or, at a minimum, all but one of them.

Step 4. Look at the list again, focusing in particular on your desire for acceptance. Eliminate from your list those jobs that would expose you to a degree of criticism you cannot handle. Examples may include jobs requiring frequent or public evaluations, or performances before audiences. Lawyers can lose many cases, athletes lose many games, politicians lose elections, and writers face frequent rejections of their manuscripts. If you think you cannot handle such setbacks, stay away from the career or job. If you have an average or low desire for acceptance, you may keep these jobs on your list.

Step 5. Eliminate from consideration any careers or job you lack the ability to perform. If the problem is a lack of credentials or education, you may want to consider going back to school to gain what you need for a fulfilling job. In the long run, you may be much better off returning to school to change careers than sticking with a career that does not fulfill you.

Step 6. Now look at your list, focusing on your desire for social contact. Eliminate any careers or jobs that require a degree of social interaction significantly greater than or less than your current level of interest or skill.

Step 7. Pick one of the jobs still remaining on your list—since they all are fulfilling, it is now okay to consider salary as a criterion for choosing.

All in the Family

When Michael Jordan won his fourth NBA title, he held up the championship trophy and told the world he had won it for his father, who was deceased. Many people are like Michael Jordan, going through adult life still desirous of pleasing their parents. When they do something they know a parent would have appreciated, they imagine the parent's approval, even after the parent has passed away.

In this chapter, I take a look at how we can fulfill the 16 basic desires through family life. I discuss positive examples of satisfaction as well as common family problems. The system of 16 basic desires suggests the following four principles of family relationships:

1. ***Principle of Family:*** The parent–child relationship is held together by two distinct basic desires, honor and family.

2. ***Principle of Uniqueness:*** Grown children sometimes have basic desires significantly different from those of their parents.

3. ***Principle of Independence:*** To be happy, children must learn how to satisfy their own basic desires, not those of their parents.

4. ***Principle of the Favored Child:*** A parent has a natural tendency to favor the child who best fulfills the parent's own basic desires.

PARENT-CHILD BONDING

The parent–child relationship is held together by two different desires (Principle of Family). The basic desire that binds children to their parents, called honor, is different from the one that binds parents to their children, called family. People who have a strong desire for honor care deeply about their parents, heritage, morality, and ethnic traditions. In contrast, people who have a strong desire for family enjoy raising their own children, and they spend a lot of time doing so. These two desires help parents and children overcome conflicts that naturally arise in their relationships. Even when parents do things that their children dislike, the children still have a basic desire to honor and remain loyal to them. Even when children upset their parents, the parents still have a basic desire to love them.

Adult children differ considerably in how strongly they honor their parents. People who have a strong sense of honor, for example, want to spend time with, and provide financial support to, their elderly parents. In contrast, people who have a weak sense of honor are nowhere to be found when their elderly parents need their help or money.

Parents with a strong desire for family love raising their children. They want to have a number of children, and they arrange their schedules to be sure they have time to be at home.

Parents with a weak need for family experience raising children as more of a burden than a joy. Author Geoffrey Canada, whose father had abandoned both his brother and him when they were babies, described his first meeting with his father and the hurt he felt when he learned how little interest his father had in him.

> I left feeling more confused than when I'd come. This man was my father, but he didn't seem to feel any particular way about me. . . . Before our visit, I imagined I would be able to feel that special parental bond that exists between a child and a parent . . . But when I met him there was nothing. No hugs, no physical contact of any kind, no words of endearment, no special glances.[1]

A third basic desire, independence, sets children on a natural course toward self-reliance. As children grow older, the parents' opportunity to mold them decreases (Principle of Independence). Freud thought that a child's basic psychological nature is determined by about age 5, and he might have been right. I would say that by the age at which a child starts to show adolescent rebellion, or about age 14, the parents' opportunity to mold the child is largely gone. As some parents have learned, at that age children are likely to do the opposite of what their parents want just to show their independence.

Another factor that affects the parent–child relationship is the degree of match between desire profiles. When a parent and a child are matched, they can use their relationship to satisfy their desires. For example, a curious parent and a curious child can travel together or play a game of chess. In contrast, both parent and child must go outside their relationship to satisfy any desires on which they are mismatched. For example, a curious parent cannot have many intellectual conversations with a non-curious adult child but instead must find somebody else with whom to converse. The same principles influence relationships between siblings—brothers and sisters can use the sibling relationship to satisfy those desires on which they are matched but not those on which they are mismatched.

Stella Chess has suggested the idea of "goodness of fit" in thinking about the parent–child relationship.[2] (This idea is similar to the idea of compatibility of desire profile.) According to Chess, parents have psychological needs that are matched with some children but are mismatched with others. When a parent's goals, values, or temperament match those of the child, Chess speaks of a good "fit." When a parent's goals, values, or temperament are mismatched with those of the child, Chess speaks of a poor "fit." The better the fit, the easier it is for parents to accept their children (Principle of the Favored Child). Some authorities think that many psychological problems in adulthood can be traced back to a poor psychological fit between parent and child.

HOW FAMILY LIFE SATISFIES OUR NEEDS

We have the potential to satisfy our desires through our relationships with our parents, children, or siblings. Let's look at ways in which family members do and do not connect on each of the 16 basic desires, beginning with the desire for power.

Power. The desire for power creates a periodic need to feel influential and competent. Although it usually takes a significant achievement of some kind to satisfy this desire, new parents can find achievement in their child's most ordinary behavior. Many new parents, for example, watch their child's first ballet steps and then brag as if it were the Nutcracker Suite. They interpret the most ordinary signs of mental development in their baby as possible indicators of genius. They watch their child catch a ball and imagine that the kid might win an athletic scholarship. In each of these examples, the parent is satisfying the desire for power through the early achievements of the child.

Sometimes parents do not attain the degree of influence or achievement in life that they would like. When this happens, the parents may pin their ambitions on their children, hoping that the children will grow up and accomplish what they themselves did not achieve. Parents may hope that their children will become great athletes, successful businessmen, renowned scientists, and so on. These parents seek a vicarious satisfaction of their own desire for power through the deeds of their children.

When achievement-oriented parents use their children to satisfy their own needs, they may not realize how much pressure they put on the children. When I coached a sixth-grade basketball team, one parent told me that his boy would win a basketball scholarship to college. His kid played very well, but only a small number of boys play well enough to win scholarships. The pressure on that boy to excel was tremendous. He could not feel happy if he played well, only if he played exceptionally well.

Significant problems can occur when ambitious parents have a non-ambitious child who rebels against their efforts to push him or her toward glory. The parents create expectations and standards that are much too high for the child, causing a significant rift in the parent–child relationship. The ambitious parent may not understand how he or she could have such an unambitious child and may even wonder if something is wrong with the child. "How can a child of mine lack willpower?" the parent wonders. On the other hand, the child may think of the parent as bossy and domineering. "Get off my back," screams the child, who may think of running away.

Tennessee Williams's *Cat on a Hot Tin Roof*[3] tells the story of a parent and child who are mismatched on ambition. Big Daddy is a powerful personality who dominates his household. He builds a business empire of such importance that governors and senators send him telegrams on his birthday. In contrast, Brick is an unambitious son who has quit his job as a sports announcer and is afraid to live his life for fear he will not live up to Big Daddy's expectations. When Brick and Big Daddy finally have a "heart-to-heart" talk, Brick tells Big Daddy that all he ever wanted was a father, not a boss, and Big Daddy finally realizes that Brick needs greater acceptance from him.

What if an unambitious parent has an ambitious child? Unambitious parents (indicating a weak desire for power) feel uncomfortable with strong feelings of power, influence, or competence; they actively avoid many achievement opportunities. They are likely to suppose that their children are similar to them and would be better off with modest aspirations; consequently, they discourage their children from pursuing ambitious dreams.

Curiosity. Parents who help their children with homework provide a common example of how curiosity can be satisfied through the parent–child relationship. The parent enjoys the homework and uses it to satisfy his or her own curiosity. Families also satisfy curiosity by travelling together on a vacation and learning about new places.

Intellectual parents generally hope that their children will like school and get good grades. For example, Kevin is the 11-year-old child of two teachers. He spends so much time reading books that the other kids on Kevin's block rarely ask him to play. The parents are not concerned by Kevin's growing social isolation but instead are pleased that he takes an interest in reading, which they think is a "natural" way for their son to behave. Their own curiosity prodded them to place a high value on education, and they are happy when Kevin behaves in ways consistent with their values.

Intellectual parents can become frustrated when they have a noncurious child who does not take a liking to school. They may see the child's attitude as a rejection of the values of their family. "The Smiths of Baltimore have always been intellectual people," they tell their child. "You should carry on this tradition and pay more attention to your grades." But the child is following a different drummer and just does not experience learning as a great joy. He is a different person from his parents and grandparents, but his family does not want a different person. Their attitude is caused by their own desire profile; it is an example of what I have called *self-hugging*.

Acceptance. The most precious gift parents can give their children is to accept them for who they are. When parents do this, the child develops a general attitude of self-confidence. When parents withhold acceptance, the child may spend the rest of his life seeking it. When parents reject their child outright, the child may lack self-confidence and be angry or depressed.

Psychoanalysts have studied how parental acceptance affects psychological development. They have concluded that a parent's rejection of a child during the first years of life can cause significant psychological problems for the child. These problems can be so difficult to overcome that they extend into adulthood.[4]

Not only do children need acceptance from their parents, but parents also need acceptance from their children. Psychologists sometimes use the word "needy" to describe parents who have an unusually strong desire for acceptance. Needy parents use their children to satisfy their own insecurities. Because they lack self-confidence, they overreact to any signs of disapproval, criticism, or rejection from their children. They demand frequent reassurances that they are loved and often point out the sacrifices they have made for their children, hoping that the children will be appreciative and approving.

Although needy parents overreact when criticized, they themselves are quick to criticize others, including their own children. They try to intimidate their children into not criticizing them because criticism denies them the level of acceptance that they need. A vicious circle of events can occur: (1) The needy parent criticizes the child; (2) the criticism makes the child angry; (3) when the child expresses anger and fights back, the needy parent reacts by becoming more insecure and even more critical of the child. The fighting can continue for years without any significant improvement in the relationship.

Needy parents want to hold on to their children as long as possible, discouraging them from growing up and leaving home. A case in point was the story of Peter Helfgott, who discouraged in every possible way his musically talented son, David, from growing up and becoming an independent adult. When David received an invitation to study music in America, Peter put his foot down, and David stayed at home. Peter later opposed his son's leaving for London to study at the Royal College of Music. When David left anyway, Peter refused to have anything to do with him. After winning an important musical competition, David suffered an emotional breakdown that required psychiatric hospitalization.

Sometimes it is the child (not the parent) who is needy. Needy children frequently seek the approval of adults and overreact to disapproval and criticism. Their need for attention often leads to behavior problems both at school and at home. Common problems include tantrums, sadness, and avoiding challenges. The behavior problems of needy children can be very difficult to manage because no matter how much love or attention the parents show it is never enough to satisfy the child. Professional help is often needed to build self-confidence and reduce the child's need for acceptance.

On the other hand, parents and children with a low need for acceptance are secure and self-confident. Parents with a low need for acceptance are satisfied knowing that their children love them; they rarely require reassurance. They are able to distinguish their needs from their children's needs, and do not react to expressions of independence as threatening. Similarly, children with a low need for acceptance rarely seek reassurance.

Order. Families are among the most important sources of stability in the lives of a great many people. For much or all of our lives, whether the symbol of constancy is the family farm, business, or home, there is a reassuring quality to the knowledge that it is still there. When the home or business is sold, the change can be unsettling because we lose an important means by which we had found order in our lives.

As these comments indicate, we have the potential to fulfill our desire for order through family life. Family habits, traditions, and rituals are motivated by the desire for order. Some families eat meals at the same time every day or spend time every Sunday together. They may gather every year at Thanksgiving or Christmas, spend every summer in the country, or play golf every Father's Day. The repetitive nature of a family activity creates a psychologically important sense of order, stability, and predictability for the family members.

Sometimes the desire for order can become a source of conflict within a family. A common mismatch occurs when a parent has a strong desire for order and the child has a weak desire. The parent creates rules, routines, and schedules but the child rebels. The parent wonders how he or she can be such a neat and organized person and the child can be so sloppy and disorganized. The child leaves clothes lying on the floor, forgets to clean up after eating, or forgets his or her schedule. The child may complain that the parent is rigid, inflexible, or "perfect."

James is an excellent example of how a parent can use the family to satisfy a strong desire for order. He makes up a rule that the family must follow for nearly everything they do. When the family computer was connected to the Internet, James determined that each child should surf the net exactly four hours a week in eight half-hour sessions. At the beginning of each week, he gave each child eight poker chips. When the child wanted to surf the net, he first turned in a poker chip, and James set a timer so that it would ring exactly one half-hour later. The children had to use all eight poker chips each week, which ensured that they would use the Internet exactly four hours every seven days.

Saving. Many parents enjoy saving for the purpose of leaving their children an inheritance. Elderly parents can derive real satisfaction from the knowledge that when they die their money and property will be passed on to their children. Families also save pictures, jewelry, and sentimental items to pass them on from one generation to the next.

Some savers hope to see their children develop similar values. It is important to them that their children learn "the value of a dollar." They make their children earn their spending money and then teach them how to save it. Another pattern of behavior is also seen, one in which the parent gives the adult child money to protect him or her from the hardships of being poor. The problem with such gifts is that they can undermine frugality. At least, that is the conclusion Thomas J. Stanley and William D. Danko drew in their book, *The Millionaire Next Door*. According to Stanley and Danko, parents who give their children money may do more harm than good. The children increase spending and get used to taking money rather than earning it. "Gift receivers are hyperconsumers and credit prone," observed Stanley and Danko.[5] Because they consume more, they save less.

Randy and Enid grew up in Appalachia, where their parents worked in coal mines. Both managed to work their way through college and land decent jobs after graduation. They worked hard to get ahead, and they adopted a highly frugal lifestyle. They gradually built a secure nest egg, and then bought a small business that made them multimillionaires.

Although Randy and Enid wanted their daughter, Alexa, to learn the value of saving, they also wanted to protect her from the hardships they had known. So they bought her the best clothes, sent her to private schools, and gave her all the money she needed. Alexa got used to the gifts and became a spender, not a saver. As an adult, she worked only part-time, accepting support from her parents. Alexa never worries about earning or saving money because she figures her parents' money will always be there for her.

Alexa married and has two children, Sasha and Ellen. Alexa's parents lavish expensive gifts on both grandchildren and have given them each a significant amount of money. Sasha has become a spender like her mother, but Ellen is a tightwad. Genes must have something to do with whether or not we become spenders or savers, because otherwise Ellen, too, would have become a spender.

Honor. We have learned that honor plays a special role in family life because it bonds the child to parents and family traditions. Here we look at other ways in which family relationships are used to satisfy the desire for honor. For example, parents satisfy their own desire for honor when they take pride in having raised a child with good moral character. Some beam when their child's integrity is recognized. They pride themselves at having raised a child with character. Beaming parents are seen at various rites of passage, such as a baptism ceremony or a bar mitzvah.

When a parent is principled and a child is unprincipled, or vice versa, they are mismatched on the desire for honor. The principled person feels that the unprincipled one lacks character, and the unprincipled person feels that the principled one is self-righteous. The mismatch can cause a rift in the relationship. An interesting example of this was portrayed in the motion picture *Hud.* Hud lives for himself, openly dates other men's wives, gets drunk, and raises hell. He believes he has to look out for himself because nobody else will. In contrast, Hud's father, Will, is a morally uncompromising man who believes in treating other people with decency. Will disapproves of his son:

> WILL: You are an unprincipled man, Hud.
>
> HUD: Don't let that bust you, you have enough for both of us.
>
> WILL: Hud, how did a man like you come to be a son to me?

A mismatch on the basic desire for honor drives Will and Hud apart. Will rejects his son because Will places a much higher value on honor than on family. In contrast, Hud places very little value on either. When events require them to make common business decisions, their desires pull them in opposite directions, and their relationship further deteriorates.

Idealism. Parents have the potential to satisfy their desire for idealism by volunteering for community services in which their own child is a participant. Common examples include parents who sponsor Boy Scout or Girl Scout troops or who coach youth-league sports. Other examples of family idealism are adopting children with special needs, participating in foreign-student exchange programs, and taking in a refugee child.

In many families, the idealism of young people can come into conflict with the realism of their parents. Such conflict was especially common during the 1960s when significant numbers of baby boomers dropped out of society and protested the Vietnam war. The generational conflict of the 1960s also included young people's opposition to racism and sexism.

Social Contact. Although parents cannot go out on double dates with their teenage children, some come close to doing just that. For example, Phyllis spent a lot of time talking with the kids with whom her daughter hung out, and she even encouraged parties at her house that she herself attended. She took an active interest in the high-school gossip, such as who would be the homecoming queen and who would break up with whom. By closely following her daughter's social life, Phyllis vicariously satisfied some of her own needs for socializing.

Another way in which families satisfy their desires for social contact is by having fun together. Common examples include family picnics, church outings, trips to the beach, and family vacations. According to the system of 16 basic desires, having fun is a bonding experience because it involves the use of family relationships to satisfy a basic human need.

A mismatch on the desire for social contact occurs when a sociable parent has a shy child or a shy parent has a sociable child. The sociable parent would like the child to join groups, have many friends, and pursue an active social life, but the shy child would prefer to spend most of his or her time alone. When people visit the home, the sociable parent may be embarrassed by the shy child. The parent does not understand why the child needs so much privacy and feels uncomfortable in a group. When the parent encourages the child to be more friendly, the child fights back.

According to a story that appeared in the *Columbus Dispatch*, Stacy Quinn was a talker.[6] She started conversations with just about anyone, and she really enjoyed meeting new people. However, her 4-year-old daughter, Annie, was shy. Annie hid behind her mother's legs when Stacy tried to introduce her to someone new. Stacy wondered how her child could be so different from her and felt helpless about how to handle the situation. She tried to "steamroll" Annie into becoming more sociable. As child psychiatrist Stella Chess commented, "Pushing a child to do something that conflicts with her temperament will make her withdraw or rebel even more . . . and that only widens the rift."[7]

Status. Parents who brag about their children's looks, dress, or social graces are vicariously satisfying their own desire for status. Some parents, for example, eagerly show baby pictures to anyone who will sit still long enough to take a look. A computer wonk was so thrilled by a new arrival in his house that he put a television camera on his personal computer so that his wife could download pictures of the baby's latest exploits. At work, he printed out the pictures and then showed them to any colleague who came near.

"Little Miss" beauty pageants provide another example of parents who use their children to satisfy their own desire for status. In these pageants, girls as young as six dress up as glamorous women. The parents derive vicarious satisfaction of their own desire for status by watching their children participate in the pageants.

Problems sometimes arise when a parent and child are mismatched on the desire for status. If the parent is status-oriented and the child is not, for example, the parent often worries about what the neighbors or friends might think, but the child couldn't care less. The child may become rebellious to express the feeling that social status is not as important as the parent thinks.

The story of Mary Cunningham provides an interesting example of a mother who used her daughters to satisfy her own desire for status. Mary could not afford to move up from the working-class, ethnic neighborhood in which she lived. Instead, she hoped that her daughters, Veronica and Margaret, would grow up and marry professional or wealthy people. She thought that their chances of doing so would be enhanced if they dressed nicely and learned proper etiquette.

Mary favored Veronica, the more socially acceptable of her two daughters. Veronica was graceful, had a soft voice, and behaved and dressed in the manner her mother thought appropriate. Veronica accepted the lifestyle her mother had chosen for her. She married a professional man and lived in a prestigious neighborhood not far from her mother's house.

In contrast, Margaret was clumsy and had a booming voice. Mary kept pressuring Margaret to be more graceful and ladylike, but Margaret did not share this desire. When her father did not intervene on her side, Margaret moved to another city to escape her mother's frequent criticism. She married a working-class man of the same ethnic background, not a professional man as her mother had wanted. When Margaret brought her husband home to meet her family, Mary declared him unacceptable and banned him from her house. At age 40, the stress took its toll on Margaret. Following an argument with her mother, Margaret entered a mental hospital.

As children grow older, they can change quite dramatically from cute little boys and girls to confused adolescents. When mommy and daddy stop doting on every little thing a child does, the loss of attention from parents (indicating a loss of status) can be devastating. Some children react by engaging in risky or attention-attracting behavior in efforts to regain lost status (attention).

Patricia, a neighbor's teenage daughter, changed from a well-behaved child to a spoiled, rebellious brat. Her grades fell from mostly A's to mostly F's in a single term, and she stopped seeing her usual friends and started hanging out with kids who frequently were in trouble with school authorities. Using foul language, Patricia complained all the time about her parents, who were at their wits' end. They finally consulted with a psychologist, who advised that Patricia was seeking their attention. Although all teenagers seek adult attention, Patricia seemed addicted to it. She engaged in reckless behavior as her best hope for getting the large amount of attention she had become accustomed to and now desired.

Vengeance. This desire can be satisfied within families in a number of ways. Perhaps the most common means are fantasies of competition or punishment. Freud believed that children fantasize about getting even with their parents for imposing limits and restricting what they can do.

When parents use their children to satisfy their desire for vengeance, an abusive situation can occur. Approximately a half-million American children are physically abused in a given year. Additional numbers of children are sexually or emotionally violated. Neglect is another common form of abuse.

The story of Rose provides an example of how a spiteful mother can use her own son to satisfy a need for revenge. In 1880 Rose's family had pressured her into an arranged marriage with her first cousin, Harry. She resented having to marry Harry, whom she did not love. For the rest of her life, she hated men, even her own son.

Rose and Harry had two daughters and a son, Andrew. Rose favored her daughters and used her son as an opportunity to get even with males. Andrew was creative, talented, and ambitious, but Rose told him he was a no-good dreamer. She did not want him to try to better himself; she wanted him to fail. She discouraged his songwriting and would not pay for him to go to college, telling him he was suited only for factory work.

When her children were grown, Rose invited her daughters to visit for holiday dinners, but she did not invite her son. She doted on her grandchildren from her daughters but had little to do with Andrew's children. Further, she complained that her son's children looked funny and openly declared that she did not care about them. When she died, she left her estate to her daughters, leaving only $1 to her son.

Sibling rivalry is probably the most common way of using family relationships to experience vindication and revenge. Young children fight with their brothers and sisters, call each other names, and tattle to parents.

The bitter rivalry between Joan Fontaine and Olivia de Havilland received a lot of publicity because the sisters were nominated for the 1941 Oscar award for best actress. When Joan won, images of her and Olivia competing as children flashed through her mind. She became so fearful of Olivia's jealousy that she was temporarily unable to move. Five years later, when Olivia won her own Oscar, Joan went over to congratulate her sister, but Olivia took one look at her and wheeled away. It was a bitter rivalry that lasted for many years.

Romance. A central assumption of Freud's theory of psychoanalysis is that family members use each other to gratify their sexual desires. According to Freud, the desire for incest can be very strong.[8] Because inbreeding weakens the gene pool, however, human societies ban it. Some societies define incest in terms of the nuclear family, but others use the broader definition of an extended family. In the United States, little is known about incest other than that it is underreported because of shame and lack of motivation.

Since incest is taboo, Freud argued that people use fantasy, imagination, wishes, dreams, and unconscious thoughts to gratify sexual impulses using family relationships.[9] In the Oedipal and Electra conflicts, for example, young boys have sexual fantasies about their mothers, and young girls have sexual fantasies about their fathers. According to the psychoanalytic school of thought, these fantasies are repressed into our unconscious mind throughout our adult lives. Although many psychologists no longer accept the Oedipal and Electra conflicts, few disagree with Freud's idea that sexual fantasies within families are normal psychological processes.

Eating. Family-oriented people satisfy their desire for eating by dining together on a daily basis. On holidays, the extended family may gather to feast or picnic. Every year the Libertellis, for example, spend Christmas Eve visiting all their nearby relatives. At the home of the paternal grandparents, they eat holiday cookies and breads. They move on to the maternal grandparents, where Polish foods are served. After Christmas mass, spaghetti is eaten at an aunt's house, and then lasagna at an uncle's. They return home several pounds heavier to serve desserts to their visiting relatives.

Parents often teach their children cherished recipes that have been passed down from grandparents. Restaurants advertise "home cooking" to capitalize on the warm feelings people have for food associated with family meals. Families also develop preferences for restaurants. For example, whenever Robert returns to Los Angeles, he likes to visit the restaurants where his father used to take him as a child.

Physical Activity. The use of family relationships to satisfy the desire for physical exercise is as common as a parent teaching a child to play ball. Families also bowl, swim, golf, and play other sports together.

Bob Griese, the former Miami Dolphins football player, is a good example of how a parent can satisfy his or her own interest in sports through a child. A former quarterback himself, Bob showed considerable pride when his son, Brian, played quarterback for the University of Michigan. Because they were matched on the desire for physical activity, football became a shared experience that strengthened their relationship. Bob helped his son learn to play, and he served as the television announcer when his son played in the Rose Bowl.

Tranquility. People can satisfy their desire for tranquility through family relationships. When some people experience stress, for example, they counteract the stress by spending some time relaxing with their families. Being with our families can provide a deep sense of comfort, especially during times when events in our lives frighten us. Human beings generally become less afraid and more tranquil when they are surrounded by their families as compared with being alone. Young children instinctively run to their parents when they are frightened. Families gather to comfort each other when a family member dies.

In his book, *Fears, Phobias, and Rituals,* Isaac Marks discussed the evolutionary significance of banding together when frightened.[10] First, animals are better able to detect danger as a group than as individuals. Second, vulnerable prey (such as females and children) can hide behind stronger prey (such as males of the species). Third, the group can post a lookout while the young are fed. Further, predators are significantly less likely to attack an entire family than an isolated animal. Even when they do so, the danger to any individual is diluted by numbers. Fourth, there is safety in numbers. Although a small animal can be no match for a larger animal, sometimes a group of small animals or a family of them can easily defeat a larger animal. For all these reasons, there is an evolutionary meaning to the feeling of tranquility that comes from family members pulling together during times of danger. Infants and young children also become emotionally upset when they are separated from their mothers, so that the desire for tranquility motivates them to reunite.

ACCEPTING THE INDIVIDUALITY
OF FAMILY MEMBERS

Parents expect their children to be like they are. Teachers often hope their children will become scholars, business people expect their children will become entrepreneurs, and farmers hope that their children will take over the family farm. Sometimes it works out this way, but children frequently pursue paths in life very different from those travelled by their parents. When a child moves in directions other than what the parents had expected, at first the parents hope that the child's behavior is only a temporary aberration of youth. Only after a long period of time do some parents realize that their children are not extensions of them.

When parents and children have significantly different desire profiles, the children may seek a lifestyle the parents do not value (Principle of Individuality). Misunderstandings, quarreling, and even everyday tyranny can occur. For example, ambitious parents may think that their child should go to law or medical school, but an unambitious child may prefer to travel around the world for a year or two and delay a career decision. Family-oriented parents may think that their child should make a greater effort to find someone to marry and raise children, but a romantic child may prefer to remain single for as long as possible. A status-oriented parent may pressure a child to move into a nice neighborhood, but an egalitarian child might feel comfortable living in the run-down section of town.

To be happy, a child must learn how to satisfy his or her own basic desires, not the parent's (Principle of Independence). The parent's duty is to nurture the child to become who the child is, not to pressure the child to be like the parent. Some children cannot be like their parents because they cannot make changes that go against their basic nature or psychological core. Nothing good can happen when a parent pressures a child to make changes that go against a child's nature.

Parents should not insist on changes in children aged 14 or older in regard to one or more of the 16 basic desires. Parents can try to change many things about their children, but not their children's basic psychological natures. Trying to do this is a losing game, and one that causes a great deal of misery. Maybe your parents have been after you to make certain changes in your life. If so, how long has it been going on—5, 10, 20, or 30 years? If your parents couldn't change you, what makes you think you can change your grown children?

How can parents tell if a problem they are having with their child is related to a mismatch of basic desires? Generally, when parents fight with their child repeatedly over the same issue, the probability is high that the root cause of the fighting is a mismatch of one or more of the basic desires. The fighting occurs repeatedly because the parents are pressuring the child to make changes that go against the child's nature. The child cannot make the changes the parent wants and still find happiness. Consequently, the fighting is futile.

Why My Father Was a Mets Fan[1]

If you think that sports are only a trifle, look at how much of people's lives are taken up by them. Every human society has offered its citizens a variety of different sports to play and watch. If a time machine were to transport you to another era of history, no matter where you end up you would still be able to find a sports team or star athlete to follow. There must be something psychologically fundamental about sports.

Sports have mass appeal because they provide people with intrinsically valued experiences that satisfy their basic desires. Although many people think that sports are primarily motivated by the need for physical activity, sports actually can satisfy nearly all basic desires. The various psychological aspects of sports—excellence, teamwork, endurance, winning, character, and leadership—satisfy different basic desires. Let's take a look at how we can use sports to satisfy our desires.

POWER

The basic desire for power creates a periodic need to experience feelings of competence. Sports provide both fans and participants with numerous opportunities to experience this feeling. When the home team scores a touchdown, for example, a surge of power goes through the stadium like a bolt of lightning. The crowd roars, people stomp up and down, and some people thrust their arms and fists powerfully into the air. The nonverbal message is, "We are powerful," "We are great," and "Glory is ours." Although it is the team on the field that scored the touchdown, the power is also experienced by the fans who saw the touchdown while rooting for the team to score.

All sports achievements—not just touchdowns—can unleash a psychological sense of power in both participants and fans. Much of America experienced a bolt of power when Brandi Chastain kicked the soccer ball into the net to win the 1999 World Cup. When an aerobic exercise is mastered, the individual derives a sense of achievement or competence. How many times have you seen Tiger Woods pump his clenched fist after sinking a putt? How many Olympic swimmers have you seen make powerful upward thrusts of their fists after winning a race?

The psychological experience of power is an apparent theme of college fight songs. According to the lyrics of these songs, the Earth itself reverberates when The Ohio State Buckeyes score a touchdown, the "echoes ring" when Dartmouth College's Big Green scores, and no fewer than "10,000 men"—an army of sorts—demand victory when the Harvard Crimson take the field. Why do college-educated people enjoy singing so much about the *powerful* nature of their sports teams? Because power, a basic desire, is intrinsically valued.

Achievement is the most common means of satisfying the desire for power. Although psychologists have studied achievement motivation mostly in terms of academic strivings and the desire to get ahead in business, athletes also are achievement-oriented. The greatest athletes not only are blessed with physical skills but also have the ambition and drive to develop those skills and achieve athletic glory. Ambitious athletes set high goals for themselves. Shannon Miller won three Olympic gold medals in gymnastics partly because she was driven by an extraordinary desire to achieve. She not only enjoyed the physical activity of gymnastics but also the challenge of reaching her goals.

Supreme Court Justice Louis Brandeis read the sports section of the newspaper before any other because it is the only section of the paper that talks about human achievement and glory. Both players and fans make frequent references to setting goals for a season, meeting challenges, win–loss records, and the Halls of Fame. What are "records" if not a history of achievements? If you go through the stacks of a good college library, you will find one sports book after another that is filled with records of past athletic accomplishments and glories.

RECORDS ARE EVERYWHERE IN SPORTS. Even non-baseball fans enjoyed watching Mark McGwire and Sammy Sosa set new records for home runs in a single season. Only once in a lifetime is such a record broken, and this one was shattered by two players in the same season. They will experience feelings of competence and pride every time they think of what they did. As fans, we try to imagine how they must have felt when they hit the record home runs, so that we can experience vicariously their sense of competence and the influence they have had on baseball.

The desire for power also can be satisfied through leadership activities. Nearly all teams have leaders, such as elected captains or senior players who lead by example. When a player has leadership qualities, any good sports announcer is quick to call this to the fans' attention. Why do the fans care? Because the basic desire for power motivates us to value leadership. When we focus on the leadership qualities of a player, we can experience vicariously the feeling of influence, thereby satisfying our own desire for power.

INDEPENDENCE

When people satisfy the desire for independence through sports, they take matters into their own hands. I cannot recall a better of example of this than an eight-year-old boy named Timmy, a member of a third-grade basketball team in a community youth league. Whenever Timmy touched the ball, the coaches would look at each other with knowing glances that Timmy would soon launch a shot at the basket. Even when most kids saw disaster—such as when they were trapped in the far corner and had lost their dribble—Timmy saw an opportunity to launch another shot. Timmy went through an entire season without throwing a single pass to another player. "When in doubt, shoot," was Timmy's philosophy.

People with a strong desire for independence hate having to rely on others to be successful. In a sports situation, therefore, they have a tendency to try to do it all on their own. Coaches call independent play "stepping up" when it works and "hot dogging" when it does not. Although such play is common in young children like Timmy, coaches work hard to develop team skills in players and reduce independent play.

We can satisfy the desire for independence by playing individual sports, such as ice skating, golf, gymnastics, skiing, and swimming. When independent-minded people play team sports, their desires will prod them to take matters into their own hands.

In contrast, people with a desire for interdependence (indicating a low desire for independence) enjoy needing and receiving help from others. They can satisfy this desire by experiencing what is called "team spirit," in which a player submerges the individual ego so that psychological identification is with the team itself. The "I" is psychologically downplayed and emphasis is given instead to the "we."

Sports-minded people generally place a high value on team spirit. Many coaches attribute success to it, and former professional basketball player Bill Bradley listed it as a core athletic value. When team spirit is absent from play, fans complain about the character of the players. Early in his stellar career, Michael Jordan was criticized for not being a team player. Under coach Phil Jackson's guidance and in Tex Winter's triangle offense, Jordan learned to rely on his teammates, after which his team, the Chicago Bulls, won six NBA championships.

CURIOSITY

Who won the championship volleyball game yesterday? Who is leading the major leagues in batting? How can I use aerobics to develop a more healthy, fit attitude? As these questions exemplify, we experience curiosity about sports. In fact, many children have been known to show much more curiosity about sports than they show about academics. The kid who does not give a hoot about what happened to Napoleon at Waterloo can wake up each morning wondering what happened last night at the ballpark.

Our curiosity is aroused when we look forward to an athletic contest. When we think about the weekend's international ice-skating competition, for example, we wonder how well our favorite skaters will do. Who will take first, second, or third place? What variation will Tara Lipinski make in her routine this time, and will she "nail" all of the triple jumps? When our curiosity is aroused, we feel we must watch or read the papers just so we can learn what actually happened.

Athletic contests between unequally skilled teams tend to be boring precisely because they do not arouse our curiosity. When unequally skilled teams or athletes compete, we think we already know who is going to win. Consequently, we tend to have little interest in the contest. Athletic stadiums empty and millions of television stations are switched off whenever an athletic game becomes a lopsided contest with an easily predictable outcome.

Learning about the strategic aspect of a game is another way in which fans satisfy their curiosity. A large part of the appeal of sports is learning the plan of how the individual athlete hopes to accomplish a goal. Tennis players must learn other players' tendencies so they can anticipate where to place the ball in their opponent's court, and baseball batters try to guess whether the next pitch will be a curveball, slider, or fastball.

Sometimes sports strategy can become so intellectually challenging that world-renowned scientists are recruited to work out the details. In 1962, the undefeated Dartmouth Indians football team played the undefeated Princeton Tigers in a game that would decide who was the best football team in the East. Princeton had a field-goal kicker, Charles Gogolak, whose soccer-style approach gave his team a significant advantage—he could kick field goals more accurately and from farther away than his Dartmouth counterpart. The Dartmouth coach consulted the Department of Physics to help him design a play that would propel a Dartmouth player into the air to block Gogolak's kicks. The calculations were done to determine the precise angle of leaning of one defensive player, while another jumped on his specially padded back so as to be moved skyward in a parabolic trajectory aimed at intercepting the kick in midair over Princeton territory. The play did not work because the defender was hurled into the air too soon; he landed before the ball was hiked. On the next play, Gogolak missed the kick, and Dartmouth fans assumed that the defender who had fallen from the sky on the previous play had "psyched him out." Although the Dartmouth Department of Physics did not deliver, the Department of Psychology did!

ACCEPTANCE

One of the reasons children play sports is to impress their parents. At scholastic athletic events below the high-school level, the audience is comprised almost entirely of parents, a few grandparents, and some siblings. When a child performs well, his or her parents show obvious pride, and the child gains the feeling of being accepted. Occasionally, a child performs poorly and reacts as if he or she has let a parent down.

The basic desire for acceptance creates a periodic need for people to feel good about themselves. Since crowds tend to accept athletes who win but reject those who lose, sports fans provide only a temporary and uncertain means of satisfying an athlete's desire for acceptance. Athletes need a source of support—usually family members or close friends—other than the roar of approval from fickle sports fans. The fickle nature of crowds is not always apparent to young athletes, who sometimes rely too much on superior play as a means of gaining acceptance.

Athletes who have a strong need for acceptance can have difficulty dealing with defeat. Many parents who have watched Little League baseball games have seen children cry or quit when they have made an out or error. Adults usually do not cry when they lose, but they sometimes throw tantrums. A number of tennis players, for example, are famous for throwing tantrums when the referee makes a call that goes against them. Psychologically, tantrums can indicate insecurity (or needy behavior), which suggests a strong desire for acceptance.

People with a strong desire for acceptance may dislike playing a sport in which judges determine the quality of a performance. These sports include competitive gymnastics, diving, ice skating, and horse shows. Gymnasts perform as individuals with all eyes on them. The judges award precise numbers to rate the performance while the athlete waits for the score. People who are sensitive to criticism and rejection (indicating a high need for acceptance) should have difficulty tolerating such an evaluation process. In contrast, sports such as walking or cross-country skiing are much less ego-threatening, and thus are better suited to the needs of people who dislike being evaluated.

ORDER

In this world of flux, sports traditions provide an important source of stability. If you left Chicago in 1970, returning to the city today would reveal many changes. Sears no longer has offices in the Sears Tower, the planes no longer run on time at O'Hare Airport, and on election day dead Democrats no longer can vote as often as they like. The Cubs still lose, however, the Sox still lose, and the Bears still lose. Thanks to sports, some things just never change in Chicago.

One of my most vivid recollections of experiencing order occurred when I was a freshman at college and attended my first Dartmouth–Harvard game in Cambridge, Massachusetts. Seating was by class, and at Dartmouth, class was a matter of identity. As a freshman, I was seated at the very top of the stadium, the farthest possible row from the field. Shortly before the game began, Harvard stadium filled to capacity, and I looked down at row after row of Dartmouth alumni and students. In the very first row were some old geezers from the class of 1902, who were introduced by the announcer just because they were so old. I realized that I could see where I would sit when I became a sophomore, skipped ten rows and saw where I would sit at age 30, and skipped 40 rows and saw where I would sit at age 60. I had a sense that my whole life was before me, revealed by the order of the stadium seating arrangements.

Baseball owners have misunderstood the psychological importance of order. In the past, star players did not move around very much. Superstars such as Willie Mays played their entire career with the same team. Today, players change clubs so often that it's hard to keep track of them. One season a player is on your team, but next season he's on an opposing team. By moving people and clubs around frequently, baseball owners have squandered the sense of stability and tradition that the sport used to provide. A lot of fans have become confused as to who's who and are unable to use baseball to satisfy their desire for order.

I should say something about the various superstitious habits commonly seen in sports. Ever wonder why a pitcher needs to rub a ball so much? It's just a ritual, or what psychologists call a compulsive behavior. Technically speaking, it is driven by the desire to impose order and structure into a situation with an uncertain outcome. The pitcher is trying to create order for the purpose of reducing anxiety. The same can be said for the batter who always wears a lucky charm or the coach who always wears a certain tie to games.

Some sports seem to be better suited to satisfying the desire for order than are others. Generally, these are sports that have many rules that must be rigidly followed. Golf is a good example of such a sport. As David Finkel wrote in the *Washington Post,*

> golf is about rules that mustn't be broken, techniques that mustn't be ignored, etiquette that mustn't be violated. It is more about what you can't do on a given day than about what you can.[2]

Further, golf satisfies the desire for cleanliness (which falls under the desire for order) because it is played on manicured lawns by people wearing clean clothes. In contrast, people with a weak desire for order may prefer sports that have few rules and allow people to get dirty. Wrestling and hunting are examples of such sports.

SAVING

We have the potential to satisfy our desire to save by collecting sports memorabilia. Some people collect trading cards, players' autographs, or uniforms, and anything else associated with memorable sports achievements or events. In 1998 there was a lot of discussion about how much money a collector might pay for the baseball Mark McGwire hit to break Babe Ruth's home-run record. Part of the reason the ball is worth so much is because collections are intrinsically valued (indicating that saving is a basic human desire).

HONOR

The basic desire for honor creates a periodic need for people to experience loyalty, including loyalty to a moral code of conduct. Sports provide both fans and participants with a means of having this experience, thereby satisfying their basic desire. Some of the most interesting games to watch are morality plays in which the two sides represent different values. The fans root for the athlete or team who best represents their values, hoping to see their version of morality triumph over evil. The first championship fight between Evander Holyfield and Mike Tyson provided a good example of this.[3] Holyfield, who represented goodness, entered the fight as a decent fellow who was deeply religious. Tyson, who represented evil, entered the fight with an arrest record and a history of trouble in his personal life. Church music was played when Holyfield entered the ring, but Tyson entered to the sounds of gangsta rap.

If you ask coaches about the purpose of playing sports at the scholastic or collegiate level, they will probably tell you that sports build character. Traditionally, athletes were expected to exemplify outstanding virtues so that society could hold them up as role models for children. They were expected never to cheat or complain, to give credit to others, be polite, and practice hard to get to where they wanted to be. The fact that things have changed has been noticed by nearly all sports fans and lamented by many sportswriters. Today we have athletes who not only cheat, they attack their coaches; who not only complain, they file lawsuits against their teams; who not only are immodest, they brag about being the greatest ever; who not only are impolite, they refuse to talk with the press; and who not only do not practice hard, but who flaunt being no-shows for training camp or preseason. It is a bit of an understatement to observe that large numbers of fans cannot satisfy their desire for honor by watching such players.

On the other hand, some players have gained the status of role models. A good case in point is Mia Hamm, the female soccer player who led the University of North Carolina to four National Collegiate Athletic Association championships in the early 90s and who won an Olympic gold medal in 1996. When asked why she likes soccer, she essentially said that it can teach you about life and build character.

Why do you think people root for teams that lose every year? If the goal in life were to maximize pleasure, adults should behave like young children and root for the team they think is most likely to win. But adults root instead for "their" team—that is, they root for the teams that represent their city, college, or nation, or at least the ones that did so when they were younger.

Rooting for a losing team is one of the ways people have of experiencing loyalty and behaving honorably. During the 1970s and 1980s, fans of the Chicago Cubs knew this feeling well. Lose, tie, or rain delay, they stuck with the Cubs, year after year. While there has been some improvement lately, the Cubs last won a World Series in 1908. So rooting for the Cubs isn't about vengeance (winning) or power (glory). It is about loyalty, about sticking with a hopeless loser and bonding with others who do the same.

Honor requires that we be loyal to our sports teams, even if they lack the talent to win. A good case in point was the New York Mets baseball teams of the 1960s. Here is the awful truth about their year-by-year performance in those years, when guys like Marvelous Marv Throneberry would blow a home run by missing not one but two bases on his trot around the infield.[4]

NEW YORK METS' PERFORMANCE

YEAR	WINS	LOSSES	GAMES BEHIND	FINISHED
1962	40	120	60½	10th
1963	51	111	48	10th
1964	53	109	40	10th
1965	50	112	47	10th
1966	66	95	28½	9th
1967	66	101	40½	10th
1968	73	89	24	9th
1969	96	61	0	1st

Year after year, the Mets contended for 9th place in a field of 10, and often fell short. In their first year they finished out of first place by a mere 60½ games, which is still a record for ineptitude. Yet my father stuck with them. By rooting for such a lousy team, he experienced the intrinsically valued feeling of being loyal. In 1969, however, a miracle happened in New York, and the Mets won the World Series. This proved that God loves New York, because nothing less than divine intervention could have made the Mets winners.

Some sports give much more emphasis to honor than do others. For example, golfers take pride in themselves for behaving honorably when they keep score, and amateur tennis players call their opponents' shots in or out of bounds. In contrast, there is much less emphasis on honor in basketball. If a male basketball player tried to satisfy his need for honor by approaching a referee to say that he committed a foul the referee did not see, the coach would probably bench him for hurting his team. The unstated rule in basketball is that the foul did not occur if the referee did not see it.

IDEALISM

The basic desire for idealism motivates us to value social justice and fairness. Sports provide us with an opportunity to work toward these values. When Jackie Robinson broke the color line in baseball, for example, our society took a significant step toward the ideal of racial justice. Many fans sensed that a higher purpose than baseball had been served. Those who lived during the time of Robinson's career experienced feelings of justice that satisfy the basic human desire for idealism.

The USA–China championship match for the 1999 World Cup of women's soccer provided an excellent example of how sports can satisfy our desire for an ideal. The game, which was the most-watched American women's sporting event up to that time, represented the ideal of equality for female athletes. When the USA won 5–4 on penalty kicks after a scoreless tie in regulation and two overtime periods, the American Broadcasting Company's announcer observed that now girls could develop their athletic skills in America without having to worry that something is wrong with them. Tiffany Millbrett, one of the key players, said, "The legacy I want to leave is that no longer can anyone take women athletes lightly."[5]

The desire for idealism can be frustrated by scandal, such as the payback fiasco that engulfed the 2002 Winter Olympic Committee. Although the International Olympics was supposed to uphold the high ideals of amateur athletics, the organizing committee members are believed to have accepted bribes when they chose Salt Lake City as the host city. Instead of an uplifting feeling of justice, we experienced the opposite feeling of injustice. Similar feelings of injustice are experienced when American Olympic basketball players, divers, ice skaters, or gymnasts are unfairly treated by Eastern-bloc referees and judges.

SOCIAL CONTACT

Sports fans can satisfy the desire for social contact in a number of ways. Simply being part of a crowd rooting for the same team can be an instant bonding experience. When the home team scores, people "high five" strangers sitting near them. One of the attractions of the large Las Vegas television screens that show sporting events is that groups gather to root for or against the teams.

The Wilsons held their first annual Super Bowl party 15 years ago, inviting friends from the neighborhood and work. About 25 couples gather to eat, talk, and hold the obligatory betting pool. Theirs is but one of thousands of such social gatherings that are held throughout the world in connection with major sporting events.

Many people participate in sports to have fun or to get to know other people. Children on a block make friends by playing ball together, and high-school students go out for teams to make new friends and enjoy the teams' social life. Friends made on playing fields can last a lifetime. Teams hold parties, and people play sports at various social gatherings such as picnics. Horseshoes, volleyball, croquet, and recreational swimming are sports that lend themselves to socializing.

FAMILY

Do you know who will be watching your local high-school girls' basketball team play this year? Or who can be counted on to be in the stands when the high-school boys' soccer team takes the field? Who can be counted on to sit through a Little League game in which the score is 25–24 after the first inning, all on walks because the pitcher can't throw a strike? If you answered parents, parents, and parents, you know your subject. Go to nearly any youth game and odds are that parents will be there in force, even when they are the only spectators.

Sports are a significant vehicle for family bonding. Parents not only watch their children perform but also teach them sports. Golfers teach their children how to play golf, bowlers teach them how to bowl, and runners teach their children to train for races. Children look up to their parents for athletic knowledge and imagine that their parents have achieved more in sports than probably was the case. A parent looks at the child and sees a young person who needs support and guidance. No matter what the final score, they are winners in each other's eyes.

Richard Williams has two daughters, Venus and Serena, who are star tennis players.[6] Richard coaches both girls. He also taught them to be respectful to other people. Because he can combine coaching and parenting, he figures he is the person to manage his daughters' careers.

Golf, bowling, boating, and camping are good examples of family sports. Many golf courses have parent-child outings, for example. Family leagues are sponsored at nearly all bowling establishments. Horseshoes, swimming, tennis, and shuffleboard also lend themselves well to participation by families.

STATUS

People can satisfy this desire by watching or playing sports that are connected to the level of status they prefer. Golf, polo, yachting, and tennis are associated with the upper class and, thus, confer status on participants. At Yankee Stadium in New York, on the other hand, there is a whole subculture of rowdy "Bleacher Bums" who pride themselves on paying little money to sit in bad seats and root for their team.

Generally, status-conscious athletes are attracted to popular spectator sports such as baseball, football, and basketball. Because these sports get the most attention, star players can enjoy a higher status than can star athletes in less popular sports. The star high school football or basketball player usually enjoys a much higher status among his or her peers than does the star swimmer.

Status-oriented people are attracted to prestigious brand names when buying sports equipment and clothing. Sneakers used to cost less than $20 and lasted for years. Today, exclusive brand names that sell for well over $100 do not last very long. Some parents are paying for more than the sneakers—they're also buying bragging rights about what type of sneaker the kid has. Since sneaker companies understand this principle, their primary method of advertising is endorsement from prestigious athletes rather than details about the quality of the product.

VENGEANCE

Because vengeance is a basic desire, victory is intrinsically valued. Even when victory produces no apparent reward or benefit, people still enjoy and value winning. Sports provide a usually harmless opportunity to satisfy this desire, which is why so much attention is paid to win–loss records. Participants compete directly against opponents, hoping for victory. Fans experience arousal of their competitive instincts, which motivates them to root for their team. People who are highly competitive hold "win-at-all-costs" attitudes partially because they enjoy experiencing competitiveness, vindictiveness, and aggressiveness.

Sports rivalries can arouse significant vindictiveness in otherwise docile people. Rivalries are common at every level of sport competition—professional, amateur, collegiate, and high school.

One of college football's greatest rivalries is between the Ohio State University and the University of Michigan. Many people in Columbus, Ohio, would rather their team beat Michigan than win a national championship. If the Devil could deliver a victory over Michigan each year, the churches in Columbus would go out of business. The OSU football coach's record is always expressed in two ways: his overall won–lost record, and his won–lost record against Michigan. Whereas a good overall record satisfies the fans' desire for power (achievement), a victory over Michigan satisfies the largely unrelated desire for vengeance.

Since sports rivalries are motivated by the basic desire for vengeance, violence is a possibility when emotions run high or expectations are frustrated. In the ancient Roman empire, for example, there was a chariot rivalry between the "blues" and the "greens" that led to revolution, the burning down of what is now Istanbul, and the mass execution of 30,000 fanatical sports fans. In recent years, violence has broken out at European soccer games, and people have been trampled to death. We have similar problems in the United States, where victories in major games have led to drunken riots in the streets.

The violence level of a sport is an overarching factor influencing our interest in participating in that sport. Boxing is perhaps the most violent of popular sports, and some of the best boxers have fought with brutal disregard for their opponents. After he knocked out Jesse Ferguson, for example, former heavyweight champion Mike Tyson said, "I wanted to hit him one more time in the nose so that bone could go up into his brain."[7] Football also is a highly aggressive sport. Dick Butkus, *Sports Illustrated*'s No. 3 favorite athlete of the century, loved the violence of football. He said that his goal was to hit the ballcarrier so hard that he knocked his head off. "What I miss," he said, "is the violence."[8]

The competitive nature of sports is a topic of controversy, especially with regard to children. Parents who enjoy competition (indicating a strong desire for vengeance) want their children to be taught to play competitive sports, but those who dislike competition (indicating a low desire for vengeance) worry that competitive sports can teach young children to be overly aggressive. Because of these concerns, some youth leagues have adopted anti-competitive rules. The rules for basketball games at our local YMCA youth league are so anti-competitive that no score is kept and the kids are not allowed to steal the ball. When my son Michael played in that league, one of his teammates stole the ball from another player, making what would be a good play in most leagues but violating the YMCA's rule against stealing the ball. The referee pulled the kid aside and explained to him that things like that aren't done in this league. I could see some of the parents take pride in the values expressed by the league and in how gently the referee corrected the boy's behavior.

When the referee told the boy not to steal the ball, what did he teach him from a psychological perspective? Did he teach the child to be sensitive to the feelings of the other boys and not to make them feel bad by stealing the ball? Not according to the viewpoint expressed in this book. In my opinion, the referee conveyed the following message to that boy: "We are non-aggressive people in this league. I am a non-aggressive person, which is a superior kind of person. You are an aggressive kid, which is a problem. If you want to associate with us, you'll have to behave the way we do. You'll have to adopt our values, and become somebody other than who you are." Whereas the referee focused on the kid's behavior, what concerned me was that the child *enjoyed* stealing the ball. Because the boy liked to make steals, I believe that the incident was more about values than behavior. I suspect that the boy concluded that there is something wrong with him because he was corrected for something he enjoys doing.

The system of 16 basic desires suggests that options should be provided to help individual children satisfy their needs through sports. Competitive children can satisfy their needs through competitive sports, whereas non-competitive children can satisfy their needs through non-competitive sports. Because one size does not fit all, communities that impose an ethic of non-competition on all children do not meet the needs of children who are competitive. Competitive children will enjoy defeating their opponents, and they should not be made to feel guilty for this basic human emotion. On the other hand, the key here is proportion. In saying that competitive children should be allowed to play competitive sports, I am not saying that a "win at all costs" attitude is appropriate. Rather, I am pointing to the need some children have for a moderate degree of competitiveness in youth-league sports.

How can a community guard against the possibility that children will learn to be overly competitive? Frans de Waal, the evolutionary biologist, has given emphasis to teaching reconciliation behavior. Kids should be encouraged to play competitive sports if that is their desire, but after the game is over they should be taught to reconcile with their opponents—perhaps by shaking hands with them after the game—so that no hard feelings remain unresolved.

ROMANCE

Sports dates are perhaps the most common way of combining athletics and romance. In several sports, men and women can team up and play as a couple. Elena Leonova and Andrei Khvalko, for example, are a husband-and-wife ice skating team, as are Sergei Ponomarenko and Marina Klimova. Skiing and hiking also are popular sports with couples. The New York Road Runners Club held a Millennium Midnight Run, which offered romantic opportunities for people to meet in an athletically festive occasion. 8,000 people ran in the very non-competitive "race." In addition to participating in sports together, some couples who are dating enjoy watching sporting events. They may attend games at the local stadium or watch together on television.

A number of sports have obvious sexual appeal for spectators. In boxing, for example, muscular men enter the ring nearly naked and put on a show of raw strength. In women's figure skating, attractively dressed women skate gracefully while music plays. These aspects of the sports are designed in part to satisfy the desire for romance.

Men and women who are courting sometimes turn to sports to impress each other with their athletic prowess. American gender roles have tended to define men as athletic and women as beautiful, creating the romantic interest of the female cheerleader for the male athlete. Many high school boys, for example, go out for sports teams to impress girlfriends. With the redefinition of gender roles in American society—more females participate in sports now, and many males are cheerleaders—macho displays of strength may no longer be seen as enough to get the girl.

EATING

Hunting, which has been practiced in every human culture of which there is a record, is the sport most closely associated with the desire to eat. Psychologically, it features adventure (curiosity), tranquility, an appreciation of the beautiful outdoors (romance), and, of course, eating. Although hunting used to be the primary means of food gathering (and still is in some cultures), today it is mostly a sport. People hunt deer, ducks, rabbits, fish, and other game.

For those of us who are less adventurous, eating and sports can be combined through such simple means as buying a hot dog at the ballpark or sitting down to watch a game on the tube with a bag of potato chips and a beer. Whether with other people or alone, many people like to snack while watching sports. The overwhelming majority of people who watch the Super Bowl, for example, consume snack food while doing so.

The pressures on athletes increase their chances of developing eating disorders.[9] A case in point is Philip, who induced vomiting after he ate because he was trying to "make weight" for wrestling. In sports in which weight is a factor, psychologists report increased frequencies of binge eating, bulimia, and other eating problems concerned with thinness or gaining weight.

PHYSICAL ACTIVITY

Sports vary in how much exertion and stamina are required. The Badwater running race in Death Valley, for example, is 115 miles long and takes a fit athlete more than 37 hours to complete.[10] Some of us have trouble staying awake for 37 hours continuously, let alone running for that long. In contrast, sports such as croquet and bird watching require so little physical exertion that some people might not even consider them sports. I assure you, however, that they are included in many books on sports. Golf, fishing, and table tennis also are among the less physically demanding sports.

Generally, we choose to participate in those sports that require an amount of physical exertion just right for our nature. We actively avoid participating in sports that require what we feel is too much physical exertion. The physical exertion required to participate in a sport, and the level of violence or aggression, are two overarching factors influencing whether or not we will play that sport.

Physical activity is more than exercise—it is also a value that parents and teachers instill in the young. Since Aristotle thought that education should be designed to teach young people how to satisfy their needs, he favored including physical education as part of the school curriculum. In recent times, the curriculum at many liberal arts colleges has been based on the philosophy of educating the "whole" person, meaning both body and mind. This philosophy recognizes physical development as an intrinsic value.

TRANQUILITY

People with a strong desire for tranquility seek to relax or achieve an inner peace, whereas those with a weak desire for tranquility can seek thrills. Sports provides a home for both groups of people.

Fishing is an excellent example of a relaxing sport. Since there is very little physical exertion, the physical signs of bodily arousal are not experienced as they are in other sports. The fisherman does not have to be constantly thinking or developing strategy as do athletes in other sports. If the fish do not bite, nothing much happens.

The martial arts are examples of sports that give emphasis to the development of an inner peace. In T'ai Chi, people learn how to gain control over their bodies and eliminate tension. The aim is a unity of mind and body that brings about a state of tranquility.

Sports that provide thrills include pole vaulting, which attracts daredevil athletes who catapult themselves as much as 20 feet into the air

VARSITY ATHLETES

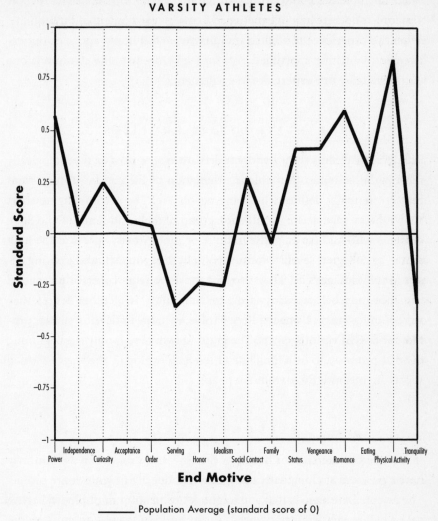

End Motive

Population Average (standard score of 0)

Participation in Two or More Varsity Sports

and who face the possibility that the pole will break or that they will miss the foam-rubber landing pad. Motorcycle races, rock climbing, skydiving, bungee jumping, and white-water rafting are other examples of sports that provide excitement, both for participants and observers.

You do not have to participate in sports to experience the thrills. Usually it is enough to simply watch. Television networks love to show games filled with excitement and sometimes the risk of injury. Why do people watch such programs? According to the theory of 16 basic desires, people aim for a moderate mix of experiences between excitement and tranquility. When we experience too much tranquility, we feel bored and seek out excitement. Watching sporting events on television or at the stadium is one way to increase our experience of excitement.

ATHLETE DESIRE PROFILES

The 16 basic desires show us why sports are experienced as psychologically meaningful activities. An athletic orientation to life can be so important that it essentially defines who some people are. The accompanying chart shows the average desire profile for a group of male and female Ohio State students who had participated in three or more varsity sports at the high school or collegiate level.[11] Not surprisingly, the group showed a strong desire for physical activity. They also had above-average scores for power and romance and a below-average score for tranquility. In all other desires, they were about average. Using the Reiss Profile, we hope to develop similar profiles for fans of various sports. The graph shown here is only the beginning of what promises to be a long line of research exploring the ways in which sports are meaningful to different people.

PERSONAL FITNESS

If you need to exercise for health or fitness—and who doesn't?—you may have a problem sticking with a program that doesn't fit your desire profile. The essential problem is that you might desire an amount of physical activity far below what your body needs for its health. One way to improve the situation is to use the information in this chapter to select a physical activity that is better suited to your desire profile than the activities you have tried in the past. Generally, you are much more likely to stick with an activity that matches your desire profile than to one that contradicts it.

In planning your fitness program, keep in mind that there are many different physical activities from which to choose. If what you are doing now feels mostly boring or unpleasant, you have probably selected the wrong activity. Maybe you think that physical workouts are supposed to feel bad, but that need not be true. You should be able to find an activity that you enjoy. If you are a sociable person who is trying to walk every day but finds it boring, maybe you would enjoy walking with a friend. If you appreciate beauty, why not find some woods or a park to walk through on your daily hike? If status is your passion, go ahead and buy those expensive athletic clothes—after all, this is your health that we're talking about, and the money will not do you much good if you don't stay healthy.

The Scientific Study of
the Human Spirit [1]

lthough Susan Havercamp and I asked no questions about spirituality
in our surveys of what is meaningful to people (see Chapter 1), the 16
basic desires that resulted from this research are closely connected to
the images of the world's great religions. Actually, these 16 basic desires are
defining attributes of many of the polytheistic gods people have worshipped throughout human history. The accompanying chart lists twelve
deities and the basic desires to which each is connected.

Although the table connects 13 of the 16 desires to gods, the remaining
three are connected to other aspects of spiritual experience. People have attributed divine significance, for example, to frugality (saving), festivals (satisfying the desire for social contact), and the Sabbath as a day of rest
(physical exercise). Further, the monotheistic God of Judaism and Christianity has characteristics that connect to many of the 16 basic desires. For
example, Christians view God as omnipotent (power), omniscient (curiosity), the savior (acceptance), perfect morality (honor), perfect justice (idealism), perfect love between father and son (family), the highest possible
status, and perfect tranquility. We experience images of God in ways that
satisfy our basic desires, which is why, from a psychological perspective,

spirituality has the potential to become so meaningful to us.[2] Let's take a closer look at how this can happen.

DEITIES	DESIRE CONNECTED TO IMAGE
gods who created the universe, the Lord, Almighty	power
gods who are completely self-sufficient	independence
omniscient (all-knowing) gods	curiosity
gods who are paths to salvation	acceptance
gods representing order from chaos	order
gods of perfect morality, gods in the image of a father	honor
gods of perfect justice	idealism
gods in the image of a son or daughter	family
gods of perfect being	status
war gods	vengeance
fertility gods	romance (and eating)
gods of perfect harmony	tranquility

POWER

We have the potential to satisfy our desire for power by experiencing the power of God. When the Bible describes God as omnipotent, Almighty, and the Lord, attention is focused on His power. Further, power is the psychological theme when God is perceived as the creator of the universe and all life within it. When we reflect on this creation, we experience a power so great that we cannot even imagine it. Psychologically, the creation of the universe is the greatest possible achievement, representing infinite influence.[3] When we relate to God as our Lord, we experience God's power, which satisfies the need to experience power. Because power is a basic desire (element of psychological meaning), we experience God's power as deeply meaningful to us.

The experience of God's power is common to many religions. Both Judaism and Christianity teach that God is omnipotent and the creator. The Hindu religion is concerned with a sacred power, called *Brahman*. The priestly caste were believed to possess this power. Even though it is invisible, Hindus believe that Brahman pervades the whole world—it sustains all life and is the force behind everything that happens. As Atman (our individual soul), Brahman is found eternally within each person. The techniques of Yoga are intended to bring us in touch with the holy power that sustains and inspires us. To experience Atman is to satisfy our desire to experience power.

We can satisfy our desire for power vicariously through the images of many stories in the Bible. In the Biblical story of the Exodus, for example, Moses repeatedly called on Yahweh (God) to show the Egyptian oppressors that His power was greater than that of all Egyptian gods. When Yahweh made the rivers flow with blood, the Egyptian gods lacked the power to undo his deed. Yahweh brought plagues upon the land, but the Egyptian gods were powerless to restore Egypt to its normal state. Yahweh took the firstborn of Egypt, passing over the Hebrew households, but the pagan gods of Egypt lacked the power to restore life. By experiencing the power of Yahweh, the Hebrew slaves satisfied their own desire to experience power.

INDEPENDENCE

God is completely independent and self-sufficient. Therefore, it may seem only natural that human beings, said in the Bible to have been created in God's image, also would desire self-sufficiency. Some clergy teach that "God helps those who help themselves." Their message is clear: Self-reliance is a virtue. When we focus our attention on this or similar messages, we experience the desire to be independent. When our attention is focused on God's independent nature, our basic desire for independence is satisfied through God.

Religious people feel dependent on God. As the theologian Rudolf Otto put it, God is experienced as a "holy other," so that humans are nothing in comparison.[4] This experience of a holy "thou" conveys a deep sense of humility and, as the theologian Schleiermacher wrote, a sense of absolute dependence on God.

How can religion satisfy our basic desire for independence if it focuses our attention on an absolute dependence on God? As we have seen throughout this book, every desire creates an opposite desire that we can use to moderate our experiences away from extremes (which is necessary to achieve value-based happiness). Because complete independence—the experience of being totally on our own—is frightening to some people, independent behavior in our secular life can create a need for dependence in our spiritual life. Psychologically, devout people are never completely on their own when they have faith in God.

Some spiritual people aim for a mystical union with God, which implies a complete loss of independence. For example, Plotinus (205–270) held that all beings yearn for unity; to return to the One from which they came. Buddhism teaches that people can reach a state of *nirvana,* the union of all consciousness. Jesus taught his followers to cultivate an inner attitude of surrender and openness to God. Christians believe that humility is a virtue and that pride (indicating inappropriate independence) is a sin. Muslims also seek to become close to God: The word *Islam* means "surrender to God." As these comments show, the idea of dependence on God is a theme found in many religions.

In a study of how religion is related to basic desires, I asked 558 people to complete the Reiss Profile and then describe themselves as *very religious, somewhat religious,* or *not religious.* The sample consisted of 344 human-service providers who had attended a regional training workshop on mental retardation and 214 students from various Midwestern colleges. The four largest denominations represented in the sample were Roman Catholic (n = 171), Baptist (n = 44), Methodist (n = 54), and Presbyterian (n = 44). Susan Havercamp administered the Reiss Profile to an additional 49 students enrolled in one of three Midwestern Protestant seminaries.

According to the results of our research studies, very religious people place a lower value on independence than do non-religious people. Religious people derive joy from the knowledge that they can trust others to meet their own needs. They seek to be dependent on God and interdependent on other people. In contrast, non-religious people are uncomfortable trusting others to meet their important needs. These people, who are much more independent-minded, do not like relying on anybody—not even a deity.

AVERAGE REISS PROFILE SCORES FOR INDEPENDENCE, N=558

GROUP	VALUE SCORE
Very religious	19.9
Somewhat religious	21.7
Not religious	23.7

Our research findings are based on statistical averages obtained mostly with Christians living in the Midwestern United States; there are many individual exceptions to the general findings. There are many independent-minded people who are religious. The statistical findings hold up for three methods of assessing very religious people (self-identification, frequency of prayer, and seminary student) and cannot be explained in terms of the age or gender of the people we surveyed. The generality of the results to other cultures has not yet been determined.

Some experts have discussed the desire for dependence on God as a negative aspect of religion. Friedrich Nietzsche (1844–1900), for example, criticized Christianity for taming people and breaking their independent spirits, transforming the proud and powerful into the shamed and weak.[5] Karl Marx wrote that the controlling classes use religion as an opiate to help working-class people accept their lack of power. For the most part, American psychologists have thought that self-reliance indicates mental health, whereas a desire to be dependent on others indicates immaturity.

Does the religious idea of dependence on God lead to acceptance of in-

SEMINARY STUDENTS

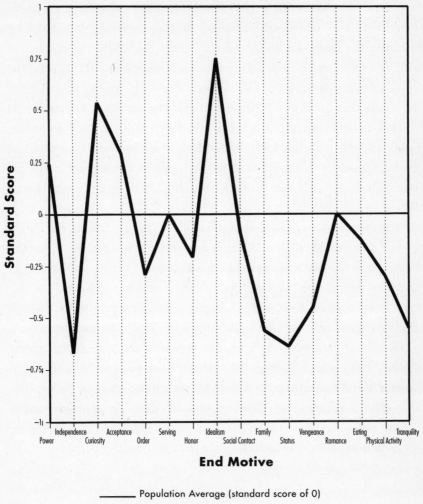

_____ Population Average (standard score of 0)

━━━ Seminary Students

terpersonal frailty and political weakness? Jesus did not think so. He taught his disciples that if they had faith, they would gain powers. "Not only would they be able to forgive sins and exorcise demons," wrote Karen Armstrong, "but they would be able to hurl a mountain into the sea."[6] Religious people consider opening themselves to God as an act of strength, not as an act of weakness. A consequence of uniting with God or One is attainment of divine power.

The results of our research supported the viewpoint that the desire for dependence on God is not a sign of psychological weakness. Our analysis differs from those conducted previously because we were able to measure separately the desire for independence versus the desire for power—in many other studies, these desires are confounded. We found that religious people value dependence on God but not submission to other people. They may desire that the distance between themselves and God be reduced to zero, but this does not imply that they have a weak will. On the *Reiss Profile*, religious people score low for independence, which indicates their desire to devote themselves to God, but they also score in the average range for power, which indicates that they are not politically or interpersonally submissive.

The system of 16 basic desires offers a new perspective on the divide between science and religion. Whereas conventional wisdom holds that the divide is caused by differences in beliefs about issues such as evolution, the theory put forth in this book implies that it is caused in part by the "not getting it" phenomenon discussed in Chapter 6. Religious people place a high value on dependence on God (indicating a low desire for independence), whereas many non-religious scientists appear to be very independent-minded. "Not getting it" may occur, so that the two groups are motivated to misunderstand each other. Beneath the surface some religious people may think that scientists deny Creation because they are prideful people, whereas non-religious scientists may believe that some religious people attack evolution partially because they are weak-minded.

CURIOSITY

The desire for curiosity can be satisfied by studying theology. Curious people have debated metaphysics, morality, and the existence of God. These and related inquiries have given rise to the field of theology. Part of what drives some people to religion is a burning desire to understand the human condition in the grand scheme of things.

Plato and Aristotle offered rational perspectives on God, suggesting that reason is a divine quality. Such views are deeply appealing to curious people, who generally are motivated to place a high value on intellectual life. However, some theologians have questioned the Greek perspective on the grounds that it provides an overly intellectual approach to God.

The results of our research studies did not show any differences in curiosity between religious and non-religious people. Religious people were no more or less likely to desire to learn than were non-religious people. Both groups placed equivalent value on reason and knowledge. From a strictly psychological perspective, religious and secular paths in life appear to be about equally effective in appealing to highly curious people.

ACCEPTANCE

Acceptance from a god can satisfy our desire for acceptance because it creates the deepest possible feeling that we are loved. Since many people use the image of God as some kind of superparent in the sky, at least for these people there is probably a similarity between how they experience acceptance from God and how they experienced acceptance from their parents when they were young children.

Christians believe that sin represents disobedience of God's will, and leads to estrangement from God, guilt, and self-criticism. Acceptance is the basic desire that motivates Christians to atone after they have sinned. Through atonement and salvation, the sinner hopes to regain acceptance from God.

From the perspective of the 16 basic desires, baptism is a religious ritual that atones for original sin, thereby satisfying the basic desire for acceptance. People who turn to Jesus as their redeemer can escape hell (indicating divine rejection) and gain heaven (indicating divine acceptance) because Jesus has paid the price of their redemption.

ORDER

The first gods of the ancient Babylonians were organized structures that emerged from a primordial soup of divine substance. These gods did not create the world and did not intervene in people's lives. They represented the human beings' yearnings for permanence, stability, organization, cleanliness, and predictability—or what I call the basic desire for order. When

Babylonians worshipped these gods, they satisfied their own desire for order by contemplating the order in the universe.

The very idea of God conveys a sense of infinite stability and permanence. No matter what might happen in life, God is always there. According to the Bible, God created the world in an orderly manner:

> And God saw everything that he had made and behold it was a unified order. GENESIS 1:31

With the Big Bang, God brought order from chaos, transforming energy into matter, organizing particles into atoms and molecules.[7] He created the day, so that the recurrence of morning and evening provides us with a sense of order. People who believe that God has a plan expect the future to unfold in an orderly manner.

Our desire for order can be satisfied through the practice of religious rituals and traditions. In fact, ancient religions were largely a matter of cult and ritual, such as rites, liturgies, hymns, dances, wearing of holy clothing, and use of holy objects. Psychologically, rituals represent an attempt to impose order, increase familiarity, and reduce ambiguity. Nations may come and go, but certain religious rites and traditions have remained constant throughout the ages. For example, at early sunrise Jews dress in talises and pray. Christian families go to church on the Sabbath and celebrate Christmas each year. Every Christian child is baptized.

Since the desire for cleanliness falls under the basic desire for order, religious practices that encourage cleanliness also satisfy this basic desire. Many religions require ritualistic baths or cleaning prior to entering a holy place or touching a holy object. In ancient Israel, men took ritualistic baths before going to the synagogue on a festival day, and women took ritualistic baths after the menstrual period to prepare themselves for the holiness of sexual relations with their husbands. The prophet Isaiah's lips were cleansed with coals so he could speak the words of God. Many religions refer to the process of atonement for sin as a cleansing process.

Freud called religion an "obsessional-compulsive neurosis." His hypothesis called attention to the fact that both religious rituals and obsessive-compulsive symptoms satisfy the desire for order. However, scientists who have studied the issue have found significant differences between religious rituals and obsessive-compulsive symptoms. Religious rituals do not interfere with the person's everyday life in the ways that compulsions do.

SAVING

Although the collecting of religious articles began as an effort to protect them from destruction, today people collect religious articles for the sheer pleasure of doing so. Collections include art, clothes, symbols, memorabilia, trinkets, and holy objects. Many Christians save Bibles or rosaries. The faithful can buy books, historical photographs, silver medals, and other religious symbols. Nine American libraries or museums specialize in Jewish collections.[8] Jews collect candelabra, Hanukkah lamps, kiddush cups, talises, and Torah items.

HONOR

The desire for honor creates a periodic need to experience feelings of loyalty to one's parents, heritage, ethnic customs, and morality. One way we can satisfy this desire is by worshipping God in the image of a father. For example, Freud said that God is a father figure, so that in worshipping God, we are psychologically honoring our father.[9]

Judaism requires loyalty to the Jewish covenant with God, which has been handed down since the days of Abraham and Moses. When Yahweh commanded that "There shall be no strange gods for you before my face," Jews became obligated to practice monotheism, recognizing Yahweh as the one true God. In return, Yahweh recognized Jews as chosen people and gave them land. Remaining loyal to the terms of the covenant is at the heart of Jewish honor. Jews also are expected to obey the Ten Commandments Yahweh gave Moses on Mount Sinai. The rabbis expanded the Jewish law to encompass 613 *mitzvot*, or commandments. Jews are expected to honor their family and ethnic group by living in accordance with all 613 mitzvot.

Another way we can satisfy our desire for honor is by observing the moral code of our religion. When we behave morally, we act honorably and are a credit to our parents and heritage. Buddhists place a high value on morality. They believe that good deeds are the means by which a person acquires merit, or karma, which determines the person's rebirth.

People can also satisfy the desire for honor by embracing the religious denomination and moral code of their parents. Studies show that the parents' religious denomination is by far the best single predictor of the adult child's denomination.[10] Further, people tend to adopt many of the moral views of their parents.

IDEALISM

Humanitarian efforts to help the poor, promote social justice, and eradicate diseases are sometimes referred to as "God's work." Because people make a connection between the ideas of God and social justice, they can satisfy the desire for idealism through spiritual and religious means.

Judaism, Islam, and Christianity are examples of religions that place a high value on social work. Jews were given this message when Yahweh said:

> *Let the weak and the orphan have justice*
> *be fair to the wretched and the destitute*
> *rescue the weak and the needy*
> *save them from the clutches of the wicked*
>
> PSALM 82

Muslims are given a duty to create a just and equitable society where the poor and vulnerable are treated decently. Islam, which is intolerant of injustice, advocates the sharing of wealth. The early Christian church taught the virtue of charity, and the Christian social gospel has been a major factor in promoting positive social change. In the United States, churches and synagogues provide more than twice the social philanthropy of foundations and organized social causes.[11]

Idealism is one of the forces that drives young people to the clergy. A sample of 49 seminary students scored very high on the *Reiss Profile* for idealism, indicating that for them religion holds potential to improve the world. Indeed, American religious leaders have been at the forefront of many social causes. The abolitionist movement of the nineteenth century, for example, was supported by clergy. The U.S. civil rights movement of the 1960s was led by eminent clergy, such as Martin Luther King. In India, Mother Teresa fought against poverty and for improvements in public health.

SOCIAL CONTACT

The desire for social contact creates a periodic need to experience fellowship and fun, both of which can be satisfied by participation in religious organizations. Fellowship is experienced when people pray together. Many religions provide morning services that are followed by breakfast and socializing.

Some religious festivals are specifically designed to provide for social contact and fun. The celebration of Christmas, for example, is accompanied by a month of good fellowship, cheer, and joyous festivities. Songs, colorful decorations, and gift-giving are among the obvious elements of fun during the Christmas season. The Jewish festival of Purim, which commemorates the ancient liberation of Jews from Persian rule, is another colorful and happy religious celebration.

Religious congregations are an important source of social support and friendship for their members. They sponsor social clubs, outings, summer camps, picnic, singles nights, softball games, bingo nights, bowling leagues, glee clubs, spaghetti dinners, and bus trips. Some sociologists have suggested that an increase in loneliness in our society has led many people to turn to religious sects and cults to satisfy their desire for social contact.

FAMILY

Since this desire creates a periodic need to experience a parent's love of a child, we have the potential to satisfy this desire by worshipping God in the image of a son or daughter. Various ancient societies, including prehistoric people who left behind artifacts such as figurines and drawings, worshipped child gods. Jesus Christ represents God in the image of a son. The idea that God would come among people in the role of a son indicates that a high value is placed on that role.

The connection between family values and organized religion dates back to antiquity. Although the Biblical Abraham was not the first person to worship a monotheistic god, he was the first to teach this concept to his children, and they taught it to their children, eventually giving rise to the nation of Israel. Today, religious ceremonies—such as baptism, communion, and bar mitzvah—bring together both nuclear and extended families. Further, organized religions generally support family values by helping

families in need. When the McCaughey family had the first living septu-
plets, for example, their church organized teams of volunteers to visit the
home and help take care of the babies.

STATUS

This desire creates a periodic need to feel important and worthy of attention. When we imagine God paying attention to us in any way, the implication is that we are important beings and worthy of God's attention. Our
desire for status is also satisfied when God listens to our prayers. The Hebrew belief that Jews represent God's chosen people implies a special status
for the Jewish covenant.

Organized religions satisfy people's desire for status by differentiating
their services and messages for people of various social classes.[12] Privileged
classes embrace religious dogma that legitimatize their lofty status. According to the doctrine of divine right, for example, the king rules by God's will.
Since the king is the head of the royal class, they, too, are legitimatized by
the doctrine of divine right. Historically, rulers have resisted the idea that
God might equally value upper- and lower-class people. For example, the
status-oriented Romans were slow to accept Christianity because they did
not want to believe that God would send his son to Earth as a poor carpen-
ter living in a remote corner of the world. It would have seemed more natural to Romans if Christ had been a Roman senator or emperor.

The idea that all people are equal before God is a powerful religious
message that holds great appeal to people who place a low value on status
or who experience some stigma. Jesus's message that kindness must be extended to all people regardless of their wealth clearly implies that poor
people are important in the eyes of God. In a sense, people in the lower class
are given a new status when looked at from this spiritual perspective.

VENGEANCE

This desire creates a periodic need to experience wrath and competition,
but it also creates a need to experience compassion, kindness, and peacekeeping as a method of governing our violent nature. People have the potential to satisfy this complex need through spirituality.

The faithful can satisfy their desire for vengeance through God's wrath. By contemplating the many stories of revenge in the Bible, for example, we experience vindictiveness. Many of the earliest gods were gods of war. Each city or tribe had its own war god, whom the people worshipped, flattered, or made sacrifices to in exchange for divine assistance in vanquishing an enemy. Since the job of the god was to deliver the enemy, war gods were agents of violence.

Vengeance is a common theme of the Old Testament. When Yahweh closed the waters of the Red Sea and destroyed the Egyptian army, he gave the Israelites their revenge for having been enslaved in Egypt. After the Israelites left Egypt, the prophet Elijah called upon Yahweh to take revenge on the Hebrews who worshipped Baal, the pagan fertility god. Baal's followers were taken to a nearby valley and slaughtered.

The Gnostics advanced the idea that vengeance was the motive for the creation of the world.[13] According to this viewpoint, the material world is too imperfect to have been created by God. Instead, semi-divine beings who descended from Heaven created the world in a fit of defiance of God. The Gnostic philosophy provides people with opportunities to experience vengeful feelings every time they focus on the question of creation.

Holy wars are an obvious example of how people can use religion to satisfy their desire for vengeance. When the first crusaders took Jerusalem, they slaughtered Jews and Muslims to avenge the death of Christ. The second crusade also was inspired by the motive of revenge against the "infidels" living in the Holy Land. Recently, we have seen brutal wars between people of different faiths in Bosnia, Northern Ireland, and the Middle East.

The modern religious view of God is complex—although God's wrath is to be feared, God is viewed as fundamentally compassionate. For example, Jesus Christ taught that charity, love, and kindness were the most important blessings. When Peter asked Jesus if it was enough to forgive a brother seven times, Jesus replied that Peter should forgive seventy times seven times. Islam also places a high value on compassion. The Koran teaches that the essence of religion is the creation of a compassionate and just society.

Thus, religion provides both a means for people to satisfy their desire for vengeance and a means for moderating that desire. Without compassion and other peacekeeping behavior, the human instinct for revenge and aggression can get out of hand. Indeed, that is exactly what happens when people show senseless violence. By using compassion and other peacekeeping behaviors, we can regulate our desire for vengeance toward a golden mean of moderation and value-based happiness.

The results of our research studies showed that very religious people place a much lower value on vengeance than do both somewhat religious people and people who are not religious. This does not mean that very religious people are less vengeful, only that they value it less. Although our study did not directly evaluate the issue, I presume that the low value that was placed on vengeance was associated with a high value on compassion and kindness.

ROMANCE

Sex within the marital union is considered holy, especially when accompanied by romantic love and aimed at procreation. Historically, many religions have prohibited sex outside the marriage. Under Jewish law, for example, adultery can be punished by death.

Religion was much more overtly sexual in ancient days than it is today. Fertility rites were practiced in nearly all ancient societies that relied on agriculture for food.[14] Although aimed at making the Earth fertile, these rites were primarily motivated by sexual desire. Rites usually included dance, ritual, drink, and in some societies, sex with little or no prohibition. The most common theme was that mother Earth is female, the sun is male, and the action of the sun on the earth gives rise to food. Another common theme is that the soil is female, the plough is a phallus, and ploughing the Earth is sexual intercourse.

Creation myths from ancient societies had apparent sexual content. An Egyptian myth, for example, expressed the idea that a primeval god created the world through some type of masturbation. Other myths viewed the world's creation as the result of sexual intercourse between gods. The idea that semen contains a vital force was expressed in many societies.

In early societies, religious leaders used sex as a means of building congregations. Many pagan ceremonies, such as those given for Baal, the fertility god, were orgies involving a fair amount of sex. As seen in the *Kama*

Sutra and ancient Indian art, some Eastern religions have obvious sexual content.

A religious ascetic cultivates hardship to minimize experiences of beauty and pleasure. This lifestyle satisfies the needs of the relatively small number of people who have an extremely low desire for romance.

EATING

Religion gives symbolic significance to the desire to eat, encouraging people to satisfy this desire in certain ways but not in others. Some primitive societies prohibit clan members from eating totem animals. When the clan comes together as a whole, however, some religions permit the sacrifice and consumption of a protected animal.

The Eucharist is a central act of nearly all Christian sects. It evolved from the Last Supper, when Christ is said to have broken bread and referred to it as his body, and to have poured wine and referred to it as his blood. Christians commemorate Christ's sacrifice through the Eucharist, which involves a breaking and sharing of bread and a pouring and drinking of wine. The Eucharist symbolizes communion with God and with the community of worshippers. Under the system of 16 basic desires, part of what makes the Eucharist a psychologically meaningful experience is the intrinsic value people place on eating.

Some religions provide strict dietary rules. The Jewish kosher laws, for example, prohibit eating pork and require that meat and milk be kept separate. Muslims also are forbidden to eat pork. Hindu rules vary with the person's caste. In the Hindu religion, ghee (clarified butter) is a symbol of dietary purity. By obeying dietary laws, the individual can simultaneously satisfy the desire to eat and practice religion.

PHYSICAL ACTIVITY

Sometimes combining physical activity with religion takes a little initiative. For example, a group of overweight religious ladies in Columbus, Ohio, did not want to work out in the local fitness club because they disliked the sexual overtones of the rock music that was played. So they arranged to work out to Church music instead. They call their group "Slim for Him."

TRANQUILITY

Buddhism and Taoism offer religious paths for gaining tranquility and coping with anxiety, pain, and suffering. Buddhists believe that people can escape from their miseries and attain perfect tranquility, or Nirvana, by living righteously. When the self becomes merged with the totality of Nirvana, there is no more suffering. In Taoism, the Way is a state of complete contentment, tranquility, and harmony with nature. The Way never acts, but nothing is undone. The Way provides a perfectly tranquil image of God which, when experienced, can satisfy the desire for tranquility.

Religions often teach that God has a purpose for everything, including human suffering. We experience suffering as much less upsetting when we believe that it has a purpose than when we believe that it is senseless or unnecessary. When suffering has no purpose, the discomfort we feel limits both our feel-good and value-based happiness. When suffering has a purpose, it can be a meaningful experience that contributes positively to our sense of value-based happiness. In a world filled with pain and suffering, people have a psychological need to fulfill their desire for tranquility by worshipping a deity who can give a divine purpose to human suffering.

Faith provides a means of overcoming fear and anxiety. Reinhold Niebuhr, the distinguished theologian, provided a Roman Catholic perspective on *ontological anxiety,* meaning anxiety arising from the nature of human existence.[15] He thought that all people become anxious when they realize how precarious their lives are. People develop fundamental fears concerning death, human insignificance, and giving in to the temptations of sin. Niebuhr thought that faith offers the best opportunity to overcome such anxieties and experience tranquility. The Christian belief in an afterlife, for example, makes death seem less terrifying. There is less of a tendency to panic over the possibility of death if you believe that the soul is headed for Heaven.

Historically, many primitive societies invented gods to control whatever frightened them. The ancient Babylonians, Syrians, Egyptians, and Hebrews, for example, worshipped war gods whom they hoped would protect them. The ancient Hawaiians invented a volcano god because they feared eruptions of the volcano on their island. Indigenous societies invented gods for the sun, Earth, wind, sea, and other natural forces. Nature seems less terrifying if it is controlled by gods who can be influenced with flattery, prayer, promises of obedience, and sacrifices.

How strong is the psychological connection between faith and the desire for tranquility? According to Freud,[16] the connection is so strong that people actually invent gods to fulfill their hope for protectors. Freud believed that fearful people turn to religion to protect them from real and imagined danger. This idea implies that religious people are fearful people, or at least people who would be fearful if they were not religious. However, the results of our research studies suggest that religion does not attract a disproportionate number of anxious and fearful people. Religious people score average on measures of fear propensity. Other studies point to the same conclusion: Anxiety and fear are not the primary psychological forces that drive most people to religion. If the Earth was discovered to be on a collision course with an asteroid, so that the world's population was threatened with annihilation in a few short years, the churches would overflow with faithful people praying for divine intervention—since religion can be a way to quell our fears—but the percentage of the population who is religious might not change. I suspect that Armageddon would send non-religious people to the science books to figure out how Earth can escape annihilation; I do not think it would cause many non-religious people to become religious.[17] I think that the saying "There are no atheists in the foxholes" is not true.

INDIVIDUALITY OF RELIGIOUS EXPERIENCE

Our desire profile influences what it is we seek from organized religion. Since each person has his or her own unique desire profile, it follows that no two people have the exact same spiritual experiences. For example, a person whose most important basic desires are low independence, idealism, and family should experience as especially meaningful religious mysticism, the social gospel, and religious family values. In contrast, a person whose most important desires are curiosity, tranquility, and order should experience as especially meaningful theology, the promise of an afterlife, and the following of strict religious rites and rituals.

Human individuality poses a significant challenge to organized religion. What can religious leaders do to meet the expectations of individuals with diverse needs and experiences in order to build the largest possible tent? In essence, the major religions may need to allow for flexibility of practice and interpretation of dogma in order to meet the diverse needs of individuals, since religions that are rigid and narrow-minded can offer meaningful experiences only to like-minded people. Narrow or strictly defined religions may turn away large numbers of people whose natures do not fit the mold.

In 1902, psychologist William James concluded that there are no common denominators to the many different varieties of religious experiences,[18] no belief all religions share, not even a belief in a god. There is no ceremony or ritual common to all religions. In James's viewpoint, all people who turn to religion do so for different reasons. About thirty years later, Gordon Allport (1897–1967) struck a similar note when he applied his psychology of the individual to the study of religion.[19] Allport also concluded that individuals turn to religion to satisfy different psychological needs.

With its emphasis on individuality, the system of 16 basic desires adds factual details to the ideas first advanced by James and Allport. For all 16 basic desires, there is a formal aspect of organized religion that can satisfy that desire. Religion is a complete psychological experience that can meet an individual's most important needs.

RELIGION AND CAPITALISM

According to some historians, people have turned to religion during times of rising capitalism. How should we explain this? Max Weber suggested that it is because Protestants have an ethic of hard work, which is consistent with the need to produce economic value in a capitalistic society. Researchers have shown, however, that Protestants are no more ambitious or hardworking than are members of other religious groups. Thus, Weber's hypothesis of a Protestant work ethic appears to be invalid.

Aristotle's concept of the Golden Mean of moderation, applied to the system of 16 basic desires, may explain the positive association between capitalism and religion. According to this idea, the desire for independence forms a continuum between autonomy and interdependence, so that each individual aims for some mix of experiences between the two extremes. In the dog-eat-dog world of capitalism, our needs for self-reliance are overly satisfied at the workplace. People in a capitalistic society may get the impression that they are on their own; they may feel as if it is sink or swim, and if they sink, they are far from certain that somebody will throw them a life preserver. Feeling uncomfortable with the degree of self-reliance that is sometimes expected in a capitalistic society, these people may need to moderate their experience of independence. Religion can fulfill this psychological need through its emphasis of a profound sense of dependence on God. The religious capitalist is never completely on his own because God is always in his heart and mind. Let's consider the example of a religious businesswoman who prays to win a lucrative business contract. When competing for the contract, the businesswoman is on her own, in dog-eat-dog mode, and there is an overwhelming sense of independence. When praying to God for assistance in winning the contract, the businessperson has an absolute sense of dependence on a force much greater than herself. The combined psychological effects of competition in the business world and faith in God is a moderated experience of self-reliance. Because the pursuit of value-based happiness motivates people to regulate basic desires toward golden means of moderation and away from extreme experiences, capitalism and religion are complementary psychological forces that in combination provide a moderate experience of independence and freedom.

In contrast, consider what might happen in a communistic society. A communist economy emphasizes dependence on the state, rather than the self-reliance of the individual. People living in such a society might seek freedom to moderate the experience of extreme dependency on the state. Religion is not well-suited psychologically to moderate the feeling of dependence because it gives emphasis to man's dependence on God. Because people are motivated to regulate basic desires toward golden means, socialism and religion are non-complementary psychological forces. Perhaps that is one reason why religion is outlawed or discouraged in communistic societies that practice dependency on the state.

Afterword

The 16 basic desires offer a way to think about yourself and others in terms you have never before used. Here are three final applications of this new way of thinking about people: self-improvement, mental illness, and consumer marketing. I have chosen these topics because I am frequently asked about them.

SELF-IMPROVEMENT

Many of us are interested in self-improvement, whether to lose weight, quit smoking, drink less, control our tempers, or worry less. The system of 16 basic desires can help you accomplish most of these goals, since we are most likely to stick with a self-improvement plan that is connected to our most important basic desires. On the other hand, we're likely to prematurely quit any self-improvement program that is inconsistent with our desire profile.

When you set out to change yourself, you need to decide if you are aiming for the short term or the long haul. In the short term, willpower and immediate incentives can provide the motivation you need. Anybody who really wants to do so can improve herself or himself for periods of months or even a year or two. It is mostly a matter of willpower and having a sensible plan. Over the long haul, however, willpower and incentives rarely work.

Lasting self-improvement usually requires either that you change your lifestyle to better satisfy your desire profile or that you change your priorities. Knowledge of the 16 basic desires can help you accomplish these goals.

The story of Rocky Graziano, the former middleweight champion prize-fighter, is an example of someone who embraced a new lifestyle that more completely satisfied his desires. As a young man, Rocky was a juvenile delinquent and petty thief. He was always getting into street-fights, using his fists against anyone who offended him. Rocky was a fighter by nature. Although he needed people to accept this fact about him, everybody tried to force the violence out of him. It didn't work. Nor was he changed when his lifestyle led to jail and left him without much money. Violence and anger were part of Graziano's core psychological nature, and provided meaning in his early life.

Graziano's life changed when he became a prizefighter. With support from his wife and children, Rocky became a responsible citizen. Although his old lifestyle of crime met his need to fight (satisfying his desire for vengeance), his new lifestyle of prizefighting satisfied a larger number of needs, including his need to fight, become somebody important (indicating a desire for status), gain romance, and raise children.

The key to effective self-improvement is to analyze how your behavior is connected to your desire profile. Your desire profile tells you what you want most from life. Unless a desired change is meaningful in the context of your life goals, I suspect that you will not change for any length of time. For Rocky Graziano, giving up violence was not an option because it was inconsistent with his most important life goal (to be accepted for who he was). He resisted others' efforts to change him because deep down he did not want to give up his violent ways. He was a fighter, and nobody could stop him from fighting. He changed only after he found a socially acceptable way of satisfying his need to fight.

If you want to change yourself to please somebody else you are unlikely to succeed for any length of time. Self-improvement works when the desired change is what you yourself want because it satisfies your desires. This sometimes requires that you change your priorities in life. If you fail at a self-improvement project, maybe you need to connect the improvement to a different set of priorities. A good case in point was my effort to quit smoking, in which I failed maybe 100 times. I was physically addicted to nicotine by the time I was 30, and figured I was headed for cancer of the throat or mouth. The thought of cancer scared me to death, so I kept trying to quit. Each time I tried, I found myself giving in to the cravings within a day or so.

When you keep failing at quitting smoking, people give you all kinds of advice. This is especially so if you are a psychologist and your friends are national experts on how to quit smoking. I tried the cold-turkey method, the gradual-reduction method, and the substitution method. None of them worked. But when my wife became pregnant with our first child, she told me that I had to quit for his sake. After having failed to quit when the reason was my health, I quit smoking the very first time I tried when the reason was my child's health. For the last 16 years, I have stuck with this self-improvement because my priorities changed.

If you have been trying to improve yourself for years without much success, maybe you need to analyze how your behavior is connected to your desire profile. People do not change permanently in response to pressure from others, and they do not stick with changes that are essentially meaningless in their lives. People stick with self-improvement only when it becomes a meaningful aspect of their lives.

The 16 basic desires teach us that the motivation for change must come from within ourselves. Pep talk and motivational gimmicks can only inspire us for short periods of time. Even the greatest coach must motivate the team before every game, because the inspirational speech given before last week's game has long since stopped motivating the players. Inspirational speeches and tips do not work over the long haul. As time goes by, you have a relentless tendency to be you. Your best hope for lasting self-improvement is to connect the new habits to your desire profile.

MENTAL ILLNESS

I suspect that unusual or extreme behavior is often a consequence of unusual or extreme desires. Nearly all therapists have noticed that people with mental disorders care about things differently than do most people. Some people with mental disorders want too much love, others want too much sex, and still others are filled with too much hatred. Some are intolerant of everyday frustration or are highly sensitive to anxiety. Some no longer care about anything. In each of these examples, we can analyze how extreme and unusual desires have led to extreme and unusual behavior.

We can review the various categories of mental disorders and analyze how many symptoms can be understood in terms of basic desires.

> **Anxiety Disorders.** These conditions are indicated by frequent or intense experiences of anxiety, stress, or fear. An abnormally high desire for tranquility precedes panic attacks. Obsessive-compulsive disorder may be associated with a high desire for order and a high desire for saving.

> **Autism.** This is a developmental disability indicated by early emotional detachment and communication problems. We have obtained some evidence that this condition is associated with a very strong desire for order and a very low desire for social contact.

> **Depression.** This condition, technically called affective disorder, is indicated by a profound sadness that does not go away. It may be associated with very low desires for independence, social contact, eating, romance, and exercise, and with high desires for acceptance, vengeance, and tranquility.

> **Schizophrenia.** This condition is indicated by false sensory perceptions (hallucinations), such as hearing voices that are not real, and by firmly held false beliefs (delusions), such as that the FBI is secretly monitoring your brain waves. Since people who have this disorder often appear unkempt and disheveled, this disorder may be associated with a low desire for status and social contact.

We are only beginning to explore the implications of the system of 16 basic desires for understanding mental illness. We already have made significant progress in understanding Panic Disorder, which affects 5 million Americans, and we have started to make progress in understanding developmental disabilities, which affect another 3 million Americans. With continued research, I hope we can make additional progress.

CONSUMER MARKETS

Now let's take a look at a very different topic, consumer marketing. The 16 desires have a powerful impact on how people react to advertisements and product images. From the perspective of consumers who are the target of advertising, it should be fun to learn how marketers use psychology to appeal to people's tastes. From the perspective of the marketer, the system of 16 basic desires can help you devise new advertisements.

The basic principles of marketing to people's desires are simple. People generally react most favorably to advertisements or product images that connect to their desire profiles. They react negatively to advertisements or product images that contradict their desire profiles.

Here are some examples of how a variety of highly successful advertising slogans connect to the 16 basic desires.

SLOGAN	CONCEPT	BASIC DESIRE
Diamonds are forever	permanence	high order
Just do it	don't think	low curiosity
We try harder	ambition	high power
Good to the last drop	perfection	high order
Breakfast of champions	competition	high vengeance
Does she . . . or doesn't she?	discovery	high curiosity
Where's the beef?	value	high saving
Look Ma, no cavities!	achievement	high power
We bring good things to life	creation	high power
Melts in your mouth, not in your hand	neatness	high order
You deserve a break today	self-worth	low acceptance
Do you know me?	no longer famous	low status

SLOGAN	CONCEPT	BASIC DESIRE
We'll leave a light on for you	friendliness	high social contact
Fast, fast, fast relief	reduce pain	high tranquility
The Pepsi generation	youth	high independence
Have it your way	individuality	high independence
Only you can prevent forest fires	responsibility	high honor
Mm-mm good	tasty	high eating
A little dab'll do ya	economy	high saving
Take the bus and leave the driving to us	relaxation	high tranquility
Ring around the collar	criticism	high acceptance
You don't have to be Jewish to love Levy's	heritage unimportant	low honor
Nothing between me and my Calvins (jeans)	sex	high romance
It's the real thing	truthfulness	high honor
Image is everything	importance of appearance	high status

Why does the system of 16 basic desires seem to match so well to effective advertising slogans? Because these desires may show the psychological structure of mass consumer markets.

IN CONCLUSION . . .

These are the 16 basic desires that make our lives meaningful. When you awaken each day, your desires start to influence your behavior automatically. They prod you to do what you do. When you satisfy them you gain value-based happiness, which is a deep sense that your life has purpose and meaning.

Your desires are what make you different from everything else in the universe—lose them and you will become what Aristotle called a thing or an object in the universe. Keep them and you remain a person. Nourish them and you grow toward self-actualization.

Appendix

WHAT DO YOU WANT AND WHY?

Here's how to create your own individual desire profile by determining how important each of the 16 desires is to you. Once you know which desires are most and least important, you can tailor your work, home life, relationships, and recreational activities to fulfill or avoid those desires.

As you answer each question below, record your response on the chart on page 261. Then turn to page 262 to graph your personal desire profile.

POWER

Rate your desire for power as *very important* to you if any of the following statements is generally true:

1. You are highly ambitious compared with other people your age.

2. You usually seek leadership roles.

3. You usually dominate in social situations with people your own age.

Rate your desire for power as *less important* to you if either of the following statements is generally true:

1. You are noticeably less ambitious than other people your own age.

2. Generally, you prefer being submissive in social situations.

Rate your desire for power as of *average importance* if you have not rated it as very important *or* less important, of if you have endorsed statements indicating that power is both very *and* less important to you. Record your response on the chart on page 261. Then graph your profile on page 262.

INDEPENDENCE

Rate your desire for independence as *very important* to you if either of the following statements is generally true:

1. You usually resist advice and guidance from others.

2. Self-reliance is essential to your happiness.

Rate your desire for independence as *less important* to you if either of the following statements is generally true:

1. Compared to other people your own age, you are noticeably more devoted to your spouse or partner.

2. You dislike being on your own.

Rate your desire for independence as of *average importance* if you have not rated it as very important *or* less important, or if you have endorsed statements indicating that independence is both very and less important to you. Record your response on the chart on page 261. Then graph your profile on page 262.

CURIOSITY

Rate curiosity as *very important* in guiding your behavior if any of the following statements is generally true:

1. You have a thirst for knowledge.

2. Compared to your peers, you ask a lot of questions.

3. You think a lot about what is true.

Rate your curiosity as *less important* in guiding your behavior if either of the following statements is true:

1. You dislike intellectual activities.

2. You rarely ask questions.

Rate your curiosity as of *average importance* if you have not rated it as very important *or* less important, or if you have endorsed statements indicating that curiosity is both very *and* less important to you. Record your response on the chart on page 261. Then graph your profile on page 262.

ACCEPTANCE

Rate acceptance as *very important* to you if any of the following statements is generally true:

1. You usually set easy goals for yourself.

2. You are a quitter.

3. You have great difficulty coping with criticism.

Rate acceptance as *less important* to you if either of the following statements is true:

1. You have a lot of self-confidence.

2. You handle criticism noticeably better than most people—that is, you do not become unduly upset.

Rate your desire for acceptance as of *average importance* if you have not rated it as very important *or* less important, or if you have endorsed statements indicating that acceptance is both very *and* less important to you. Record your response on the chart on page 261. Then graph your profile on page 262.

ORDER

Rate your desire for order as *very important* in your life if any of the following statements is generally true:

1. You are noticeably more organized than most people.

2. Your have many rules and try to follow them religiously.

3. You enjoy cleaning up.

Rate your desire for order as *less important* in your life if either of the following statements is generally true:

1. Your office/workplace is usually a mess.

2. You hate planning.

Rate your desire for order as of *average importance* if you have not rated it as very important *or* less important, or if you have endorsed statements indicating that order is both very *and* less important to you. Record your response on the chart on page 261. Then graph your profile on page 262.

SAVING

Rate your desire for saving as *very important* to you if any of the following statements is generally true:

1. You are a collector.

2. You are a miser.

3. You are noticeably more tight with your money than other people are with their money.

Rate this desire as *less important* to you if any of the following statements are generally true:

1. You are a free spender.

2. You rarely save anything at all.

Rate your desire for saving as of *average importance* if you have not rated it as very important or less important, *or* if you have endorsed statements indicating that the desire to save is both very *and* less important to you. Record your response on the chart on page 261. Then graph your profile on page 262.

HONOR

Rate your desire for honor as *very important* to you if either of the following statements is generally true:

1. You are known as a highly principled person.

2. You are known as a very loyal person.

Rate your desire for honor as *less important* to you if either of the following statements is generally true:

1. You believe that everyone is out for him- or herself.

2. You do not care much about morality.

Rate your desire for honor as of *average importance* if you have not rated it as very important *or* less important, or if you have endorsed statements indicating honor is both very *and* less important to you. Record your response on the chart on page 261. Then graph your profile on page 262.

IDEALISM

Rate your desire for idealism as *very important* to you if any of the following statements is true:

1. You make personal sacrifices for a social or humanitarian cause.

2. You have repeatedly volunteered time to community-service organizations.

3. You have repeatedly made generous contributions to the needy.

Rate your desire for idealism as *less important* to you if either of the following statements is generally true:

1. You pay little attention to what is going on in society at large.

2. You do not believe in charity.

Rate your desire for idealism as of *average importance* if you have not rated it as very important *or* less important, or if you have endorsed statements indicating that idealism is both very *and* less important to you. Record your response on the chart on page 261. Then graph your profile on page 262.

SOCIAL CONTACT

Rate your desire for social contact as *very important* to you if either of the following statements is generally true:

1. You feel that you need to be around other people a lot to be happy.

2. You are known as a fun-loving person.

Rate your desire for social contact as *less important* to you if any of the following statements is generally true:

1. You are a private person.

2. You hate parties.

3. You do not care much about other people except for family and a few close friends.

Rate your desire for social contact as of *average importance* if you have not rated it as very important *or* less important, or if you have endorsed statements indicating that social contact is both very *and* less important to you. Record your response on the chart on page 261. Then graph your profile on page 262.

FAMILY

Rate your desire for family as *very important* to you if either of the following statements is generally true:

1. Raising children is essential to your happiness.

2. Compared with other parents you know, you spend much more time with your children.

Rate your desire for family as *less important* to you if either of the following statements is generally true:

1. You find being a parent mostly burdensome.

2. You have abandoned a child.

Rate your desire for family as of *average importance* if you have not rated it as very important *or* less important, or if you endorsed statements indicating that family is both very *and* less important to you. Record your response on the chart on page 261. Then graph your profile on page 262.

SOCIAL STATUS

Rate your desire for status as *very important* to you if any of the following statements is generally true:

1. You almost always want to buy only the best or most expensive things.

2. You often buy things just to impress other people.

3. You spend a great deal of time trying to join or maintain membership in prestigious clubs or organizations.

Rate your desire for status as *less important* to you if any of the following statements is generally true:

1. You usually do not care what most people think of you.

2. You are significantly less impressed by wealth than most people you know.

3. You are not at all impressed by upper-class status or royalty.

Rate your desire for status as of *average importance* if you have not rated it as very important *or* less important, or if you have endorsed statements indicating that status is both very *and* less important to you. Record your response on the chart on page 261. Then graph your profile on page 262.

VENGEANCE

Rate your desire for vengeance as *very important* to you if any of the following statements is generally true:

1. You have trouble controlling your anger.

2. You are aggressive.

3. You love to compete.

4. You spend a lot of your time seeking revenge.

Rate your desire as *less important* to you if any of the following statements is generally true:

1. You are slow to feel anger compared to most people.

2. You often "look the other way" when insulted or offended.

3. You dislike competitive situations.

Rate your desire for vengeance as of *average importance* if you have not rated it as very important *or* less important, of if you have endorsed statements indicating that vengeance is both very *and* less important to you. Record your response on the chart on page 261. Then graph your profile on page 262.

ROMANCE

Rate your desire for romance as *very important* to you if any of the following statements is generally true:

1. You spend an unusual amount of time, compared to other people you know who are about the same age as you, in the pursuit of romance.

2. You have a long history of sex with many partners.

3. You have trouble controlling your sexual urges.

4. Compared to most people you know, you spend much more time appreciating beauty.

Rate your desire for romance as *less important* to you if any of the following statements is generally true:

1. You spend little time pursuing or thinking about sex.

2. You think that sex is disgusting.

Rate your desire for romance as of *average importance* if you have not rated it as very important *or* less important to you, or if you have endorsed statements indicating that romance is both very *and* less important to you. Record your response on the chart on page 261. Then graph your profile on page 262.

EATING

Rate your desire for food as *very important* to you if either of the following statements is generally true:

1. You spend an unusual amount of time, compared to other people you know who are about the same age as you, eating.

2. You spend an unusual amount of time, compared to other people you know who are about the same age as you, dieting.

Rate your desire for food as *less important* if either of the following statements is generally true:

1. You have never had a weight problem.

2. You rarely eat more than you should.

Rate your desire for food as of *average importance* if you have not rated it as very important *or* less important, or if you have endorsed statements indicating that eating is both very *and* less important to you. Record your response on the chart on page 261. Then graph your profile on page 262.

PHYSICAL ACTIVITY

Rate your desire for physical activity as *very important* to you if either of the following statements is generally true:

1. You have exercised regularly all your life.

2. Playing a sport is an important part of your life.

Rate your desire for physical activity as *less important* to you if either of the following statements is generally true:

1. You have a history of being physically lazy.

2. You have a sedentary lifestyle.

Rate your desire for physical activity as of *average importance* if you have not rated it as very important *or* less important, or if you have endorsed statements indicating that physical activity is both very *and* less important to you. Record your response on the chart on page 261. Then graph your profile on page 262.

TRANQUILITY

Rate your desire for tranquility as *very important* to you if any of the following statements is generally true:

1. You strongly agree with at least two of the four ASI statements:
   a. It scares me when I feel "shaky" (trembling).
   b. It scares me when my heart beats rapidly.
   c. When I notice that my heart is beating, I worry that I might have a heart attack.
   d. It embarrasses me when my stomach growls.

2. You have a history of recurring panic attacks.

3. You are generally fearful and timid.

Rate your desire for tranquility as *less important* if either of the following statements is generally true:

1. You are a brave person.

2. You have noticeably fewer fears than your peers.

Rate your desire for tranquility as of *average importance* if you have not rated it as very important *or* less important, or if you have endorsed statements indicating that tranquility is both very *and* less important to you. Record your response on the chart on page 261. Then graph your profile on page 262.

Record of Basic Desires

In the blanks below, enter the ratings for yourself and others whom you would like to analyze in terms of the 16 basic desires.

For every question you answered with: *Please record below:*

Very Important   V

Average Importance   A

Less Important   L

	Example: Susan	*Me*	*My Partner*	*Family (child/parent)*	*My Employer*
Power (p. 36)	V				
Independence (p. 38)	A				
Curiosity (p. 41)	V				
Acceptance (p. 43)	A				
Order (p. 46)	A				
Saving (p. 49)	A				
Honor (p. 52)	A				
Idealism (p. 55)	A				
Social Contact (p. 57)	A				
Family (p. 60)	A				
Status (p. 62)	L				
Vengeance (p. 66)	A				
Romance (p. 70)	V				
Eating (p. 73)	A				
Physical Activity (p. 76)	L				
Tranquility (p. 78)	A				

Now turn to the chart on page 262 and graph your answers in the appropriate column. For each desire you rated "very important," place a dot at the level indicated by "need to have." For every desire you rated as "less important," place a dot at the level indicated by "need to avoid." For all other desires, place a dot at the middle level labeled "average importance."

Example:

Susan rated power, curiosity and romance as "very important." She rated physical activity and status as "less important." Susan then marked the remaining 11 desires as being of "average importance."

SUSAN'S DESIRE PROFILE

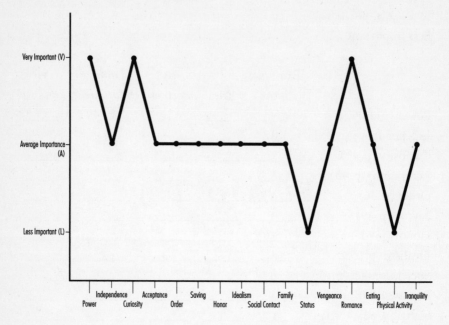

YOUR PERSONAL DESIRE PROFILE

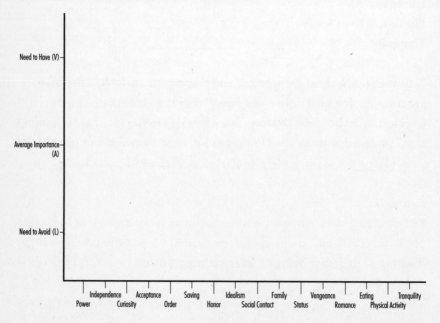

Bibliography

The following sources had significant influence on the development of the theory of 16 basic desires.

Adler, A. (1964) *The Practice and Theory of Individual Psychology*. New York: Harcourt Brace Jovanovich.

Allport, G. W. (1961) *The Individual and His Religion*. New York: The Macmillian Company.

Aristotle (350B.C./1953) *The Nicomachean Ethics* (trans. by J. A. K. Thomson). New York: Penguin Books.

Armstrong, K. (1993) *A History of God*. New York: Ballantine Books.

Blood, R. O., Jr. (1969) *Marriage*. New York: The Free Press.

Chess, S., M.D., and Thomas, A., M.D. (1996) *Goodness of Fit: Clinical Applications from Infancy Through Adult Life*. New York: Bruner/Mazel Publishers.

Darwin, C. (1872/1965) *The Expression of the Emotions in Man and Animals*. Chicago: The University of Chicago Press.

de Waal, F. (1989) *Peacemaking Among Primates*. Cambridge, MA: Harvard University Press.

Ebenstein, A. O. (1991) *The Greatest Happiness Principle: An Examination of Utilitarianism*. New York: Garland.

Flugel, J. C. (1961) *Man, Morals and Society*. New York: The Viking Press.

Frankl, V. E. (1984) *Man's Search for Meaning*. New York: Simon & Schuster.

James, W. (1906) *The Varieties of Religious Experience*. London: Longmans, Green, and Co.

James, W. (1890/1918) *The Principles of Psychology (vol. 2)*. New York: Dover Publications.

Maslow, A. H. (1954) *Motivation and Personality*. New York: Harper & Row.

Masson, J. M. (1995) *When Elephants Weep*. New York: Dell Publishing.

McDougall, W. (1921) *An Introduction to Social Psychology*. Boston: John W. Luce.

Niebuhr, R. (1949) *The Nature and Destiny of Man*. New York: Charles Scribner's Sons.

Ramsay, G. (1843) *An Inquiry Into the Principles of Human Happiness and Human Duty*. London: William Pickering.

Russell, B. (1977) *A History of Western Philosophy*. New York: Simon & Schuster.

Wittgenstein, L. (1953/1967) *Philosophical Investigations* (2nd ed.). New York: The Macmillan Company.

Endnotes

INTRODUCTION

1. Carol D. Ryff (1989), "Happiness is Everything, or Is It? Explorations on the Meaning of Psychological Well-being," *Journal of Personality and Social Psychology* 57: 1069–1081.
2. In the *Republic*, Plato wrote the following: "Well, then, you know that most people identify the Good [the end goal of human life] with pleasure, whereas the more enlightened think it is knowledge." See Francis MacDonald Cornford (1945), *The Republic of Plato*, New York: Oxford University Press, 225.
3. Also in the *Republic*, Plato wrote, "Then only the just man is happy; injustice will involve unhappiness." Ibid., 39.
4. When he lectured at Clark University, Freud said the following: "The male genital organ is symbolically represented in dreams in many different ways. . . . The sacred number *three* is symbolic of the whole male genitalia. . . . The penis is symbolized primarily by objects which resemble it in form, being long and upstanding, such as *sticks, umbrellas, poles, trees . . . knives, daggers, lances, sabres . . . guns, pistols, and revolvers . . . taps, water-cans, or springs . . . pulley lamps, pencils, penholders . . . are undoubtedly male sexual symbols.* . . . The female genitalia are symbolically represented by all such objects as share with them the property of enclosing a space or are capable of acting as receptacles: such as *pits, hollows and caves . . . jars and bottles, and boxes . . . chests, coffers, pockets . . . cupboards, stoves and, above all, rooms . . . wood, paper . . . tables and books . . . snails and mussels . . . apples, peaches and fruit.*" From Sigmund Freud (1924–1960), *A General Introduction to Psychoanalysis*, New York: Washington Square Press, 161–164.

5. Alfred Adler (1927), *The Practice and Theory of Individual Psychology*, New York: Harcourt Brace Jovanovich.

6. Erik H. Erikson (1950/1963), *Childhood and Society*, New York: W. W. Norton & Company.

7. K. W. Spence (1956), *Behavior Theory and Conditioning*, New Haven: Yale University Press.

8. In a paper entitled "Behaviorism at Fifty," which was delivered for the Rice University Semicentennial Series, B. F. Skinner (1964) said: "If psychology is a science of mental life—of the mind, of conscious experience—then it must develop and defend a special methodology, which it has not yet done successfully." In T. W. Wann (ed.), *Behaviorism and Phenomenology*, Chicago: University of Chicago Press, 79–108.

9. Carl R. Rogers (1961), *On Becoming a Person*, Boston: Houghton Mifflin.

10. William James (1890/1950), *The Principles of Psychology*, New York: Dover Publications.

11. William McDougall (1921), *An Introduction to Social Psychology*, Boston: John W. Luce & Co.

12. Henry A. Murray acknowledged the origins of his famous list of needs when he wrote: "This classification of needs is not very different from lists constructed by McDougall, Garnett, and a number of other writers." Henry A. Murray (1938), *Explorations in Personality*, New York: Oxford University Press, 84.

13. Henry A. Murray (1943), *Manual of the Thematic Apperception Test*, Cambridge, MA: Harvard University Press.

14. Abraham H. Maslow (1954), *Motivation and Personality*, New York: Harper & Row.

15. We combined Aristotle's philosophical idea of end motive with the psychological method of factor analysis, producing what may be the first factor studies of end motivation.

16. Harvard University psychologist David McClelland and his students produced a large body of research on human motivation, especially on achievement motivation and power. They based their entire body of research on psychological interpretations of themes in stories made up in response to drawings, a technique called the *Thematic Apperception Test* (TAT). Although the TAT or related techniques are still used in clinical assessments, today very little research is conducted using these techniques. A quick check of recent issues of prestigious journals, such as the *Journal of Abnormal Psychology*, shows that the TAT is dead as a research instrument. The authoritative reference source on the validity of the TAT and related techniques is Joseph Zubin, Leonard Eron, and Florence Schumer's (1965), *An Experimental Approach to Projective Techniques*, New York: John Wiley & Sons.

17. Steven Reiss and Susan M. Havercamp (1998), "Toward a Comprehensive Assessment of Fundamental Motivation: Factor Structure of the Reiss Profile," *Psychological Assessment* 10: 97–106.

CHAPTER ONE

1. William James (1890/1918), *The Principles of Psychology (vol. 2)*, New York: Dover Publications.
2. William McDougall (1921), *An Introduction to Social Psychology*, Boston: John W. Luce & Co.
3. Ibid., 443.
4. Actually, only 14 of the 16 basic desires are clearly seen in animals. For two basic desires—acceptance and idealism—scientific authorities are still debating the issue. Some authorities say that because animals do not have language, they cannot have a self-concept. This implies that they do not have the desire for acceptance or self-worth in the same sense that people do. Some authorities say that idealism is seen in animals in the form of altruistic behavior, but others question whether or not true altruism is seen very often in animals.
5. Strictly speaking, I am referring to the strength or intensity of motivation. Although I sometimes use the word "pleasure" for the sake of simplicity, what I really mean is "motivation."
6. Diane Ackerman (1994), *A Natural History of Love*, New York: Vintage Books, 251–252.
7. James W. Vander Zanden (1995), *Human Development*, New York: McGraw-Hill, 348–350.
8. John W. M. Whiting and Irwin L. Child (1953), *Child Training and Personality*, New Haven: Yale University Press.
9. Albert Ellis (1962), *Reason and Emotion in Psychotherapy*, New York: Lyle Stuart.
10. In factor-analytic studies of the kind Susan and I conducted, sample size of 300 or more—as well as diversity of research participants—are often considered sufficient.
11. A noteworthy exception is a statistical tendency for people with a strong need for power also to have a strong need for status.
12. Each of the 16 basic desires can serve as a means as well as an end, depending on the goal that is ultimately motivating the behavior. The 16 basic desires can function as means because each can be used as a stepping stone toward some other goal. In sexual harassment, for example, power is a means, and romance is an end. In achievement situations, however, power is an end. Although all ends can be means, not all means can be ends.

CHAPTER TWO

1. Richard Grid Powers (1987), *Secrecy and Power: The Life of J. Edgar Hoover*, New York: The Free Press.
2. Ibid., 393.
3. Ibid.
4. George Ramsay (1843), *An Inquiry Into the Principles of Human Happiness and Human Duty*, London: William Pickering.
5. Alfred Adler (1964), *The Practice and Theory of Individual Psychology*, London: Routledge & Kegan Paul.

6. Independence and power are often confused with each other, but they are distinct desires.

7. Kenneth L. Dion and Karen K. Dion (1988), "Romantic Love: Individual and Cultural Perspectives," in R. J. Sternberg and Michael L. Barnes (eds.), *The Psychology of Love,* New Haven: Yale University Press, 264–292.

8. L. Takeo Doi (1962), "Amae: A Key Concept for Understanding Japanese Personality Structure," in R. J. Smith and R. K. Beardsley (eds.), *Japanese Culture: Its Development and Characteristics,* New York: Viking Fund Publications.

9. Based on Louis K. Wechsler (1976), *Benjamin Franklin,* Boston: Twayne Publishers.

10. Carl Sandburg (1926), *Abraham Lincoln,* New York: Harcourt, Brace & Company.

11. Stella Chess and Alexander Thomas (1996), *Goodness of Fit: Clinical Applications from Infancy Through Adult Life,* New York: Bruner/Mazel Publishers.

12. Edward Zigler (1971), "The Retarded Child as a Whole Person," in H. E. Adams & W. K. Boardman (eds.), *Advances in Experimental Clinical Psychology,* New York: Pergamon, 47–121.

13. William James (1890/1950), *The Principles of Psychology,* New York: Dover.

14. Mrs. Child (1828), *The American Frugal Housewife,* Boston: Carter, Hendee, and Co.

15. M. Spence (August 1997), "Money Mad," *Biography* magazine, 50–53.

16. "When a Love of Books Means a Life in Stacks," *The New York Times,* 6 July, 1997.

CHAPTER THREE

1. "Diary Breaks Silence of Disgraced Titanic Survivor," *Columbus Dispatch,* 23 December, 1997, 4A.

2. J. C. Flugel (1961), *Man, Morals, and Society,* New York: The Viking Press.

3. J. M. Masson (1995), *When Elephants Weep,* New York: Dell Publishing.

4. M. K. Gandhi (1951), *Non-Violent Resistance,* New York: Schocken Books.

5. According to the theory of 16 basic desires, self-discipline is a means to other goals rather than an end goal. As in the example of Gandhi's philosophy, self-discipline is often a means to the end of honor.

6. Gabrielle Glaser (1997), *Strangers to the Tribe: Portraits of Interfaith Marriage,* Boston: Houghton Mifflin.

7. Masson, *When Elephants Weep.*

8. David L. Lewis (1978), *King: A Biography,* Urbana, IL: University of Illinois Press.

9. Ibid.

10. Alexandre Dumas (1844), *The Three Musketeers* (trans. W. Robson), New York: Heritage Press.

11. "Though many say they're shy, some truly cut themselves off," *The Columbus Dispatch,* 10 August, 1998, 3E.

12. Masson, *When Elephants Weep.*

13. For example, see Henry A. Murray (1938), *Explorations in Personality,* New York: Oxford University Press.

14. "A Mother First," *The Columbus Dispatch,* 23 April, 1998, 8G.

15. William A. Henry III (1993), *The Great One: The Life and Legend of Jackie Gleason,* New York: G. K. Hall and Co.

16. Paul Fussell (1964), *Class: A Guide Through the American Status System*, New York: Touchstone.

CHAPTER FOUR

1. J. M. Masson (1995), *When Elephants Weep*, New York: Dell.
2. Tennessee Williams (1975), *Cat on a Hot Tin Roof*, New York: Dramatists Play Services.
3. L. H. Huesmann and Leonard D. Eron (1989), "Individual Differences and the Trait of Aggression," *European Journal of Personality* 3, 95.
4. The absolute level of aggression changes with age—adolescents 16 years old are more aggressive than middle-aged men 45 years old—but how aggressive a person is relative to same-aged peers is fairly stable.
5. "In Unabomber's Own Words," *The New York Times*, 29 April, 1998, a16.
6. Susan Jacoby (1983), *Wild Justice: The Evolution of Revenge*, New York: Harper & Row.
7. Fred Goldman, *Newsweek*, 7 July, 1997, 23.
8. Frans de Waal (1989), *Peacekeeping Among Primates*, Cambridge, MA: Harvard University Press.
9. Martin S. Lindauer (1981), "Aesthetics Experience: A Neglected Topic in the Psychology of the Arts," in David O'Hare (ed.), *Psychology and the Arts*, Atlantic Highlands, NJ: Humanities Press.
10. Diane Ackerman (1995), *A Natural History of Love*, New York: Vintage Books, 77.
11. Aristotle, *The Nichomachean Ethics* (trans. J. A. K. Thomson), New York: Penguin.
12. *Newsweek*, 1 September, 1997, 23.
13. In Benjamin Wolman (1982), *Psychological Aspects of Obesity*, New York: Van Nostrand Reinhold, 30.
14. William A. Henry III (1993), *The Great One: The Life and Legend of Jackie Gleason*, New York: G. K. Hall and Co.
15. "From the Wide World of Golf, Singh Emerges a Winner," *The Columbus Dispatch*, 3 June, 1997, 1G.
16. "Tara Lipinski: Enjoying Her Destiny," *International Figure Skating*, February 1999.
17. Richard J. McNally (1994), *Panic Disorder: A Critical Analysis*, New York: The Guilford Press.
18. Sherry H. Stewart, Sarah Barton Samoluk, and Alan B. MacDonald (1999), "Anxiety Sensitivity and Substance Use and Abuse," in Steven Taylor (ed.), *Anxiety Sensitivity*, Mahwah, NJ: Erlbaum.
19. Steven Taylor (Editor, 1999), *Anxiety Sensitivity*, Mahwah, NJ: Erlbaum.
20. Norman B. Schmidt, D. R. Lerew, and R. J. Jackson (1997), "The Role of Anxiety Sensitivity in the Pathogenesis of Panic: Prospective Evaluation of Spontaneous Panic Attacks During Acute Stress," *Journal of Abnormal Psychology* 106: 355–364.

CHAPTER FIVE

1. The method of analyzing biographies as an initial test of concept validity was used by many previous psychologists, including Freud and Maslow. The limitations of this method are significant: the interpretation is subjective, the biographies them-

selves are incomplete, and some of the biographical material may not be accurate. Nevertheless, this analysis of biographical material is still a reasonable initial method of evaluating both the relevance and comprehensiveness of the system of 16 basic desires.

2. Based on Peter Harry Brown and Pat H. Broeske (1997), *Howard Hughes: The Untold Story,* New York: Penguin.

3. Ibid., 129.

4. Ibid., 137.

5. Ibid., 327.

6. Ibid., 140.

7. Ibid., 27.

8. Ibid., 27.

9. Ibid., 114.

10. Peter Maas (1997), *Underboss,* New York: HarperCollins. This analysis was written prior to Gravano's arrest in 2000 for selling drugs.

11. Ibid., 254.

12. Ibid., 50.

13. Ibid., 18.

14. Ibid., 88.

15. Ibid., 51.

16. Ibid., 49.

17. Ibid., 51.

18. Ibid., 129.

19. Ibid., 300.

20. C. David Heymann (1989), *A Woman Named Jackie,* New York: Signet (Penguin).

21. Ibid., 91.

22. Ibid., 211.

23. Ibid., 253.

24. Ibid., 259.

25. Based partially on J. Meyers (1997), *Bogart: A Life in Hollywood,* New York: Houghton Mifflin.

26. Based partially on A. M. Serber and E. Lax (1997), *Bogart,* New York: William Morrow and Co.

27. Abraham Maslow (1970), *Motivation and Personality,* New York: Harper & Row.

28. Maslow distinguished between the needs for romantic love and sex—he thought that sex was a biological (Stage 1) concern but that romantic love was a higher (Stage 3) concern.

29. Maslow, *Motivation and Personality,* 382.

30. Maslow wrote in 1970: "And yet it [Maslow's theory of motivation] still lacks experimental verification and support. I have not yet been able to think of a good way to put it to the test in the laboratory" (p. xii). Since Maslow developed no objective measures of self-actualization or human needs, his theory has not been verified. Further, a number of scientific reviews of Maslow's theory have observed the absence of factual support, such as the review by C. N. Cofer and M. H. Appley in their 1964 book, *Motivation: Theory and Research,* New York: John Wiley & Sons.

31. Ibid., 159.

CHAPTER SIX

1. George Ramsay (1843), *An Inquiry into the Principles of Human Happiness and Human Duty,* London: William Pickering, 25.
2. Tennessee Williams (1975), *Cat on a Hot Tin Roof,* New York: Dramatists Play Services.
3. Michael White and John Gribbin (1995), *Darwin: A Life in Science,* New York: Plume.
4. "He Traded Career for Family Wealth," *Columbus Dispatch,* 15 June, 1997.
5. Alfie Kohn (1993), *Punished by Rewards,* New York: Houghton Mifflin.
6. Francis MacDonald Cornford (trans., 1966), *The Republic of Plato,* Book IX, London: Oxford University Press, 312.
7. William Shakespeare, *Henry IV.*

CHAPTER SEVEN

1. F. Scott Fitzgerald (1925), *The Great Gatsby,* New York: Charles Scribner's Sons.
2. Christopher Reeve (1998), *Still Me,* New York: Random House.
3. Bertrand Russell (1977), *A History of Western Philosophy,* New York: Simon & Schuster.
4. D. S. Hutchinson, "Introduction," in Brad Inwood and L. P. Gerson, *The Epicurus Reader* Indianapolis: Hackett.
5. "Motivation" is beyond pleasure and pain. The thesis of this book is that our life goals are motivated by factors not directly connected to pleasure or pain. Scientifically, this is the thesis that psychologists can explain and predict more behavior through the idea of 16 end motives than the idea that pleasure and pain are overarching end motives.
6. Alex Haley (1964), *The Autobiography of Malcolm X,* New York: Ballantine.
7. Viktor E. Frankl (1984), *Man's Search for Meaning,* New York: Touchstone.
8. How can psychologists provide a scientific analysis of human meaning if meaning refers to no physical or biological event? Well, every day, scientists study truths outside the "real world." For example, physical science is based on mathematics, and philosophers have proven logically that mathematics does not exist, at least not as an abstraction from reality (see the critique of referential theories of language in L. Wittgenstein, *Philosophical Investigations*). Besides, what could seem more fantastic or "unreal" than the theory of Big Bang, which says that space, time, and the universe were created in a gigantic explosion? We cannot intuitively understand how "time" can be relative to motion. The idea that behavioral science cannot deal with the human spirit because "spirit" does not refer to a physical thing existing in time and space is invalid, especially since "time" and "space" do not "exist" as Newton had supposed.
9. John Stuart Mill (1873/1964), *Autobiography of John Stuart Mill,* New York: New American Library, 112.

10. Aristotle, *The Nicomachean Ethics* (trans. J. A. K. Thomson), New York: Penguin.
11. Suzanne Somers (1998), *After the Fall*, New York: Crown.
12. Ibid., 3.

CHAPTER EIGHT

1. Robert O. Blood, Jr. (1969), *Marriage*, New York: The Free Press.
2. Since the desire for curiosity was discussed in the introductory comments, we are moving directly to a discussion of acceptance.
3. Two people with a strong desire for acceptance are each insecure and will *not* bond easily. In this regard, the desire for acceptance is an important exception to the principle that like-mindedness attracts.
4. Clinton E. Phillips and Roger J. Corsini (1982), *Give In—or Give Up*, Chicago: Nelson–Hall, 143–144.
5. Partners who do not elect to have children can strengthen their bonds through the mutual fulfillment of other desires.
6. Blood, *Marriage*, 419
7. Roger A. Harper (1949), *Marriage*, New York: Appleton-Century-Crofts.
8. "A Cold Dose of Vengeance," *Time*, 12 July, 1999, 31.
9. Ibid.
10. We are skipping the desire for physical exercise because it is redundant with the discussion on the desire for romance in Chapter 11.
11. Sherry H. Stewart, Sarah Barton Samoluk, and Alan B. MacDonald (1999), "Anxiety Sensitivity and Substance Use and Abuse," in Steven Taylor (ed.), *Anxiety Sensitivity*, Mahwah, NJ: Erlbaum.

CHAPTER NINE

1. Based on the motion picture *Amadeus*.
2. J. McBride (1997), *Steven Spielberg: A Biography*, New York: Simon & Schuster.

CHAPTER TEN

1. Geoffrey Canada (1997), *Reaching Up for Manhood*, Boston: Beacon Press, 35.
2. Stella Chess and Thomas Alexander (1996), *Goodness of Fit: Clinical Applications from Infancy Through Adult Life*, New York: Bruner/Mazel.
3. Tennessee Williams (1975), *Cat on a Hot Tin Roof*, New York: Dramatists Play Services.
4. Norman Cameron (1963), *Personality Development and Psychopathology*, Boston: Houghton Mifflin.
5. Thomas J. Stanley and William D. Danko (1996), *The Millionaire Next Door*, New York: Pocket Books, 157.
6. "How to Make the Pieces Fit When You're Raising a 'Mismatch,' " *The Columbus Dispatch*, 8 January, 1998.
7. Ibid.

8. Sigmund Freud (1924/1961), *A General Introduction to Psychoanalysis*, New York: Washington Square Press.
9. Ibid.
10. Isaac M. Marks (1987), *Fears, Phobias, and Rituals*, New York: Oxford University Press.

CHAPTER ELEVEN

1. An original theory of sports motivation is put forth in this chapter. Surprisingly, psychologists have presented few such theories and perhaps none with the breadth of the theory of 16 desires. Noteworthy features of this theory are the recognition of the multifaceted nature of sports motivation, the effort to explain why we like some sports and not others, and the effort to explain the motivation of both participant and fan.
2. David Finkel (1998), "Golf's Saving Grace," in Bill Littlefield (ed.), *1998: The Best American Sports Writing*, Boston: Houghton Mifflin.
3. David Remnick (1998), "Kid Dynamite Blows Up," in Littlefield.
4. "In the Beginning, the Mets Were a Symbol of Ineptness," *The New York Times*, 26 September, 1969, 71C.
5. According to the Associated Press, millions of Chinese saw the game as an opportunity to avenge the May 7, 1999, accidental bombing of China's embassy in Yugoslavia. "I really hope they lose face," said Wang Zhanjun, a Beijing factory worker. "Economically, militarily, we can't punish America, so we have to use soccer."
6. Linda Robinson (1998), "On Planet Venus," in Littlefield.
7. Remnick, "Kid Dynamite."
8. *Sports Illustrated*, 12 July, 1999, 80.
9. Ron A. Thompson and Roberta T. Sherman (1993), *Helping Athletes with Eating Disorders*, Champaign, IL: Human Kinetics.
10. David Ferrell (1998), "Far Beyond a Mere Marathon," in Littlefield.
11. Ohio State University Psychology graduate student Jim Wiltz collected these data.

CHAPTER TWELVE

1. On first consideration, the scientific study of religious experience may seem like an oxymoron. Since God is ineffable and beyond comprehension, how can scientists study God? The ancient rabbis taught that God comes to each person commensurate with that person's ability to receive Him. They thought that each individual's personality influences how he or she perceives God. Thus, psychologists can study spiritual experience, or how people perceive God, even though they cannot study God Himself.
2. We asked people what is meaningful to them, but we did not ask specific questions about spirituality. We analyzed the results mathematically. The fact that many of the 16 desires are attributes of gods people have worshipped suggests that we have truly identified basic psychological elements of meaning.
3. The Old Testament says that God created the universe in six days; modern physics suggests that the universe is 12 to 15 billion years old. In his book *Genesis and the Big*

Bang, Gerald L. Schroeder uses Einstein's theory of relativity to reconcile these statements. Based on the measured rate of expansion of the universe, Schroeder argues that six days in God's time can equal about 15 billion years in ours.

4. Rudolf Otto (1936), *The Idea of the Holy* (trans. John W. Harvey), New York: Oxford University Press.

5. Bertrand Russell (1945/1972), *A History of Western Philosophy,* New York: Simon & Schuster, 760–772.

6. Karen Armstrong (1993), *A History of God,* New York: Ballantine, 83.

7. Gerald L. Schroeder (1990), *Genesis and the Big Bang,* New York: Bantam Books.

8. Penny Forstner and Lael Bower (1996), *A Guide to Collecting Christian and Judaic Religious Artifacts,* Florence, AL: Books Americana.

9. Sigmund Freud (1913/1958), *Totem and Taboo,* London: The Hogarth Press.

10. J. Milton Yinger (1970), *The Scientific Study of Religion,* New York: Macmillan.

11. Ibid.

12. Ibid.

13. Armstrong, *A History of God.*

14. Ibid.

15. Reinhold Niebuhr (1949), *The Nature and Destiny of Man,* New York: Charles Scribner's Sons.

16. Freud, *Totem and Taboo.*

17. Of course, addressing fear through science versus religion is not an either/or proposition: Religious people can deal with fears through both prayer and science.

18. William James (1902), *The Varieties of Religious Experience,* New York: Longmans, Green, and Co.

19. Gordon W. Allport (1961), *The Individual and His Religion,* New York: Macmillan.

Index

social contact (*cont.*)
   relationships and, 150–51
   spirituality and, 233
   in sports, 212
   value-based happiness and, 138–39
   in work, 174–75
Somers, Suzanne, 135
Sosa, Sammy, 203
Spence, Kenneth, 6–7
Spielberg, Steven, 173
spirituality, 32, 222–41
   basic desires in, 223–39
   capitalism and, 240–41
   individuality in, 239–40
sports, 201–21
   athlete desire profiles and, 220
   basic desires in, 201–20
   personal fitness and, 220–21
   See also physical activity
Stanley, Thomas J., 191
Starr, Kenneth, 61
status, 62–65
   in family life, 194–95
   "not getting it" and, 114–15
   relationships and, 152–53
   spirituality and, 234
   in sports, 213
   value-based happiness and, 139
   in work, 176
Stein, Murray, 81
Stewart, Sherry L., 162
survival, desire for, 32–33, 130–31

Teresa, Mother, 56, 232
Three Musketeers, The (Dumas), 57–58
Titanic (movie), 103
Titanic (ship), 53, 62
tranquility, 78–82
   aging and, 96
   in family life, 198
   gender differences in, 162
   "not getting it" and, 119–20
   relationships and, 155–56
   spirituality and, 238–39
   in sports, 218–20
   value-based happiness and, 141

   in work, 177–79
Tripp, Linda, 53
Turner, Ike and Tina, 154
Turner, Ted, 56
Tyson, Mike, 209, 214–15

Unabomber, 68
Uniqueness, Principle of, 184

value-based happiness, 12, 123–41
   as available to all, 126–27
   basic desires and, 136–41
   as enduring, 124
   Nazi concentration camps and, 131–33
   reality of, 133–34
   search for, 134–36
   vs. will to survive, 130–31
vengeance, 66–70
   aging and, 95
   in family life, 195–96
   gender differences in, 162
   "not getting it" and, 115–16
   relationships and, 153–54
   spirituality and, 234–36
   in sports, 214–16
   value-based happiness and, 139
   violence and, 30–32, 67–68
   in work, 176–77

Weatherby, W. J., 74
Weber, Max, 240
Whiting, John, 24
Williams, Richard, 213
Williams, Serena, 213
Williams, Tennessee, 101, 187–88
Williams, Venus, 213
Woods, Tiger, 202
work, 163–83
   basic desires in, 166–79
   and changing jobs, 179–80
   and choosing fulfilling career, 180–83
   relationships at, 163–65

York, Duchess of (Sarah Ferguson), 73

Zigler, Edward, 46